The Definitive Guide to the Doomsday Phenomenon

SCIENCE or SUPERSTITION

Alexandra Bruce

www.2012sos.net

Published by:
The Disinformation Company Ltd.
220 East 23rd Street Suite 500
New York, NY 10010
Tel.: +1.212.691.1605
Fax: +1.212.691.1606
www.disinfo.com

Library of Congress Control Number: 2009933971

ISBN: 978-1-934708-28-6

Designed by Greg Stadnyk

Distributed in the U. S. and Canada by:
Consortium Book Sales and Distribution
34 Thirteenth Avenue NE, Suite 101
Minneapolis MN 55413-1007
Tel.: +1.800.283.3572   Fax: +1.612.746.2606
www.cbsd.com

Distributed in the United Kingdom and Eire by:
Turnaround Publisher Services Ltd.
Unit 3, Olympia Trading Estate
Coburg Road
London, N22 6TZ
Tel.: +44.(0)20.8829.3000   Fax: +44.(0)20.8881.5088
www.turnaround-uk.com

Distributed in Australia by:
Tower Books
Unit 2/17 Rodborough Road
Frenchs Forest NSW 2086
Tel.: +61.2.9975.5566   Fax: +61.2.9975.5599
Email: info@towerbooks.com.au

Printed in USA

10 9 8 7 6 5 4 3 2 1

Managing Editor: Ralph Bernardo

For my father, Roger Alan Bruce

ACKNOWLEDGEMENTS

I am very grateful to Gary Baddeley for giving me the opportunity to root around in the woolly worlds of human beliefs.

I would like to thank the on-camera interviewees of the film version of *2012: Science or Superstition*, courageous people who have the temerity to challenge the orthodoxies—or to defend them, as their consciences see fit. In particular, I'd like to thank Graham Hancock, Dr. Anthony Aveni, John Major Jenkins, Alonso Mendez, Daniel Pinchbeck, Alberto Villoldo and Walter Cruttenden for the work they do and for their wonderful insights.

I wish to express my gratitude to Michael Cremo and to Bernhard Steinberger for being generous with their time and for their thoughtful responses in our interviews. Colossal thanks to Alex Kochkin, for his lifework and the Global Awakening Press—and for making sure I didn't miss anything—and a shout-out to his friends at the Web Bot project. A million thanks to the brilliant Laura Knight-Jadczyk for everything she does. Big-ups the community of tenured rebels within the scientific establishment, all over the world who are working to defragment our understanding of the Earth, the cosmos and ourselves. Here's to the Holocene Impact Working Group—and all that's like 'em!

Major thanks to the Legendary Literary Lion, Peter Miller, who treats me better than anyone and big love to the three wonderful men who've made my life possible over the past couple of years: the unstoppable and magnificent Demian Lichtenstein, Dave Sokolin and Glen Baietti.

Alexandra Bruce

TABLE OF CONTENTS

CHAPTER THREE

THE PRECESSION OF THE EQUINOXES & COSMIC INTERLOPERS

CHAPTER FOUR
WORLD AGES

CHAPTER FIVE
THE SCIENCE OF APOCALYPSE

CHAPTER SIX

THE HISTORY OF THE 2012 MEME

CHAPTER SEVEN

REVELATION, SURVIVAL, ASCENSION OR ... ?

FOREWORD

As well as being the publisher and editor of this book, I'm also the writer and producer of the companion documentary film that shares the book's title. In fact, the film came first and originally I had not thought the world really needed another 2012-themed book. That was before I made the movie.

In the course of preparing to make the film I read an enormous amount of books, essays and other materials relating to 2012. It became clear to me that there was no single book that even attempted to investigate and report on the broad range of research, opinions and debates that continue to rage around this most imminent of esoteric subjects.

I started talking about this with my close friend Alexandra Bruce, who is also the author of two previous books that my company has published, *Beyond The Bleep* and *Beyond The Secret*, which investigated in great detail the New Age movie and book phenomena *What The Bleep Do We Know!?* and *The Secret*, respectively.

One of Alexandra's great talents is to be able to understand and simply convey complex empirical science just as easily as she can boil down esoteric spiritual, shamanic or other "touchy-feely" theories and ideas. In discussing the different themes that I planned to include in the movie, it was clear to me that she was able to dig far deeper into, for example, astrophysics or Hindu theology, than I was ever going to, and besides there just wasn't room for everything in the film.

This book is the result of those conversations. Alexandra has taken the ball and run far and wide with it. Included in the book are excerpts from interviews that the film's director, Nimrod Erez, and I conducted with many of the best minds available, talking about 2012, including Graham Hancock, Daniel Pinchbeck, John Major Jenkins,

Lawrence Joseph, Anthony Aveni, Alberto Villoldo and several others. But Alexandra has been able to go far beyond the scope of our film, conducting new interviews with the likes of Michael Cremo and Bernhard Steinberger as well as reviewing the work of thinkers like Terence McKenna, José Argüelles, Barbara Hand Clow, Gregg Braden, Carl Johan Calleman, Jay Weidner and many others who have made important contributions to our understanding of the possible meaning(s) of 2012.

I hope and expect that anyone whose imagination or curiosity has been piqued by the non-stop media hype building up to December 21, 2012 will find much in this book that will surprise and delight them, as so little information is really purveyed by the typical cable TV "special investigation" or Hollywood movie. I should warn the reader now, though, that despite Alexandra's very accessible writing style, there are many terms, both scientific and esoteric, that the reader may be unfamiliar with, depending on his or her previous reading. To that end I would encourage you to review the **Glossary** contained at the back of the book *before* reading the main text. You probably won't want to read the Glossary from beginning to end, but once you know the terms are there, you can go back and review them as they appear in the book.

I hope you enjoy the book as much as I did. We would love to hear from you—feedback is always welcome and you can leave comments on our website at www.2012sos.net, where you will also find copious additional information about the book, the film and, of course, December 21, 2012.

Gary Baddeley

CHAPTER ONE

Catastrophobia 2012

"If you don't know about 2012 doomsday predictions by now, you don't have enough woo-woo friends."[1]

—Dwight Garner, *New York Times*

CHICXULUB DOOMSDAY & THE "TAIL OF THE DEVIL"

Here's a woo-woo story for you. While working on this book late one evening, I read that the Chicxulub impact crater, the scene of the most notorious mass extinction event in history, was named after the small fishing village located near its epicenter in northern Yucatán, Chicxulub, which translates loosely from Mayan into English as "Tail of the Devil."

Moments after I'd read this factoid, a friend of my colleagues, actor Rudy Youngblood dropped by the studio and we had an impromptu cocktail party. Rudy played the lead role in the film *Apocalypto*, so I commented to him about how eerie it was that "Chicxulub" means "Tail of the Devil." He nodded slowly and looked me dead in the eye. He said, "They *knew*."

Rudy told me that he'd spent almost a year in the Yucatán filming *Apocalypto* and during that time he'd befriended some local shamans. They told him about a practice that has existed for ages in Maya culture, where the shamans go into deep states of meditation and as Rudy described it, they would "time travel," to see the land in the future and in the past, to lead their communities towards the most auspicious areas, for settlement, for planting, for building. The modern-day shamans told Rudy that the ancient shamans of 1,500 years ago had astrally "seen" the cataclysm at Chicxulub and that was how the village had come to be given the name "Tail of the Devil," in the Mayan language of the Classic period.

The Chicxulub impact was one of the biggest doomsdays in the history of this planet. An object about 6 miles wide came in out of the sky and slammed into the beautiful Caribbean. The impact literally shook the Earth to its core. The massive shock waves generated global earthquakes, volcanic eruptions and megatsunamis thousands of feet high. The super-heated pyroclastic dust fanned out in every direction for millions of miles, broiling Earth's surface, setting most of the world ablaze. For almost a decade, the sky was blacked-out, with a rain of ash dust and sulfuric acid, accompanied by freezing temperatures. The photosynthesis of plants came to a halt, affecting the entire food chain of whatever survived the initial blast.

Today, the crater is buried beneath a kilometer of sediments. From the ground, no one would guess that such unimaginable devastation could ever have taken place in this tropical paradise, yet the Chicxulub impact is generally viewed to be the cause the Cretaceous-Tertiary extinction event that wiped out 75% of all Earth's species and 100% of the dinosaurs—which brings us to the apocalypse at hand ...

THE 2012 PHENOMENON

How did fragmentary glyphs carved into the rocks of the Maya ruins seize popular imagination, spawning myriad cottage industries and a literary sub-genre?

Once you wade through the oceans of shameless snake oil and past the gatekeepers at the Ivory Towers, you may be surprised to find the concepts encompassed by 2012 to be the most vital in existence. 2012 concerns the mysterious past, present and future of the Earth and of every being upon it.

2012 has gone from being an obscure artifact from an ancient calendar that fell out of use 1,000 years ago into a mass conversation about the different ways people relate to each other and to everything else. How do we relate to the Earth and to the cosmos? How do we measure time, how do we conceive of history and of personal identity? What are our values, our ideals and our faiths? How do we countenance our personal deaths? How do we feel about mass extinction? How can we avoid mass extinction?

Contrary to the New Age mantra about "You Create Your Own Reality," of which *The Secret* has been the most lucrative exemplar yet, a salient feature of the 2012 mythos is this sense of a complete loss of control. This is especially evident in the weird urban legend that has insinuated itself to the meme, about a "Planet X" bogeyman that's going to barrel through our solar system and wreak all kinds of unscientific-sounding havoc.

The proliferation of books and films that contain "2012" in their titles, range from the reasonably speculative to the totally kooky but all speak to a sense that modern humanity has lost touch with something essential and that we've thus become sitting ducks. We fear that we've given our power away to the authorities and that now they won't tell us about a comet cluster that's coming to clobber us or about an imminent single-ply Earth crustal displacement cataclysm—none of which we could do anything to prevent or would have any chance of surviving—if they were really happening and should we desire to live in a post-Apocalyptic world, without clean sheets, creme rinse or Chinese delivery ...

We've been told since childhood that an asteroid extinguished the mighty dinosaurs in a single day. When we look out at our pock-marked celestial neighbors, we know that something similar could happen here again. Recent discoveries at the bottom of the seas seem to bear this out and the "Planet X" rumors probably stem from these new scientific observations. "In 1980, only 86 Near-Earth asteroids and comets were known to exist ... [today] NASA estimates that there are perhaps 20,000 potentially hazardous asteroids and comets in the general vicinity of Earth."[2] So far, the technology to adequately view and track these potential threats simply didn't exist. With the November 2009 launch of NASA's WISE (Wide-field Infrared Survey Explorer), it is hoped that we'll be able to see any hazards that we've missed.

This book carefully examines the latest discoveries in astrophysics and geophysics and determines the probability of the many alleged imminent extinction-level catastrophes that have been injected into the 2012 mythos.

THE 2012 BLOCKBUSTER

2012® has been developed as a brand target-marketed to a demographic that is overwrought with dread, panic and anxiety, a demographic that is increasingly distrustful of the ability of officialdom to respond to matters of vital consequence. This demographic represents the larger number of people in the overdeveloped areas of world today.

The rumblings in the noösphere of today's mega 'burbs are summed up quite well in the 30-second preview for the ultimate "2012" product to date, the $200 million Hollywood disaster film by Director Roland Emmerich:

EXT. TIBETAN HIMALAYAS—The Highest Mountains In The World

YOUNG MONK runs up a mountainside towards a BELL TOWER at the top.

INT. TIBETAN BELL TOWER

YOUNG MONK bursts through the doors. OLD MONK rings a huge, ancient GONG.

TITLE CARDS

HOW WOULD THE GOVERNMENTS OF OUR PLANET PREPARE SIX BILLION PEOPLE FOR THE END OF THE WORLD?

EXT. OCEAN RISES UP OVER THE ENTIRE HIMALAYAN RANGE, CASCADES OVER THE PEAKS, PULVERIZES BELL TOWER

TITLE CARDS

THEY WOULDN'T
2012
FIND OUT THE TRUTH
GOOGLE SEARCH 2012[3]

Roland Emmerich does have a point. No government would really want to admit that they don't have the situation handled—and because scientists and universities must rely on government grants to subsidize their research, those who don't toe the line of the uniformitarianist establishment may find it difficult to get funding. Uniformitarianism "holds that the same fundamental geological processes operated in the past as do today ... originally proposed in contrast to catastrophism, which states that the distant past 'consisted of epochs of paroxysmal and catastrophic action interposed between periods of comparative tranquility.'"[4] The so-called "catastrophists" have tended to work with fewer resources and their theories have tended to remain in the background, under a pall of crankdom.

GEOMYTHOLOGY: AN INTEGRATED VIEW OF LIFE ON EARTH

A new subdiscipline of science is emerging, called geomythology, practiced by people like Los Alamos National Laboratory environmental archaeologist Bruce Masse, who was given access to over 4,000 myths from South America east of the Andes in the UCLA database and to which he applied the same rigorous standards that he applies to his other areas of scientific study. We will take a look at the fascinating discoveries being made in the cutting edge of astrophysics, dendrochronology, marine geology and geomythology, which bring a new level of holism to our understanding of life on Earth, as their interdisciplinary efforts reveal how Earth history *is* human history— and that *Earth's astrophysical history* is also human history.

MAYA MYSTERIES

The fascinating and mysterious remains of the classical Maya civilization represent a relatively new field of study for archaeologists. The bulk of Maya hieroglyphics were not decoded until the 1980s and the job is presently just three quarters complete. Maya mathematics and astronomy amaze everyone for being more advanced than that of their Roman contemporaries and Maya timekeeping methods were perhaps their most stunning achievement.

In the 7th century BCE the Maya built magnificent pyramids, temple complexes and cities with beautiful bas-reliefs and sculptures. During the 21st century CE, the Maya also "mysteriously" built many of the McMansions in upscale areas of the United States, as undocumented workers ... Like its Roman counterpart, the Maya empire collapsed and tens of thousands have migrated to North America, but about 6 million Maya living in their traditional lands speak Mayan as a first language and in certain remote highland areas of Guatemala they still use their ancient calendrical system, in an unbroken tradition of over 2,000 years.[5]

What is one to make of a pre-telescopic civilization that was so obsessed with keeping time, that they would carve glyphs into monuments, representing increasingly huge units of time, the largest, equal to 10,331,233,010,526,315,789,473,682,240,000 days, found engraved in a stele at the large temple complex at Cobá?

If these were just numbers, that would be one thing, but these multi-billion-year chunks are *units of time.*

BASICS OF THE MAYA CALENDARS

It is said that in their heyday, the Maya of the Classic period regularly made use of twenty-four different calendars. The Maya created almanacs based on every celestial body whose movements they could consistently observe and record but for everyday use, they kept time with two interlocking cyclical calendars, one lunar and the other solar. These were called the *T'zolk'in* and the *Haab'*, respectively, which were synchronized to form a cycle of 52 years that was called a "Calendar Round" and which consisted of 18,980 distinctly-named dates. With everything these calendars did identify, they did not specify years, which is a bit strange for a Western mind to figure.

For longer periods or for identifying when distant events occurred in relation to others, Mesoamericans developed Long Count calendars, which unlike the *T'zolk'in* and the *Haab'* were linear and therefore theoretically infinite and never-ending. The Gregorian calendar is similar, in that it can be extended to refer to any date in the future or in the past. We will get into the details of Maya Long Count calendar in the next chapter.

Among the most mind-boggling features of Maya timekeeping are the enormous units of time to which they gave names. The longest of the named units exceeds the estimated age of the universe, according to modern cosmology and the biggest time unit discovered so far at an archaeological dig in Cobá, Mexico is unnamed and is simply called the "Cobá number," which is in the ten nonillions!

UNITS OF TIME LARGER THAN THE *B'AK'TUN*

These were usually noted by placing 13 in the counts larger than *b'ak'tun*: 13.13.13.13.13.0.0.0.0

13 *b'ak'tun* = 5,125 years

13 *pik'tun* = 102,000 years

13 *kalab'tun* = 2,000,000 years

13 *k'inchil'tun* = 42,000,000 years

13 *alau'tun* = 820,000,000 years

13 *habla'tun* = 16,400,000,000 years

WERE THE MAYA FROM OUTER SPACE?

The impressive time units, in conjunction with the dazzling accuracy of Maya timekeeping and the mysterious abandonment of their beautiful temple complexes have helped give rise to some rather outlandish allegations among New Age entrepreneurs.

A number of enterprising entertainers have declared that the ancient Maya were actually extraterrestrials who have since returned to their "home world," a view which can be interpreted as insulting to the modern-day Maya, who have been contending with cultural oppression and genocide for over five centuries, as it is. It's almost like saying that the Romans were really from outer space and that they went back to their abode in the stars, resulting in the Fall of Rome. (Because Italians couldn't possibly have built the Roman Empire ...)

100% PURE MYTHOMANIA

Yes, these were the Galactic Maya, great civilizers of the Pleiadian beyond who brought their time science to a planet which they knew was devoid of it, and hence incapable of entering the great tournament of time traveling athletes whose wanderings and mental exploits mark the annals of the galactic saga of spiritual and mental evolution. So here on Earth they infiltrated, partook of the Olmec shamanic rites, became jaguar priests, tamed naguals, and erected cosmic temples upon which they inscribed inscrutable star histories, episodes occurring hundreds of millions and even billions of years in the past—or the future. Finally they set up their dynasties and rivalries which marked the end of their time on Earth.[6]

It's one thing to be amazed at these massive units of time and to have a "sci-fi moment" and to wonder if the Maya could really be from this planet or even from this universe, playing with units of time that were longer than the universe is old. What in the world were they doing with units of time that had 10,331,233,010,526,315,789,473,682,2 40,000 days in them? I really can't blame anyone for "going there," in one's imagination, as a thought experiment, as entertainment, as fiction—but as a career?

These time units could well have been a mathematical exercise or a way to allege massive ancientness and legitimacy to the lineage of the local ruler. To really "go there" and put a shingle up and make a cottage industry out of saying that the "galactic" or "seed" ET Maya have gone home and that the Maya living in Mesoamerica today aren't the real deal ... ?

I'm not saying that there hasn't been any interplanetary or interdimensional weirdness in Earth's history but there's got to be a better way to make a living than by dissing the Maya! The ET narrative also functions as a bizarre form of denial. As if our own civilization couldn't be brought to its knees, after severe economic and environmental collapse and cataclysm, followed by a violent conquest at the hands of brutal, ignorant, weapon-toting ideologues—like what happened to the Maya.

The only function that this mind-rotting ET narrative seems to serve is to distract from the fact that every single empire that has ever risen has also fallen, because empires are unsustainable. The Maya now living the traditional, low-impact way in the Guatemala highlands have since found a way to live that is sustainable. Hopefully, we'll find a way to do the same—and still keep our iPods. (Actually, I'm pretty sure they have those in the Highlands ...)

THE DIFFERENCE BETWEEN A "MAYANIST" & "MAYANISM"

Mayanists are scholars who have specialized in the study of the pre-Columbian Maya civilization. Mayanism is something different, altogether. It is a blend of New Age beliefs and pre-Columbian Maya mythology. Prior to the 1970s, Mayanism was largely influenced by the works of Charles Étienne Brasseur de Bourbourg and was associated with the idea that the survivors of the "lost continent" of Atlantis could be found in modern-day Mesoamerica. More recently, Mayanism also came to include speculations that the Maya either originated from outer space or they were influenced by off-planetary intelligence or that the reason they abandoned their pyramids was to return to the stars. (We will discuss more about Mayanism in upcoming chapters).

13 B'AK'TUNS

The December 21, 2012 "doomsday" derives from the Maya Long Count calendar. The interpretation of the date's significance is based on ancient Maya belief that the end of a 13-b'ak'tun cycle signifies the end of a "World Age" and the beginning of a new one.

Many Westerners are looking to ancient sources and to the wisdom of the indigenous peoples, in hopes of "reconnecting" with a lost "Unity Consciousness" that is poorly understood. It's ironic, considering that Westerners had almost completely stamped Native Americans out of existence. The Maya managed to escape total physical decimation and are today among the largest populations of Native American groups, living mostly in Southern Mexico, Guatemala, Belize, Honduras and El Salvador.

The incredible precision of ancient Maya timekeeping and their mysterious shamanic approach to life has prompted many Westerners to wonder whether the Maya knew or know something that Westerners don't. Many believe that ancient and modern-day indigenous cultures hold vital information that has long been forgotten in the West, ranging from how to live in harmony with the Earth to detailed knowledge about vast cosmic cycles—in particular, those related to astrophysical events of a cataclysmic order.

2012 IS NOT THE "END OF THE MAYA CALENDAR"

The Maya Long Count calendar had fallen out of use hundreds of years before the Spaniards arrived in Mesoamerica. It was later rediscovered and painstakingly correlated to the Gregorian calendar by archaeologists and epigraphers over the greater part of the 20th century.

Technically, 2012 is NOT the "end of the Maya calendar" because the Long Count is linear and theoretically infinite, with the ability to express any date in the past or future, much like the calendar used in the West. Also, there are many ancient Maya inscriptions with dates beyond 2012, notably one with a date that corresponds to October 21, 4772, where Lord Pakal of Palenque predicted that people would celebrate his coronation on the eightieth Calendar Round of its anniversary.[7]

December 21, 2012 does correspond to the end of the current World Age and the beginning of the next World Age, as described in the ancient Maya creation myth, the *Popol Vuh* ("Council Book" or "Book of the Community"), which was translated directly from *K'iche'* Maya to English for the first time in 1986 by Dennis Tedlock.[8]

According to Mayanist John Major Jenkins, the ancient Maya viewed an epochal cycle to be akin to a cosmic pregnancy, where the most important part was at the end or the "birth." Academics who specialize in this culture that are willing to engage the topic are virtually unanimous in their assessments, that from the ancient Maya perspective, the most important aspect of 2012 was that it marked the beginning of a new era.

While it is true that the 2012 date marked the end of a World Age for the ancient Maya, most modern-day Maya do not believe that this date is particularly significant. According to Robert K. Sitler, a professor of modern languages and Maya culture at Stetson University in Florida "... [contemporary], authentic indigenous beliefs ... point to an approaching period of significant, even catastrophic, world change and subsequent renewal but without explicit reference to 2012."[9]

HOW DID 2012 COME TO MEAN "THE END OF TIME"?

Discoveries about ancient Maya civilization were some of the biggest news in archaeology throughout the 1980s and 1990s. Around that time, two spellbinding performance artists, José Argüelles and Terence McKenna, seized public attention with their ingenious-sounding screeds and spiels that invoked these fascinating new discoveries about the Maya and the Mesoamerican Long Count calendar. Both men were academic types who'd wandered off the "rez" and who'd had their minds blown by Maya civilization (with considerable psychedelic assistance).

It appears that, as innate showmen, they knew that it wasn't catchy enough to say, "Twenty-odd years from now, a cyclical eon conceived of by an obscure, ancient Mesoamerican culture will be drawing to an end." This was not entertainment and it just wasn't selling. Instead, they said things like, 2012 was "the end of history," "the end of time," "the dominion of time," "the singularity of novelty," and "time is art."

"The end of time" really caught on but it probably derives from the period McKenna spent in the Amazon tripping on a variety of rainforest ingredients with Peruvian shamans, who to this day have a tradition that is called "stepping out of time."

Argüelles and McKenna acted independently of each other and they had different agendas. McKenna's vision was of a cosmic singularity that would precede the technological singularity touted by futurists like Ray Kurzweil. Argüelles to this day remains adamant that the world should adopt his 13-Moon *Dreamspell* calendar, as "the correct and biologically accurate calendar for the whole planet." [10]

2012 has been simmering on the backburner in the minds of those who ever read the works or who were ever present at the electrifying public speaking events given by either Argüelles or McKenna. Their startling pronouncements regarding 2012 have had the effect of a slow-acting retrovirus in the body of urban legend over the succeeding decades, recently morphing into a souvenir T-shirt for the "End of the World."

Whatever it was or will be—the 2012 date is finally upon us.

CHAPTER TWO

The Maya

"We have to pay due respect to the Maya themselves and to their astonishing knowledge of the heavens and to their mastery of time."
—Graham Hancock, On-Camera Interview in *2012: Science or Superstition*

"COSMOVISION"

I ronically, the collapse of several key urban centers five hundred years prior to the arrival of the Spaniards helped to preserve much of the Maya archaeological legacy, which lay hidden under thickets of luxuriant tropical vegetation well into the 20th century. Of all the Native American cultures, the ancient Maya civilization of Southern Mexico and Central America is among the most studied by scholars today.

The material culture of the Maya shares similarities with that of the great ancient civilizations in the Old World but any similarities between the ambitions of the ancient Maya and their European conquerors screech to a dead stop when it comes to their spiritual outlook. The Maya were shamanistic and divinatory in all of their pursuits; the boundaries between the phenomenological and spiritual worlds were to be opened and navigated—in complete contrast to the strict prohibitions against "necromancy" by the religion of the Holy See.

SHAMANISM IN ANCIENT MAYA CULTURE

"The Maya King was the High Shaman. It was the Kings' responsibility to commune with the cosmic center and in so doing, they could sustain the kingdom and they could also convey sacred information and sacred insight to keep the society running smoothly ... the sacred traditions that you find fragmented in Europe today or surviving in underground ways—they reflect a very profound ancient paradigm that has become eclipsed by a modern materialistic and debased worldview."

—John Major Jenkins, On-Camera Interview in *2012: Science or Superstition*

NATIVE AMERICAN SPIRITUALITY

"They were the keepers of this ancient body of knowledge that has remained intact for 100,000 years. The ancient knowledge is not like modern science. It doesn't get better every year. It's not an incremental body of knowledge. You don't keep adding to it. It has been complete from the beginning—from before the beginning. The task of the shaman was to tap into this body of wisdom that has remained intact since before the beginning of time. To do that, they had to step outside of ordinary time, as we know it. They had to step into infinity.

"If we look at the field of molecular archaeology, which traces genetic variations, we can tell that there were twelve to fourteen people that crossed the Bering Strait about 32,000 years ago.

"Of those, four were women. Three of those women remained in the Northeast of North America. A single woman came down with the peoples that later became the Maya, the Inca and the

Hopi; a single Eve ... you can trace this back to Tibet, 60,000 years ago, to the Himalayas where people settled after leaving Africa close to 100,000 years ago. So we look at this ancient body of wisdom as being an infinite one that has always existed that was brought intact across the Bering Strait and into the Americas. They've acquired flavors, acquired the Hopi flavor, the Inca flavor, the Mayan flavor, but at its core its essence was unique and singular and the same for all of these peoples."

—Alberto Villoldo

On-Camera Interview in *2012: Science or Superstition*

MAYA PRIME & COLLAPSE

At its height, Maya civilization was one of the most densely populated and culturally dynamic societies in the world. Maya civilization is studied as the pre-Classic period between circa 1800 BCE to 250 CE; the Classic period between ca. 250 CE to 900 CE; and the post-Classic period, which officially ended in 1502, with the first known encounter between the Maya and the Spaniards.

During the 8th and 9th centuries, many urban centers in the south mysteriously collapsed. This was recently determined to be the result of soil erosion and a prolonged drought.[11] There is evidence that in the Maya centers of the Guatemala highlands, the people literally starved to death.[12] However, throughout the post-Classic period cities in the northern lowlands, like Chichén-Itzá, flourished through the late 1400s.

Despite the genocidal campaigns against them and the wholesale destruction of their literature and culture over the next 200 years, some Maya city-states remained independent until the Spanish finally overpowered them in 1697.

The history of the pre-Classic Maya is often simplified to depict them as an offshoot of the preceding Olmec culture. The Olmecs were a civilization thought to have informed virtually all subsequent Mesoamerican cultures and which itself experienced a sudden population decline and a virtual disappearance around 400 CE, possibly due to catastrophic earthquakes. There was unquestionably a cross-pollenization between the early Maya, the Olmec and the Mixtec and Zapotec–speaking peoples of southern Mesoamerica. Many of the earliest significant inscriptions and buildings appeared in this overlapping zone and evidence suggests that these cultures and the formative Maya influenced one another.[13]

The pyramid of *K'uk'ulkan* at Chichén-Itzá.

THE MAYA CALENDARS

The Maya's assiduous, accurate tracking of several celestial cycles and their penetrating perception of the mathematical relationships among them were uncanny. They didn't have telescopes or computers! Working knowledge of Maya calendrics is a daunting undertaking that requires serious devotion, like that of the communities who continue, to this day to practice these unbroken traditions of over 2,000 years—and like that of the modern scholars who have dedicated their lives to decoding the ancient Maya glyphs. Readers interested in a fuller understanding in this area are encouraged to review the works of Michael Coe, Linda Schele and others listed in the **Resources** section at the end of this book.

A calendar used throughout pre-Hispanic Mesoamerica was the 260-day "sacred calendar" with 13 day-numbers and 20 day-signs. The *trecena* of 13 day-numbers goes sequentially from 1 to 13 then starts again at 1, while the named-day sequence of 20 day-signs continues onwards. Every possible combination of day-number/day-sign takes 260 days to complete in this interlocking 13- and 20-day cycle. This calendar is called the *T'zolk'in* in the *K'iche'* Mayan language of the Guatemalan Highlands and is called the *Cholquij* in the *Yukatek* language spoken in the lowlands of Mexico's Yucatán Peninsula. There are a total of 29 recognized Mayan languages spoken by indigenous Maya, which all descend from the proto-Mayan language thought to have been spoken about 5,000 years ago.[14]

As Mayanist John Major Jenkins explains, "Each day-sign has an oracular meaning, with many layers of linguistic puns and metaphysical references to provide a rich database for Mayan calendar-priests to weave their interpretations."[15] Mayan shamans would consult the *T'zolk'in* to answer yes/no questions, to schedule marriages on favorable dates and to determine the personalities and talents of newborns, similarly to how modern-day Western astrology is practiced but far more central to the everyday lives of members of Classic Maya society.

260 = THE MAGIC NUMBER

"The Maya calendars also encode an insight into the interwoven nature of reality. What we might call a fractal model, or a quantum model of reality. We see this most clearly in the 260-day calendar, the *T'zolk'in*, which is the core building block of all the Maya calendar systems. It consists of 13 numbers combined with 20 day-signs. 13 times 20 equals 260. Two-sixty is a key number for the Maya because it corresponds to the human gestation period.

"There's this nine-month process of human unfolding that we all share. This is the philosophy behind the Maya calendar. Time unfolds like a flower, and it's unfolding the inner essence of consciousness out of the Earth matrix, you might say. Another use for the 260-day calendar is that it corresponds to the interval between planting and harvesting of corn in the highlands, so that's an agricultural metaphor.

"Most incredibly, the 260-day calendar is used as a key in the Maya almanacs. The Maya almanacs are calendars that schedule the appearance of Venus and Mercury and Mars. There's this very, very important astronomical reference in the 260-*T'zolk'in* calendar, as well. What we see in all this is the use of 260 as a key to different dimensions in human experience. It unites the cycles in the heavens and the cycles here on Earth, including cycles that human beings experience. So it's an insight into that paradigm of 'as above so below,' how the microcosm reflects the macrocosm."

—John Major Jenkins, On-Camera Interview in *2012: Science or Superstition*

THE "CALENDAR ROUND"

The *T'zolk'in* has been in continuous use in some communities of the Guatemalan highlands since the 6th century BCE. It was and is used in conjunction with the 365-day solar calendar called the *Haab'*. These two calendars being based on 260 days and 365 days, respectively, were synchronized to form a cycle of 52 *Haab'* years, referred to as a "Calendar Round," which features 18,980 distinctly-named dates. Other important divisions of time in the Maya calendar include, as already mentioned, the twenty 13-day *trecenas* of the *T'zolk'in* and the 20-day *tuns* or "months" of the 18-month *Haab'*.

A 584-day Venus cycle was also tracked, especially to determine auspicious times to conduct warfare or coronations. A "Venus Round" consisted of 104 years, or two "Calendar Rounds," which was an important ceremonial date that marked the realignment of the *Haab'*, *T'zolk'in* and Venus cycles. The lunar phases and cyclical positions were also diligently recorded and noted on their monuments.

All of these calendars are considered remarkable for their incredible accuracy, demonstrating the extraordinary abilities of astronomical observation and timekeeping of the pre-Hispanic, pre-telescopic Mesoamericans. However, the Western preoccupation with these calendars' accuracy causes grievous annoyance to John Major Jenkins because it fails to comprehend the exquisite sophistication of the Mesoamericans' holistic, multidimensional worldview or what he calls their "cosmovision."

[T]hat misses the whole point of the Mesoamerican calendar being designed as a holistic system of nested cycles that harmoniously embrace the commensuration of planetary and eclipse cycles. It's not about precise accuracy, it's about comprehensive comprehension. The Mesoamerican calendar embraces not only different astronomical cycles, but different dimensions of human experience, from human biology to agriculture to astronomy. THAT is the wonder and miracle of Maya time philosophy. Mere accuracy is an irrelevant offshoot of the grand *cosmovision* attained by the Maya.[16]

Accurate as they were, the combined calendars did not identify years. Since the average lifespan of the ancient Maya person was below 52 years and the combined *T'zolk'in* and *Haab'* dates wouldn't recur for another 52 years, this system of identifying days was satisfactory for the uses of most of the people back then.

THE MAYA LONG COUNT CALENDAR

The Long Count calendar is a framework that utilizes nested periods with five place values. Unlike Western numbering, which uses a base-10 number scheme, the Long Count days were tallied in a base-20 scheme. Therefore, 0.0.0.1.5 would be equal to 25, and 0.0.0.2.0 would be equal to 40. However, the Long Count gets a bit tricky, in that it is not consistently base-20: the second digit rolls over to zero when it reaches 18. For that reason, 0.0.1.0.0 does not represent 400 days, it represents 360 days. The following table shows the period equivalents as well as the Mayan names for these time periods:

Representation	Long Count Subdivisions	Days	~Solar years
0.0.0.0.1	1 k'in	1	1/365
0.0.0.1.0	1 winal = 20 k'in	20	1/18
0.0.1.0.0	1 tun = 18 winal	360	1
0.1.0.0.0	1 k'atun = 20 tun	7,200	19.7
1.0.0.0.0	1 b'ak'tun = 20 k'atun	144,000	394

The Long Count calendar contains several cycles, which interlink with one another. A very important cycle is a period of 13 b'ak'tuns or 5,125 years, considered by the ancient Maya to be the equivalent of a human epoch or a World Age. The Long Count calendar is a key to understanding the Maya doctrine of the World Ages that we find in the creation myth in the Popol Vuh, which was akin to the Old Testament for the ancient Maya.

After a century of academic trial and tribulation, the start-date of the Maya Long Count is today generally agreed to correspond to August 11, 3114 BCE in the Gregorian calendar. Although the Long Count calendar was established "only" 2,000 years ago, its start-date precedes its creation by almost 3,000 years, to mark the beginning of the 13-b'ak'tun cycle that is now ending.

POPOL VUH: THE MAYA BIBLE

The *Popol Vuh* describes the creation and destruction of previous versions of humankind, even predicting the means by which the current
version of human beings—you and I—will meet either its demise or
its transformation, depending on your woo-woo factor. The previous
version of humankind was destroyed by flood, which is eerily reminiscent of the biblical Flood in Western tradition. The current version
of humankind is prophesied to be destroyed by "earthquakes" at the
end of the current age: December 21, 2012.

The Maya World Age doctrine, as expressed in the *Popol Vuh*,
has significant commonalities with those of many indigenous groups
throughout the Americas. Even ancient Greek mythology has a tradition of the "Five Ages of Man" and it even shares some stunningly
specific details to those found in the *Popol Vuh*. The Hindu tradition
has its cyclical ages or *yugas*. These World Age doctrines will be discussed in greater detail in **Chapter 4** of this book.

The remnant of a World Age doctrine that has managed to survive in the West is the 12-sign zodiac of astrology, which is based
on an ancient Babylonian system but it is not taken very seriously
by most. Christian fundamentalists actually warn that "astrology and
sorcery are forbidden by the Bible. [Astrology] is a religious system
which originated from Satan." [17] (Who knew?)

DID THE MAYA KNOW SOMETHING WE DON'T?

"Perhaps [the Maya] may have known something that we don't know.
There are objects called long-period comets. It's quite common to
find a comet that has an orbit of more than 12,000 years and when
the Maya speak directly and specifically of a cataclysmic end, a gigantic flood, an overthrow of the world as we know it now, I don't think

we should rule out the possibility that they may be speaking of real physical events and that perhaps they had information about a very dangerous comet which intersects the orbit of the Earth at intervals of thousands of years and perhaps it's coming back in our time. Our astronomers would know nothing about it today. Typically, when these Near-Earth asteroids or comets pass the Earth very closely, we only know about them after they've gone by and I often wonder whether the Mayan warning concerns the cyclical return of some object in the sky, which may be on a collision course with Earth."

—Graham Hancock, On-Camera Interview in *2012: Science or Superstition*

DOES THE MAYA CALENDAR PREDICT APOCALYPSE IN 2012?

The Long Count calendar was created within a Mesoamerican cultural context ca. 200 BCE, in which there were very specific beliefs about the existence of cyclical World Ages. By their very definition, the beginnings and endings of human epochs or "World Ages" are accompanied by cataclysm, according to the *Popol Vuh*.

Modern-day speculation that an apocalypse may accompany the end of the current 13-*b'ak'tun* cycle is largely seen as a New Age urban legend that arose in the mid-1980s, so it may come as a surprise that this idea made its first 20th century appearance in the 1966 book *The Maya*, written by one of the most respected Mayanist scholars in the world, Michael Coe, Professor Emeritus of Anthropology at Yale University, among his many other impressive positions and titles:

There is a suggestion ... that Armageddon would overtake the degenerate peoples of the world and all creation on the final day of the thirteenth [*b'ak'tun*]. Thus ... our present universe ... [would] be annihilated ... when the Great Cycle of the Long Count reaches completion.[18]

If Maya mythology is cross-referenced with scientific findings in archaeology, astronomy and geophysics, this could well lead to an interpretation that the 5,125-year epoch in Maya Long Count calendar is related to cataclysmic cycles on Earth.

For example, the Maya Long Count calendar's start-date of August 11, 3114 BCE occurred during a timeframe that happened to coincide with the collapse of several Bronze Age civilizations in the Fertile Crescent, which some theorize was caused by meteorite impacts from the breakup of a larger body that is today known as Comet Encke and its accompanying Taurid complex, a stream of matter that is the largest in the inner solar system.[19] Taurid meteor showers occur twice per year but the stream has a cycle of activity that peaks every 2,500 to 3,000 years, when there are larger impactors. The Royal Observatory in Scotland estimates that the next peak involving large-sized meteors from the Taurids will begin sometime between the years 2400–3000 CE.[20]

The Maya creation myth describes what happened the last time the *b'ak'tun* cycle ended—a Great Flood, which destroyed the last version of the human race. This is spooky, as the West has its own traditions about a Great Flood in which almost all humans and fellow creatures perished. Of course, these could have all been local accounts—or is it possible they were referring to a global catastrophe?

THE LAST APOCALYPSE: CORRELATING MYTH WITH EARTH SCIENCE

Among the Maya groups that left behind written testimonies ... we find different accounts that revolve around the existence of a flood that wiped out the previous world and allowed for the creation of a new cosmological order.[21]

Given these Maya accounts, it is only natural to suspect that the early days of the current 13-*b'ak'tun* cycle might recall an actual, historical period of cataclysmic flooding. When the ancient Maya created the Long Count calendar, they set it up to begin on a very specific date 3,000 years *in their own past*, which coincided with a zenithal passage of the Sun. This astronomical event signified "New Year's Day" to the Maya, because it was the day where one would "cast no shadows." Thus, the 5th Maya era retroactively began on August 11, 3114 BCE or as the date was known in the Long Count, 13.0.0.0.0; 4 *Ahaw* 8 *Kumk'u*.

In 3114 BCE, the Maya were in their "Late Archaic" stage, having long since succeeded in domesticating animals and hybridizing local grasses into maize. In the timeline below, the period around 3100 BCE appears to have been a "watershed" moment for many civilizations, according to archaeological findings all over the world.

3114 BCE	Start-date of a 13-*b'ak'tun* epoch of the Meso-american Long Count calendar (correlated to Gregorian calendar), used by the ancient Maya civilization to record the post-Flood epoch, which ends on December 21, 2012.
3102 BCE	Beginning of the *Kali Yuga* era, as correlated to Gregorian calendar. Date may commemorate the "Flood of *Manu*" in Hindu *Puranas*.[22]
ca. 3100 BCE	The Indus Valley civilization constructs the first advanced system of drainage. Menes unifies Upper and Lower Egypt, and a new capital is erected at Memphis
ca. 3050 BCE	The beginnings of Iberian civilizations, arrival to the peninsula, dating as far back as 4000 BCE.

ca. 3000 BCE   *Umm al Binni* lake in the *Al Amarah* region of Iraq may be an impact crater, as suggested by satellite imagery, (Master 2001, 2002). Age of the crater estimated to be < 5,000 years. During that time, the region was under the Persian Gulf at a depth of approximately 10m (Larsen & Evans 1978: 237). The alleged *Umm al Binni* impact could be responsible for producing the energy equivalent to thousands of Hiroshima-sized bombs. The impact-induced tsunamis would have devastated coastal Sumerian cities. This may provide an alternate origin of the 2.6 m sediment layer dis-covered during an excavation of the Sumerian city of Ur by Leonard Wooley in 1954. Descriptive pas-sages in the *Epic of Gilgamesh* may describe such an impact and tsunami, suggesting a link to the Sumerian Deluge (Matthews 2001; Britt 2001).

Neolithic period ends, Aegean Bronze Age starts, Minoan civilization starts, Troy is founded.

Stonehenge construction begins. In its first ver-sion, it consists of a circular ditch and bank, with 56 wooden posts.[23]

2807 BCE   A very large-scale comet or meteorite impact event in the southern Indian Ocean, caused enormous megatsunamis. It is theorized that the legends of the "Great Flood" in the Bible, the Maya *Popol Vuh*, the Hindu *Puranic* story of *Manu*, the *Deucalion* in Greek mythology and the story of *Utnapishtim* in the *Epic of Gilgamesh* may be associated with this event, which created the 18-mile wide Burckle crater, under 12,500 feet of ocean.

Is it just a coincidence that there are several traditions worldwide of cataclysmic flooding during the same time period, flooding which was so destructive that a line of demarcation separates everything that occurred before this time with a word was invented specifically to describe it: "antediluvian"? Is it a coincidence that roughly a century after this time, worldwide, we see new civilizations founded and the start of new dynasties or the beginnings of "new eras" in pre-existing cultures?

THE START-DATE OF THE MAYA CALENDAR

This date [August 13, 3114 BCE, a.k.a., 13.0.0.0.0; 4 *Ahaw* 8 *Kumk'u*] appears over and over in ... inscriptions throughout the Maya world. On that day the creator gods set three stones or mountains in the sky after lifting it with the sacred tree of life, *from the dark waters that once covered the primordial world*. These three stones formed a cosmic hearth at the center of the universe. The gods then struck divine new fire by means of lightning, which charged the world with new life.[24]

PLATO'S *TIMAEUS* & *CRITIAS*

Greek philosopher Plato wrote the books *Timaeus* and *Critias,* which are often cited as the earliest historical references to the antediluvian civilization of Atlantis. Its location and identification remain unsolved mysteries to this day and Atlantis is generally regarded by the mainstream to be a mythical place that never physically existed. In the account of *Critias*, the Athenian statesman, Solon visits Egypt and asks the learned priests about their knowledge of ancient history. He then recounts to them the Greek "history" about the Deluge caused by Zeus as a punishment for the practice of human sacrifice and cannibalism among the Pelasgians (pre-Hellenic, antediluvian inhabitants of Greece). According to this legend, there'd been two survivors, Deucalion and his wife, Pyrrha, who had followed the instructions of Deucalion's father to build an ark. Deucalion's story is virtually the same as that of the biblical Noah and of the Sumerian Utnapishtim in the *Epic of Gilgamesh*.

In response to Solon's recitation, the Egyptian priest Sonchis deadpans that Greek knowledge of history is pathetically limited, saying there have been more than just one Deluge, and that, "There have been, and will be again, many destructions of mankind."

> There is a story, which even you have preserved, that once upon a time Phaëton, the son of Helios, having yoked the steeds in his father's chariot, because he was not able to drive them in the path of his father, burnt up all that was upon the Earth ... Now this has the form of a myth, but really signifies a declination of the bodies moving in the heavens around the Earth, and a great conflagration of things upon the Earth, which recurs after long intervals ... just when you ... are beginning to be provided with letters and the other requisites of civilized life, after the usual interval, the stream from heaven, like a pestilence, comes pouring down, and leaves only those of you who are destitute of letters and education; and so you have to begin all over again like children, and know nothing of what happened in ancient times ... [25]

The Chiemgau impact, which occurred around 500 BCE in Bavaria, Germany, left behind a large debris field and formed Lake Tüttensee, which is believed by some to be the final resting place of the Phaëton comet.

HOLOCENE IMPACT WORKING GROUP

Columbia University geophysicist Dr. Dallas Abbott and her Holocene Impact Working Group are working to correct our collective amnesia by proving that bodies larger than half a mile long have impacted Earth fairly regularly in historic times and that these have in turn regularly affected the development of civilization:

> Although conventional astronomy suggests that large (>1 km) impactors hit the Earth once every 300,000 years we have assembled evidence for at least 3 large oceanic impacts during the last 11,000 years. The ~1.5 km "Deluge comet" produced the 29 km Burckle crater, which is astronomically estimated to be 4,800 years old. This impact may be responsible for ancient legends about torrential rainfall, hurricane force winds, and coastal megatsunamis. The deluge was followed by a period of dim sunlight and colder climate.[26]

One of the group's members, Bruce Masse from Los Alamos National Laboratory in New Mexico, thinks he can name the precise date of the impact of the comet which caused the biblical Deluge: the morning of May 10, 2807 BCE.

> Dr. Masse analyzed 175 flood myths from around the world, and tried to relate them to known and accurately dated natural events like solar eclipses and volcanic eruptions. Among other evidence, he said, 14 flood myths specifically mention a full solar eclipse, which could have been the one that occurred in May 2807 B.C.

> Half the myths talk of a torrential downpour, Dr. Masse said. A third talk of a tsunami. Worldwide they describe hurricane force winds and darkness during the storm. All of these could come from a megatsunami.[27]

(**Chapter 5** contains a table of 16 Holocene impacts and references to the myths associated with them.)

2012 & THE PRECESSION OF THE EQUINOXES

For his part, Mayanist John Major Jenkins believes that the creators of the Long Count calendar were less concerned with its start-date than they were with setting an auspicious end-date, as he explains in his 1994 essay, "The How and Why of the Mayan End-date In 2012 AD." He credits epigrapher Linda Schele's decoding of the Mayan glyph which signifies the "Sacred Tree," a key figure in Maya mythology that she realized was also an astronomical reference to the crossing point of the Sun with the plane of the ecliptic, i.e., the path the Sun traces across the sky with the band of the Milky Way.

Linda Schele was influenced by the work *Hamlet's Mill*, written by MIT's Giorgio de Santillana and Hertha von Dechend. The authors famously argue that mythology has been misunderstood for centuries because scholars have failed to understand that myths were a coded language used by the priestly classes in ancient times to describe their astronomical observations—an idea with which the ancient Egyptian priest Sonchis, cited before, would have completely agreed. Today nearly everyone involved with this kind of study agrees with this premise.

Rendering of the "galactic alignment," a rare astronomical conjunction of the path of the winter solstice Sun with the band of the Milky Way—or "galactic equator."

Jenkins' main thesis hangs on the idea that over two millennia ago, the Maya were able to calculate an end-date that would coincide with a very rare astronomical conjunction; that of the path of the winter solstice Sun with the band of the Milky Way—or the galactic equator, to be exact. At 11:11 a.m. on December 21, 2012, the Sun will appear at the very center of the Maya's "Sacred Tree."

> We couldn't have hoped for a closer conjunction. 1 day before or after will remove the Sun a noticeable distance from the crossing point ... the creators of the Long Count knew about and calculated the rate of precession over 2,300 years ago. I can conceive of no other conclusion. To explain this away as "coincidence" would only obscure the issue.
>
> For early Mesoamerican skywatchers, the slow approach of the Winter Solstice Sun to the Sacred Tree was seen as a critical process, the culmination of which was surely worthy of being called 13.0.0.0.0, the end of a World Age. The channel would then be open through the Winter Solstice doorway, up the Sacred Tree, the *Xibalba Be'* [the Road to the Underworld], to the center of the churning heavens, the Heart of Sky.[28]

Jenkins has spent nearly his entire adult life studying ancient Maya civilization and he has also lived for periods of time in the Guatemala highlands, studying the traditional culture of the modern-day Maya. His lifework is about proving the importance of the December 21, 2012 calendar end-date, its relationship with what he deems a rare galactic conjunction that will occur on that date, and how this proves that the Maya were aware of the "precession of the equinoxes" (see **Chapter 3** for a full explanation). Other Mayanists, such as Dr. Anthony Aveni and Alonso Mendez who were also interviewed in this book's companion documentary film, *2012: Science or Superstition*, are not so convinced.

A MAYA POINT OF VIEW

Alonso Mendez has been working at the Palenque site for almost a decade, helping to decode the stele and to map the site. He was born in the highlands of Chiapas, of *Tzeltal* Maya heritage and his mother worked as a secretary for renowned explorer and archaeologist Frans Blom in the 1970s. Mendez grew up surrounded by anthropologists, botanists and ethnographers and he went to high school and college in the United States before returning to Mexico with his wife. He disagrees with Jenkins' view that the ancient Maya were aware of the Milky Way Galaxy and that the end-date was timed to correspond with a "galactic alignment."

Mendez has been involved in very interesting discoveries about astronomical events relating to the start-date of the 13-*b'ak'tun* cycle. On August 11, 3114 BCE, the Sun crossed the zenith of the Maya skies and at the same time the Orion constellation was in a nadir passage, directly beneath the feet of the ancient Maya.

THE NADIR PASSAGE

"Orion was coincidently passing through the center of the Underworld, with one of its principal stars of Orion's Belt as the marker of the center of the Underworld ... [this] may explain one of these primordial axes and concepts of an axis being dedicated on that primordial date. The constellation of Orion does play an integral part in the creation mythology, as the center of the sky. The axial relationship between the zenith and the nadir now functioned as a kind of conduit, if you will, between these three distinct realms [Heaven, Earth, Underworld]."

—Alonso Mendez, On-Camera Interview in *2012: Science or Superstition*

POPOL VUH PREDICTIONS & END-DATE DISPUTES

According to the *Popol Vuh*, we are currently living in the "Fifth Sun" or "Age." The previous World Age ended at the start of a 13th *b'ak 'tun*, on a date numbered 12.19.19.17.19 almost 5,125 years ago. Another 12.19.19.17.19 is coming up on December 20, 2012, followed by the start of the fourteenth *b'ak 'tun*, 13.0.0.0.0, on December 21, 2012.

There is some disagreement among Mayanists about this Gregorian end-date. Two respected academics in this field, archaeologist Michael Coe and epigrapher Linda Schele, both placed the end-date on December 23, 2012, while Swedish author Carl Johan Calleman has very personal ideas about the "acceleration of time" and has placed the Gregorian end-date at October 28, 2011.

John Major Jenkins is perhaps the most vocal supporter of the December 21, 2012 end-date. According to his research, the two-day discrepancy between his count and that of the two respected academics is based on a misconception in the work of Schele's mentor, Floyd Lounsbury. Jenkins adds:

> The misconception was also noted by Dennis Tedlock and Victoria Bricker. I discussed this issue at length in an appendix in *Maya Cosmogenesis 2012*, and it was a primary focus of my book *Tzolkin*. Suffice it to say that December 21, 2012 remains the best candidate for the end-date.[29]

DID PSYCHEDELICS FACILITATE THE MAYA "COSMOVISION"?

"At the site of Izapa, the place where the Long Count calendar was invented, we have two main factors. Besides the invention of the Long Count calendar, and it was also the place that originated the creation mythology, the *Popol Vuh*. There's a third very important factor for understanding how all of this was accomplished that has to do with the use of hallucinogenic plants, vision-producing plants.

"The shamans would avail themselves of these tools of consciousness-expansion in the environment. And in so doing, I believe that it allowed them to see the integrated, whole picture of the universe. In other words, these substances can convey universal insights—very deep, universal insights into the true architecture of the world ...

"This was really a kind of spiritual science for expanding consciousness and perception. The idea was that the person can come into an understanding of the outer universe by venturing within. If you can venture deep within the spiritual psyche and access the universal principles that way, then you can have an understanding of the universe, at large ...

"Izapa really was a kind of New World Eleusis. In the Old World, Eleusis was a place where seekers were initiated into the sacred mysteries. And at Izapa, those seeking knowledge were brought through a process of understanding this new galactic cosmology, because it was at Izapa where the galactic alignment was discovered and put in place with the Long Count calendar pointing to the 2012 end-date, how that was integrated into the creation mythology as a prophecy and a spiritual teaching ...

"Dimethyltryptamine [DMT] is a powerful hallucinogenic that can be harvested from the glands of the *bufo* toad. Stele 6 at Izapa depicts the *bufo* toad, it actually shows the toad's glands with vision scrolls coming out of the glands. This is actually very clear proof that they were aware of the vision-producing effects of the gland secretions ... Izapa was an initiatory center that utilized hallucinogenic plants and substances, in order to facilitate expansion of consciousness so that larger perspectives could be embraced."

—John Major Jenkins, On-Camera Interview in *2012: Science or Superstition*

SHOULD THE U.S. PRESIDENT TAKE PSYCHEDELICS?

"I believe that our spiritual leaders and our political leaders should be practiced in being able to access Universal Wisdom. And if utilizing a sacred plant is a way to do that, I would definitely advocate that. In my book, *Maya Cosmogenesis 2012*, I tongue-in-cheek suggested that the president of the United States should take hallucinogenic mushrooms eight hours before giving the State of the Union address. The idea here is that political power in the Earthly sphere should come packaged with direct spiritual insight.

"In other words, there should be an interest in having the whole picture involved in decision-making. It's so easy for consciousness to get wrapped up in the concerns of individual ego, the self-serving concerns of ego, when it does not have recourse to having a direct experience of one's relationship to the Whole.

"And shamans for thousands and thousands of years, certainly longer than our own science has been around, have been using sacred plants in the environment as tools for accessing this kind of Unity Consciousness.

"So yes definitely, our political and spiritual leadership today are

> often simply mouthpieces for an exoteric dogmatic religion. The problem here is that all religions have at their root a direct spiritual revelation, you might say. But through the ensuing centuries that direct spiritual revelation gets lost and instead the religion becomes a system of codified rules that are often designed to control people."
>
> —John Major Jenkins, On-Camera Interview in *2012: Science or Superstition*

HARD EVIDENCE: 2012 WAS SIGNIFICANT TO THE ANCIENT MAYA

Aside from engineering it to be the end-date in their 5,125-year, 13-*b'ak'tun* epoch, which signified a cycle of creation, destruction and the recreation of mankind, there is also a carving on Monument 6 at the archaeological site at Tortuguero in Mexico. It contains a partially decoded reference to the 2012 end-date in conjunction with the deity called *Bolon Yokte K'u*. This deity is associated with war, conflict, and the Maya "Underworlds" of night-time and death. *Bolon Yokte* is also a god who is often present during "creation events," so we could deduce from this that 2012 was thought of by the Maya as a creation or recreation of the world, likely during a time of war, conflict and death.[30]

CHAPTER THREE

The Precession of the Equinoxes & Cosmic Interlopers

"We might envision that over this great 26,000-year period that there are seasons ... This is an insight into this larger cycle and how it actually does affect Earth phenomena, including life on Earth."

—John Major Jenkins, On-Camera Interview in *2012: Science or Superstition*

THE DOMINANT "WOBBLE" THEORY

If we could film the Earth from a geosynchronous satellite for thousands of years in time-lapse photography and then play back the footage in fast motion, the Earth would look like a spinning top, with a teetering wobble. From the Earth's surface, the visual byproduct of this wobble is a slow shifting of background stars in the night sky, at a rate of 1° every 72 years. The "wobble" takes a total of 26,000 years to complete. An accepted cause of this wobble are the complex gravitational workings of the Moon and the Sun or the "lunisolar" forces upon the Earth's movements, creating oscillations in Earth's elliptical orbit around the Sun (from zero to 5° in a roughly 100,000-year cycle), as well as oscillations in Earth's axial tilt or "obliquity," (from 21.5° to 24.5° in a 41,000-year cycle). This interplay of lunisolar forces has resulted in the "Milankovitch cycles" of changes in the Earth's climate and is theorized to be the cause of the Earth's cyclical Ice Ages.

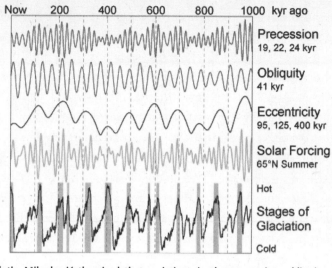

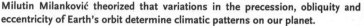

Milutin Milanković theorized that variations in the precession, obliquity and eccentricity of Earth's orbit determine climatic patterns on our planet.

For example, the Northern Hemisphere is currently experiencing less contrast in summer and winter temperatures, with the opposite being the case in the Southern Hemisphere because Earth is currently in a cycle of perihelion (closest to the Sun in its eccentric orbit) during the Northern winter and at its aphelion (furthest from the Sun) during the Northern summer. In roughly 13,000 years, the situation will be reversed and seasonal extremes in the Northern Hemisphere will be exacerbated by Earth's position in it cycle of eccentricity. There are additional complexities in Earth-Sun motions, including a slow rotation of the orbit of the Earth itself about once every four precession cycles. This creates shorter precessional cycles of 19,000 and 24,000 years that average out to 22,000 years. This is the generally accepted view.

Because precession is so gradual, in order for a culture to be aware of it requires two or three generation's worth of good astronomical observations—and good calculations based on those observations. In the West, the ancient Greek astronomer Hipparchus is generally credited with discovering precession in the 2nd century BCE, though there is some debate that another Greek had discovered precession in the previous century. Hipparchus accomplished this by comparing his own observations of the brightest stars in the sky with those of two Greek astronomers who lived before him, one- and two-hundred years respectively, leading him to calculate that the full 360°-cycle of precession of the sky above would take approximately 36,000 years— over 10,000 years longer than has since been determined.

In the view of the modern scientific establishment, knowledge of this cycle was not achieved prior to the Greeks of Hipparchus' time. It should also be pointed out that Hipparchus' understanding of precession was geocentric, as all astronomers at that time still believed that Earth was motionless and that the celestial sphere was moving above them.

DID THE ANCIENTS KNOW ABOUT PRECESSION?

Western astrology is based on the ancient Babylonian system, developed in the 2nd millennium BCE, which divided the precession of the equinoxes initially into thirteen and later to the twelve signs of the zodiac, with "ages" of about 2,000 years each. I believe that this would adequately prove the Babylonians' knowledge of precession. The ancient Egyptians moved the temples at Karnak, as the stars drifted out of the strict alignments in which they had been carefully erected, but as Jenkins notes this kind of "evidence is ultimately deemed 'circumstantial' by hard-core empiricists," [31] because it technically only proves that they'd noticed that the stars had shifted.

The Egyptians did, however keep accurate calendars and it can be argued that if they'd recorded the dates of temple reconstructions, it would have been simple enough to determine the rate of precession. Officially, no ancient Egyptian astronomical texts specifying knowledge of the precession of the equinoxes have been found.

HAMLET'S MILL

Hamlet's Mill was a seminal book first published in 1969, written by Giorgio de Santillana, a professor of the history of science at MIT, and Hertha von Dechend, a scientist at Johann Wolfgang Goethe University in Germany. Though initially scorned by academics, it became an influential book in anthropology and archaeo-astronomy.

Hamlet's Mill proposes that many of the stories of ancient mythology are a coded priestly language for expressing astronomical observations and knowledge. The book also proposes that the precession of the equinoxes was discovered long before the accepted date of the Greek discovery, perhaps as early as 4000 BCE. The authors do not identify the original discoverers except to say that the civilization was of "unsuspected sophistication." The authors suggest that the ancients held the belief that the rise and fall of civilizations and of human achievement were inextricably related to the precession of the equinoxes. The authors propose that ancient mythology both encodes this astronomical knowledge and symbolically transmits this belief through the mythical archetype of the "hero's journey." [32]

Mayanist John Major Jenkins was very influenced by *Hamlet's Mill* and the premise of his own book, *Cosmogenesis 2012: The True Meaning of the Maya Calendar End-Date*, is that:

> Precession was at the foundation of cosmological and calendric science in Mesoamerica ... the Mayan Long Count calendar, which ends in 2012 AD, highlights a precession-related alignment between the Solstice Sun and the Milky Way. [33]

Jenkins says that knowledge of precession is also expressed in one of the central myths in the *Popol Vuh* of the ancient Maya, that of the Hero Twins and their father, *Hun-Hunahpú*.

PRECESSIONAL MYTH OF THE HERO TWINS & *HUN-HUNAHPÚ*

"The Hero Twin myth is about the fall and resurrection of the father, *Hun-Hunahpú*. *Hun-Hunahpú* did battle with the Lords of Darkness and he was tricked and his head was cut off ... he got disconnected from his Wholeness. *Hun-Hunahpú* represents the December solstice Sun, so it's basically a metaphor for the death and resurrection of the December solstice Sun Lord.

"This makes sense because the December solstice is that day of the year that ends the previous year and begins the New Year, so it is like a day of death and rebirth.

"However, it's really a precessional myth because for many hundreds of years, the December solstice Sun has been shifting ... very slowly towards the 'Rebirth Place' in the sky. The Rebirth Place in the sky is the Dark Rift in the Milky Way at the celestial crossroads, the 'Sacred Tree.'

"These features are also encoded into the Maya creation mythology. For example, the Dark Rift is called the *Xibalba Be*', the 'Road to the Underworld.' *Hun-Hunahpú* takes that 'Road to the Underworld,' when he does battle with the Lords of Darkness and he dies.

"At the end of the Maya creation mythology, the Hero Twins are successful in facilitating the demise of the Lords of Darkness, and then they resurrect their father, *Hun-Hunahpú*. When he's resurrected he reappears into his Wholeness through the Rebirth Place in the sky, which is the Dark Rift in the Milky Way. The entire creation mythology is a metaphor for the astronomical galactic alignment that culminates in the years around 2012."

—John Major Jenkins, On-Camera Interview in *2012: Science or Superstition*

Author Graham Hancock similarly believes the ancient Maya looked way into the future to our current epoch. He says this is suggested by the alignment of the stunning pyramid at Chichén-Itzá, which points to a zenithal conjunction of the Pleiades constellation exactly and only during the 2012 time period.

CHICHÉN-ITZÁ & THE PLEIADES

"At the pyramid of *K'ulk'ulkan* at Chichén-Itzá, there are 363 days of a year when you can visit it and see nothing particularly special happening. But on two days, the spring equinox and the autumn equinox, 21st of March and 21st of September in our calendar, you discover that the pyramid is so perfectly positioned on the ground that it creates a shadow effect with the Sun, at that time only, which produces the appearance of a gigantic serpent undulating up and down the north stairway of the monument.

"Clearly, they were drawing our attention to that particular time of year, the spring and the autumn equinoxes ... [were] regarded as most important. The cleverness of Mayan astronomy is that vertically above the apex of the pyramids in our time—and our time only—60 days after the spring equinox, it's as though that serpent effect on the northern staircase is to alert you to something else that is coming.

"60 days later, the Pleiades, which was a very significant constellation in Maya astronomy, sits directly overhead the apex of the pyramid in our epoch. Not in any previous epoch. So again, it's like a signal that is drawing our attention to our own time using the universal language of astronomy and the positioning of monuments to bring about that effect."

—Graham Hancock, On-Camera Interview in *2012: Science or Superstition*

Dr. Anthony Aveni, professor of astronomy and anthropology, takes the strict scientific view of such things:

KNOWLEDGE OF PRECESSION REFLECTED IN MAYA CODICES?

"Could these ancient cultures have known about the precession of the equinoxes? I might sound like our ex-President Clinton by saying it depends what you mean by 'known' ... is there evidence in the codices, in the alignments, even in the mythology that they were aware of or concerned about a 26,000 year period? My answer would be no."

—Dr. Anthony Aveni, On-Camera Interview in *2012: Science or Superstition*

FINGERPRINTS OF THE GODS & MESSAGE OF THE SPHINX

Like the authors of *Hamlet's Mill*, Graham Hancock ascribes a much greater antiquity to human civilization than is generally accepted. He is a big promoter of the idea that vital astronomical information was encoded not only in the myths of the ancients but also in the construction of temples, such as the Giza complex in Egypt with its three pyramids and the Sphinx.

In his book *Fingerprints of the Gods*, Hancock proposes that an as-yet unidentified, pre-historic civilization was the common ancestor of all ancient historical civilizations, who were given profound knowledge about astronomy, architecture and mathematics sometime after the end of the last Ice Age. The evidence or "fingerprints" of this are reflected in the ancient traditions one finds on every continent that feature "teacher-deities," as exemplified by Quetzalcoatl, Hermes, Thoth and Oannes, among many others.

In Hancock's collaboration with engineer turned bestselling

author Robert Bauval, *The Message of the Sphinx,* they propose that the Sphinx was originally constructed as long ago as 10,500 BCE according to their astronomical software, which was programmed to display the celestial sphere at any given date. Their claim about the Sphinx was supported to some extent by the statements of geologist Robert Schoch, who determined that the erosion patterns on the Sphinx were caused by prolonged exposure to rainfall:

> Though we continue to refine our knowledge of the details of the paleoclimatic history of the Giza Plateau over the last 10,000 years, we already know enough to associate certain dominant modes of weathering with certain parts of that climatic history.[34]

Schoch gave the date for its original construction at 7000–5000 BCE, which is significantly older than the 4,500-year age generally espoused by Egyptologists.

Using computer simulations of the ancient skies, Hancock and Bauval built on the latter's earlier work in his bestselling book *The Orion Mystery.* The "Orion Correlation theory," as it became known, proposes that the pyramids were built to represent the arrangement of the three stars of Orion's Belt during the vernal equinox in the skies of the era around 10,500 BCE. They proposed that this specific era represented *Zep Tepi,* or the "first time," that is constantly referenced in Egyptian hieroglyphics.

Professional archaeologists dismiss their work, claiming there is no evidence supporting the existence of a great civilization in 10,500 BCE. The astronomical claims of Bauval and Hancock were completely savaged by Ed Krupp of the Griffith Observatory in Los Angeles and Anthony Fairall, professor of astronomy at the University of Cape Town, South Africa[35] on BBC2's 1999 show, "Horizon: Atlantis Uncovered and Atlantis Reborn."

BATTLE WITH THE STATUS QUO

In fact, their on-air treatment was so egregious that a year later, in November 2000, Hancock and Bauval succeeded in getting the UK's Broadcasting Standards Commission to make a judgment against BBC2, as:

> Guilty of unfairly representing alternative history authors Graham Hancock and Robert Bauval in a programme broadcast in November of last year ... Krupp's criticism was also rejected by two prominent British astronomers, Dr. Percy Seymour of Plymouth University and Dr. Archie Roy, professor emeritus at Glasgow University. But neither of these astronomers was given an opportunity to appear on the programme. Moreover, the programme-makers cut out Hancock's and Bauval's own rebuttals of Krupp from the documentary. Consequently, "the Commission considers that the omission of Mr. Hancock's arguments was not justified. It therefore finds that this was unfair to Mr. Hancock." Likewise, "as the originator of the Giza-Orion correlation theory, Mr. Bauval had a reasonable expectation that his own views of Dr. Krupp's argument would be included. They were not, and the Commission finds that this was unfair to Mr. Bauval." [36]

Incredibly, BBC2 took the unprecedented step of broadcasting a re-edited and corrected version of the documentary the month following the verdict.

GRAHAM HANCOCK: CHAMPION OF UNORTHODOX VIEWS

Hancock's popularity stems not only from his phenomenal gifts of articulation and storytelling but also from his keen sense of where the hot buttons are in the various disciplines of science—and he presses them! He has coaxed the kind of debates and controversies around his material and has known how to stand his ground, generating loads of publicity and selling lots of books. Hancock sees himself as providing a counterbalance to what he perceives as the "unquestioned" acceptance and support given to orthodox views by the educational systems, the media, and by society at large.

For example Hancock makes a big point of giving credence to the scientifically-unpopular Earth crustal displacement theory (which we discuss further in **Chapter 5**), as he writes on his personal website, "a massive one-piece displacement of the Earth's crust, is a very plausible explanation of the worldwide cataclysm that did indeed occur."[37] Well, them's fightin' words, in the view of modern geophysics! Hancock mitigates this statement with his subsequent avowal of the more accepted possibility that meteor or comet impacts during that time are "strong contenders for the mysterious cataclysmic agency that ended the Ice Age." Personally, Earth crustal displacement only makes sense to me if it involves an impact by something really big, that's moving at a very high speed, as proposed in 1999 by Italian naval engineer, Dr. Flavio Barbiero, and restated very convincingly in his 2006 article on Hancock's site.[38]

"ATLANTIS-IN-ANTARCTICA"

Hancock is unbowed in his support for the viability of another theory that is controversial on three counts: that the lost continent of Atlantis (A) existed; (B) corresponds with what is today known as Antarctica; and (C) was moved from its former geographic coordinates by means of scientifically "discredited" Earth crustal displacement.

In their book *When the Sky Fell*, authors Rand and Rose Flem-Ath advance the theory that the legendary continent of Atlantis was previously located in a temperate Antarctica, at a time when there was also more land above sea level, as sea levels have since risen 400 ft. globally due to the melting of polar ice. This idea was based on Charles

Hapgood's "pole shift" theory, which is really a theory of Earth crustal displacement. Hapgood names several geographic coordinates where the land masses at Earth's rotational axis of the poles had rapidly "wandered," the last movement occurring at the end of the last Ice Age, when the entire surface of the Earth quickly slipped. The land formerly sitting at the rotational axis of the North Pole shifted to what is now Hudson Bay, at 60°N 83°W. On the Flem-Ath's site, there is a calculator where you can find the "Atlantean" latitudes and longitudes for present day locations, to see if they are close to sites that the Flem-Aths allege were important to the Atlanteans.

The Flem-Aths point to the evidence showing that Siberia and its polar opposite or "antipodes," Antarctica, were previously located at more temperate latitudes before they were abruptly shifted into their current polar positions and turned into frozen wastelands. The Flem-Aths make a persuasive, though not necessarily bulletproof, case for this with the graphics on their website.[39] It is certainly well worth a look and a fun thought experiment, if nothing else. A revised and expanded ebook edition of *When The Sky Fell* is being released in 2009.

This map shows the antipodes of each point on the Earth's surface—the points where the light and dark overlap are land antipodes—most land has its antipodes in the ocean.

For his part, Hancock says, "I believed then, and believe still, that the Flem-Aths' ["Atlantis–in-Antarctica"] theory is a ground-breaking one and that it is immensely important to any proper consideration of the possibility that there may have been a lost civilization."[40] The Flem-Aths propose that the few survivors of the cataclysm in Antarctica went on to inform the Sumerian, Egyptian, Olmec and Maya cultures, accounting for their many commonalities, such as pyramid construction, astronomy, divinatory priesthoods, etc.

Hancock's content-rich website—with a really good search engine—is full of persuasive alternative science articles that challenge mainstream views in geophysics and archaeology, along with other interesting developments in science news.

FLASH-FROZEN MAMMOTHS

It is commonly known that during the last Ice Age, while northern Europe and North America were covered with glacial ice caps, Siberia was not glaciated and was heavily populated with several different kinds of megafauna, including the European woolly rhinoceros—and five distinct species of mammoth. Millions upon millions of megafauna fossils, bones and well-preserved fleshy remains have been found "flash-frozen" in Siberia, such as the baby woolly mammoth discovered in May of 2007:

> The 4-foot gray-and-brown carcass, **believed to be between 40,000 and 10,000 years old**, was discovered in May by a reindeer herder in the subarctic Yamal-Nenets region.

> It has **its trunk and eyes virtually intact** and even some fur remaining, said Alexei Tikhonov, deputy director of the Russian Academy of Sciences' Zoological Institute.[41]

When one considers that the daily nutritional requirement for a small-ish adult 6-ton mammoth was roughly 400 lbs. per day, one wonders what could have sustained five different species of mammoth in a vegetation-weak tundra environment for almost 5 million years—unless conditions during the Pliocene and Pleistocene were more temperate and there were more trees for the mammoths to eat.

The staggering preponderance of frozen, rather than fossilized mammoth and other megafaunal remains in Siberia has opened my mind to the possibility that there might have been some kind of shift in Earth's axial tilt at the end of the last Ice Age, but I haven't found a single scientific authority supporting this idea.

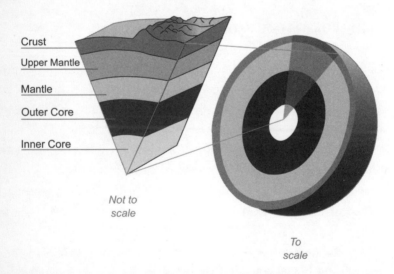

Cutaway views showing the widely-accepted, mainstream view of the Earth's internal structure. Above left: A view not drawn to scale to show its three main layers (crust, mantle, and core) in detail. Above right: This view drawn to scale illustrates that Earth's crust literally is only skin deep.

FEAR & LOATHING OF EARTH CRUSTAL DISPLACEMENT

Innumerable impact scenarios have been advanced to explain the existing evidence for global catastrophe at the end of the Pleistocene epoch. The most contentious explanations, however, all include the idea that there was a catastrophic, mass slippage of Earth's entire crust.

In **Chapter 5**, I interview a respected geophysicist, Bernhard Steinberger, who specializes in the movements of the Earth's crust, which is called "true polar wander" in the business. TPW involves the movement of the entire lithosphere, whereas continental drift describes the movement of individual continents (which move in different directions). Based on his years of study in this field, Steinberger holds the view of accepted, mainstream geophysics, that the rate of TPW does not exceed 1° every million years. Proponents of Earth crustal displacement, on the other hand, believe that movements of 30° have regularly taken place over the course of a day or as "long" as a week, with unimaginably cataclysmic effects for those living at certain latitudes and especially for those living near large bodies of water, where they would get creamed by the massive inertial "slosh."

Earth crustal displacement, which some would contend is a suppressed theory, may be the biggest source of fear mongering associated with 2012. The images of a great ocean sloshing over the Himalayas in the preview for Roland Emmerich's film is a depiction of the topsy-turvy weirdness that one would witness in the hypothetical event of Earth crustal displacement. However, people whose intelligence I respect insist that new discoveries about the makeup of Earth's crust and of the instability of Earth's inner mantle strongly support Charles Hapgood's Earth crustal displacement theory.

Canadian science blogger A. Robert Clein claims that subducted slabs of Earth's crust are composed of graphene, better known as pencil lead, which is used in pencils precisely because of its properties of slipperiness under pressure, as it leaves behind one-atom-thick "sheets" of itself.

Logically ... a complete movement of the crust can only occur if it is possible for a layer to exist whose viscosity approaches zero or whose contact layer exhibits friction approaching zero ... This deal breaker problem became resolvable when I began to take an interest in the properties of elemental carbon. Recent discoveries regarding graphene have allowed us to become even more confident ...

Fundamental to this conjecture is that carbon has the highest melting point of any element ... That means that unmelted carbon can be dragged down to a melt layer below all the crust yet to just above the metallic core ... The bulk of [a subducted slab] is likely in the form of graphene, now that we know that exists. **This layer does have a viscosity approaching zero ...**

Therefore, our conjecture that the moderately unbalanced crust will respond to a nudge in the right direction appears to be well founded ... **That it shifted thirty degrees is necessary to resolve a range of logical impossibilities in the geological record ...** [42]

WHEN THE EARTH NEARLY DIED

When the Earth Nearly Died: Compelling Evidence of Catastrophic World Change in 9500 BC is a book describing how Earth crustal displacement, among other disasters, occurred in the not-too-distant past. Barbara Hand Clow's company republished the book in 1997 and it's been endorsed by the Flem-Aths. Written by Derek S. Allan, a researcher specializing in paleogeography, and J. Bernard Delair, a geological surveyor,[43] it describes a cosmic catastrophe for which they found written evidence on an ancient Akkadian cylinder, referring to a cosmic interloper called "Marduk."

The ancient cylinder describes how Marduk initially crashed into a planet formerly located between the orbits of Mars and Jupiter, which the Mesopotamians called "Tiamat." This planet was completely shattered, creating what is today the asteroid belt. Marduk continued careening sunwards, dragging a trail of Tiamat's debris, as well as that of its satellite, nearly destroying both Mars and Earth, with collateral bombardments.

Marduk, which the authors refer to as "Phaëton" was no ordinary comet. They conjecture that it must have had an extremely intense electromagnetic field in order to be capable of such destruction and that it was most likely a high-velocity stellar fragment from the Vela Supernova explosion.

According to Allan and Delair, the terrestrial impact of this stellar fragment was so powerful that it altered Earth's rotational axis and caused massive crustal displacements, creating the great mountain ranges of today, in addition to enormous seismic and volcanic eruptions, the rearrangement of the coastlines and the Pleistocene mass extinction.

The face of the Earth was completely changed, violently, rapidly and comparatively recently. This scenario offers a possible explanation for the many mythological references to the former "Eternal Spring" of the Golden Age. Relatively unchanging global weather conditions would be the result of a previously perpendicular or near-perpendicular alignment of Earth's rotational axis.

PAUL LAVIOLETTE'S "GALACTIC SUPERWAVES"

Physicist Paul LaViolette believes that the melting of the polar ice caps and the extinction of the megafauna around 16,000–12,000 BP (Before Present) was caused by a cyclical gamma ray burst from our Galaxy's core, which resulted in a "nuclear winter" of darkness, freezing cold, severe solar storms, periodic heat and cataclysmic floods that were the scourge of humanity for several generations. He reckons that these "galactic superwaves" occur in 10,000-year cycles and he deadpans, "It is estimated that approximately one or two superwaves strong enough to trigger an Ice Age are presently on their way to us from their birth place 23,000 light-years away. There is a finite chance that one such event could arrive within the next few decades." [44]

LaViolette sees a connection between the December 26, 2004 Indonesian Earthquake/Tsunami and the incident of the brightest gamma ray burst (GRB) ever recorded at the time, which emanated from a "soft gamma ray repeater" star in our Galaxy, SGR 1806-20. He says that although the light from this GRB was detected 44.6 hours after the earthquake, that the gravity wave from the GRB may have reached Earth at "a superluminal speed." [45]

He asserts that gamma ray bursts or "superwaves" are preceded by powerful gravity waves, which "during their passage ... could induce earthquakes and cause polar axis-torquing effects," which he describes at length in his Ph.D. dissertation and in his book, *Earth Under Fire*.

BARBARA HAND CLOW: PROBLEMS WITH QUATERNARY HISTORY

Barbara Hand Clow is the writer and publisher of some of the most influential New Age books over the past twenty years. Though Clow acquires some of her material from psychic "channeling," one might be surprised to learn that Clow is in agreement with mainstream paleontology. Where Clow diverges from the mainstream is in her view of history over the past 15,000 years:

> During my entire life, I've watched science try to avoid looking at the recent and most important cataclysm, the Pleistocene Extinction. Instead, they focus on extinctions way into the past,

such as the demise of the dinosaurs 65 million years ago. Maybe this is because we know that hunter-gatherers wandered Earth 11,500 years ago. That is, we resist knowing about the recent cataclysm because humans experienced the nearly complete annihilation of life on Earth. Evidence of this catastrophe lies in the intact frozen bodies of oxen, bison, horses, sheep, tigers, lions, hairy mammoths, and woolly rhinoceroses found interred in the Sibero-Alaskan permafrost ... [46]

Clow believes that there was a cataclysmic extraterrestrial impact at the end of the last Ice Age. She agrees with Allan and Delair that "the Monster," as she calls it, was a fragment of stellar material from the Vela Supernova (the timing for a possible arrival of a stellar fragment from Vela to Earth is around 9500 BCE). She says the results of this impact were absolutely brutal, "the Earth's lithosphere was dislocated both vertically and horizontally and tectonic plates formed that caused the planet to become a polyhedron of twenty faces—an *icosahedron* ..." [47]

Clow believes that a driving factor in modern humanity's mindless destruction of the ecosphere has to do with the incredible trauma of this 9500 BCE impact event. Trauma which she believes is still locked in our DNA and/or past-life memories, blocking our view of that era as well as preventing the spiritual/psychological/cultural integration of those events, which is the subject of her book, *Catastrophobia*.

The "Man vs. Nature" theme that has dominated much of Western literature may have, at its core, the frantic experience of going from a Golden Age of "Eternal Spring" to one where Earth's surface was covered in a holocaustal mélange of decaying marine and land animal body parts, piled up as far as the eye could see and stinking to high heaven.

THE #1 WOO-WOO EXPLANATION ...

Astrologer, author, lecturer and Internet phenomenon Michael Tsarion believes the story was actually much more involved:

> The answer lies in the ancient records of our forefathers and in the myths and legends of the pre- and post-diluvian epochs, that speak of the visitation of the "gods" or "angels" ... [who] instigated a hybridization program lasting centuries. Their genetic interference of the Earth Races resulted in several hybrid creatures, one of whom I will refer to as *Homo Atlantis.*" ... **Its greatest proof, one can argue, lies in the mysteriously destructive behavior that we, modern humans, have adopted toward our own home planet, the animal kingdom and the indigenous peoples who have lived in relative harmony with the planet.**[48]

Tsarion makes a great point at the end of that statement but his other claims could lead one to suspect that this British subject is courting David Icke's readership. Admittedly, his story is astounding—as are his public speaking abilities. He claims that after failing twice to make faithful servants out of their genetic hybrids, the "gods" grew vengeful and unleashed a nuclear war upon them, which he claims was the actual cause of the Pleistocene extinction and that this event is recorded in several books of the Bible, including Genesis 6–8:

> And the Lord said, I will destroy man whom I have created from the face of the Earth; both man, and beast, and the creeping thing, and the fowls of the air; for it repenteth me that I have made them.

THE GLITCH IN GEOLOGICAL TIME

Geology certainly appears to have an odd relationship with the time period spanning 15,000 to 7000 BP. There is an unresolved academic dispute as to whether or not the Quaternary period, which straddles the time of the first Pleistocene glaciation, through the extinction of the megafauna, to the present should be classified as a geologic "epoch" or an "era."

Like Graham Hancock and others whose works we've discussed, Barbara Hand Clow believes that until around 9500 BCE, the Earth was host to a global civilization that was more technologically advanced than that of today.

> ... most ... do not pay enough attention to what the 9500 BC cataclysm did to the global civilization, creating conditions where survival was precarious and often worse than death. Even though three writers are sure (as am I) that humanity was once more advanced, they don't provide for ... the massive regression of civilization, because they don't use 9500 BC as a dichotomy in the timeline. Without this divider, it is much more difficult to see what was happening: *We need to comprehend the regression of our own species, or humanity will commit ecocide.*[49]

Clow proposes that these three separate disasters have been conflated in modern memory into a single "Great Deluge": 1. The 9500 BCE impact event; 2. The 5600 BCE Black Sea cataclysmic flood and 3. The 4000 BCE "Noah's Flood" of the Tigris and Euphrates. Clow believes it is very important to distinguish these calamities as separate events, so that we may better understand our own history and the realities of life on Earth.

JOHN MAJOR JENKINS' *GALACTIC ALIGNMENT*

As we've discussed, John Major Jenkins' central claim is that the ancient Maya carefully designed the 13-*b'ak'tun* cycle of their Long Count calendar so that it would roll over to begin the next age during the December solstice of 2012, which he says coincides with a solar alignment with the galactic center or what he says the Maya called the "Rebirth Place" in the sky. Jenkins claims that the Maya would only have been able to calculate this alignment by having full knowledge of the precession of the equinoxes, which he claims was known to the ancient Maya at least 2,300 years ago.

In his book, *Galactic Alignment: The Transformation of Consciousness According to Mayan, Egyptian and Vedic Traditions*, Jenkins introduces us to Sri Yukteswar, the early 20th century Indian Kriya Yoga guru who wrote *Holy Science*, published in 1894. In this book, Sri Yukteswar proposed replacing the traditional Hindu calendar with one that is based on our Sun's 24,000-year orbit around a companion star, making Sri Yukteswar perhaps the first person in modern times to allege that our Sun is part of a binary star system. Moreover, Yukteswar claimed that it is this binary orbit that is responsible for what is perceived from the surface of Earth to be the precession of the equinoxes—not a subtle wobble of the Earth caused by lunisolar forces, as mainstream science would have us believe.

... the Sun, with its planets and their moons, **takes some star for its dual and revolves around it in about 24,000 years of our Earth**—a celestial phenomenon which causes the backward movement of the equinoctial points around the zodiac. The Sun also has another motion by which it revolves round a grand center called *Vishnunabhi*, which is the seat of the creative power, Brahma, the universal magnetism. Brahma regulates dharma, the mental virtue of the internal world.[50]

Sri Yukteswar is saying a mouthful here. Not only is he suggesting that our solar system is part of a binary star system, he says we are also orbiting around the galactic center and/or the center of the universe and that our orbital position with respect to "the seat of the creative power" has a direct relationship with our inner lives and with the manner in which we are expressed, as civilizations and as individuals.

BINARY STAR THEORY

Research into Sri Yukteswar's proposal is currently being conducted by the Binary Research Institute, founded by Walter Cruttenden, author of the book *Lost Star of Myth and Time* and writer/producer of a documentary on the topic entitled *The Great Year,* narrated by James Earl Jones.

PRECESSION: NOT A LOCAL "WOBBLE"; A GRAND ELLIPSE THROUGH THE HEAVENS

"The new explanation [for precession] is it's not a wobble on the axis of the Earth, they're suggesting that our Sun revolves around a companion star. Like 80% of all the stars in the heavens, our Sun is in a binary system and therefore is on a great orbit through the heavens and dragging, of course all the planets with it. That journey through the heavens would produce exactly the same observable effects of the changing positions of the stars down through the ages."

—Graham Hancock, On-Camera Interview in *2012: Science or Superstition*

THE "NEMESIS THEORY": OUR SUN'S EVIL TWIN

Research between the early 1800s and today suggests that many stars are part of either binary star systems or star systems with more than two stars, called multiple star systems. A binary star system consists of two stars orbiting around their common center of mass. The brighter star is called the "primary" and the other is its "companion" or "secondary."

Speculation about the existence of a mysterious twin to our own Sun abounds. The twin is thought to be a brown dwarf, a "substar" that is too low in mass to sustain stable hydrogen fusion. Brown dwarfs are difficult to find, as they emit almost no light and have cool outer atmospheres. Their strongest emissions are in the infrared spectrum and their composition is characterized by the presence of lithium and sometimes methane.

Walter Cruttenden at the Binary Reasearch Institute, Professor Richard Muller at UC Berkeley and Dr. Daniel Whitmire of the University of Louisiana, amongst several others, have long speculated on the possibility that our Sun might have an as-yet undiscovered small companion with a highly elliptical orbit.

In 1983, Richard Muller, prompted by his guru at UC Berkeley, Luis Alvarez, came up with the "Nemesis theory" that a brown dwarf companion to our Sun makes its closest approach to the edge of our solar system every 26 million years, perturbing the orbits of the comets in the Oort cloud, sending them in our direction and accounting for the regular intervals of mass extinctions on Earth. Daniel Whitmire had simultaneously come to a similar conclusion with computer scientist Albert Jackson, as did New York University's Michael Rampino. (More on the 1998 "Shiva Hypothesis," billed as a "unifying concept in Earth sciences," in **Chapter 5.**)

Whitmire is co-author with John J. Matese of the 1999 peer-reviewed paper, "Cometary evidence of a massive body in the outer Oort cloud,"[51] which notes the anomalous distribution and behaviors of comets at the edge of our solar system and predicts a brown dwarf "perturber" at a distance from Earth of approximately 25,000 AU (Astronomical Units), which "acting in concert with the galactic tide" is causing certain comets to be more easily observable from Earth.

On his website, Whitmire opines that the "perturber" is a "t-dwarf," which is a class of even lower-mass, lower-temperature and lower-luminosity dwarfs than regular brown dwarfs, with the coolest one measured so far at around 388 K or 240 °F, just a bit hotter than a pot of boiling water at sea level.

The 2003 discovery of Sedna, a small planet-like object at the edge of the solar system, was first detected by Cal Tech astronomer Dr. Michael Brown. Cruttenden believes that this may provide indirect physical evidence of a solar companion. Matching the recent findings by Dr. Brown showing that Sedna moves in a highly unusual elliptical orbit, Cruttenden has determined that Sedna moves in resonance with previously published orbital data for a hypothetical companion star.[52] However, the scientific community currently classes Sedna as a dwarf planet, akin to Pluto, due to its size and to the spectral analysis of its composition, which shows that it is a rocky planetoid, rather than a gassy substar.

DOES PRECESSION AFFECT THE EVOLUTION OF CONSCIOUSNESS?

"There are 200-plus myths that talk about this movement of the stars, causing some change in the history of the Earth. And it just seemed that if [precession] is only what modern scholars say it is, just a simple wobbling of the Earth, that it shouldn't be related to any change in history or consciousness. So, we really dug into the Vedic teachings about precession. Which gave us a whole different meaning ... the whole solar system going around another star, we believe is the cause of why we see this precession of the 12 constellations of the zodiac over roughly 24,000 years.

"We believe that the precession cycle is actually closer to 24,000 years rather than 25,669 years, which is the accepted rate. The reason is, if it is due to an orbit, as we suspect and that all orbits conform to Kepler's Laws, they move in a great ellipsis, rather than a circle. That means the bodies speed up when the two masses get closer to each other, when the gravitation is stronger—and then they slow down when they get farther away from each other. The Moon does this, going around the Earth. The Earth does this, as do all the planets, as they go around the Sun. This is just the way that the cosmos works.

"So if precession is the observable aspect of our solar system in motion around another star, it too would have to obey Kepler's Laws and speed up and slow down. We've had really, really good scientific data from the last 100 years, going back to the great Simon Newcomb. He kept precise records of precession and he noticed that it's speeding up every year. Exponentially.

"Therefore, if precession actually takes 26,000 years, then we must be in the slow part of the orbit or far from the companion star right now. So we plotted on a curve what should the precession rate be over this last 100 years, and we came out with the exact curve that we've seen historically. From that, we were able to predict that the precession rate will continue to accelerate ... until we reach a periapsis [the point of least distance of an object from its center of attraction in an elliptical orbit]."

—Walter Cruttenden, On-Camera Interview in *2012: Science or Superstition*

In the interview with Walter Cruttenden for the film *2012: Science or Superstition,* it is clear that Cruttenden's scientific investigation into the undiscovered "companion" star is at least partly driven by his faith in Sri Yukteswar's controversial teachings about the World Age doctrine (which we discuss in **Chapter 4**).

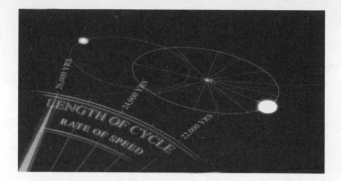

Precession described by means of a proposed binary star for our solar system.

EVIDENCE OF OUR "DARK COMPANION"

Cruttenden presents some compelling evidence that precession is caused by a force outside of our solar system. He argues that if the lunisolar forces play the biggest role in causing Earth's wobble, i.e., the accepted cause of precession, then how come our planet's "wobble" doesn't affect our view of objects *within* the solar system? As Cruttenden explains in an article he wrote for *Atlantis Rising* magazine:

> You would expect the observation date of the Perseids to change at the same rate that the Earth precesses relative to the fixed stars ... at 1° every 72 years, or almost a full week since the Gregorian calendar reform. The Perseids [debris within the solar system that cause yearly meteor showers] should have done the same (relative to the wobbling Earth). This means the shower should now be peaking around August 5 or earlier. But the fact is the Perseids have moved very little if at all in those 423 years ... Why hasn't it precessed through the calendar like everything else outside the solar system?
>
> ... [a] logical conclusion is that we can't measure precession relative to objects within the solar system because ... the major change in orientation that we experience ... is likely not due to

any large wobbling of the axis—but rather the whole Solar System ... gently curving through space ...

If our Sun is part of a binary (or multiple star) system it would be gravitationally bound to a companion star, resulting in the Sun's curved motion through space around a common center of gravity ...

The ancients hinted in their myth and folklore of a lost star and they implied it drove the rise and fall of the ages. If we discover that we are in a binary system, with waxing and waning influences from another star ... we might prove the ancients right![53]

Cruttenden believes that knowledge of our Sun's binary status, like that of so many other things, was lost as a result a of our descent into the *Kali Yuga*, the "Age of Vice" of the Hindu calendar. Cruttenden clearly subscribes to Sri Yukteswar's controversial *yuga* model, so he believes that Earth and its inhabitants are now on an ascending cycle towards greatness, instead of just barely getting started on a 400,000+ year descent into Hell-on-Earth, as luridly described in ancient Hindu texts.

It seems to me that *any* agency that could effect major cyclical climactic changes on our planet, such as Ice Ages, would be sufficient cause for there to have been distinct epochs in both Earth and human history, regardless of whether produced by the lunisolar forces or the tug of a brown dwarf. My "consciousness" would certainly be different right now, if we were in the middle of an Ice Age!

But if it's true that precession is caused by a much grander movement through the cosmos around our companion star, rather than the nervous wobble of our planet, this would endow an even more profound significance to the hundreds of ancient myths from around the world that allegedly demonstrate an understanding of the precession of the equinoxes—and perhaps an even deeper knowledge of the cosmos than that of modern astronomers. These are a lot of big "ifs."

NASA'S WIDE-FIELD INFRARED SURVEY EXPLORER

So far, the technology to detect our hypothetical brown dwarf simply hasn't been there. As Dr. Daniel Whitmire says on his website, "Currently, I am searching the half billion point sources in the 2MASS database for evidence of this object. This survey covered 99% of the sky at near-infrared wavelengths of 1–2 microns. The optimum wavelength for our search is 5 microns but no such full sky survey exists, as yet." [54]

However, there is some cause for excitement, as Whitmire tells us that he, along with UCLA's Ned Wright, will conduct a survey with NASA's new space telescope, the WISE (Wide-field Infrared Survey Explorer), which is scheduled for launch in November 2009. Whitmire is confident that "[t]his instrument should easily detect the conjectured solar companion." So, if the Sun has a little dark companion, we should be able to see it very soon!

Either way, John Major Jenkins' all-important 2012 date will be unaffected by the possible discovery that our Sun might have a secret companion.

BINARY STAR THEORY DOES NOT AFFECT 2012 DATE

"I believe that the thesis put forward by Walter Cruttenden at the Binary Research Institute is very interesting to look at ... this challenges the wobble theory, the idea that the Earth wobbles on its axis. I'm all for open-mindedness in scientific discourse, but it doesn't really matter whether it's the binary star model or the wobble model in terms of the length of precession. We know that the length of precession is basically 26,000 [years]. So it doesn't really affect the thesis of the 2012 end-date. It doesn't affect the location of that date or anything else really about Maya cosmology."

—John Major Jenkins, On-Camera Interview in 2012: *Science or Superstition*

CHAPTER FOUR

World Ages

"So if there was a Golden Age in the past, then the ancient system of ideas would suggest that a full cycle ... would bring us back to that Golden Age again."

—Graham Hancock, On-Camera Interview in *2012: Science or Superstition*

THE WORLD AGE DOCTRINE

There is an idea from antiquity of World Ages that stealthily survives in the West. Anyone with a passing awareness of astrology has been hearing that we're moving out of the Age of Pisces and moving into the Age of Aquarius. The World Age doctrine of Western astrology is based on the precession of the equinoxes. It is therefore cyclical, with each sign of the zodiac dominating the night sky for just over 2,000 years, adding up to a full round of 26,000 years and then starting over again. People who believe in astrology believe that the attendant qualities or "personality traits" of each sign affect the character of society during the 2,000+ years that each sign "rules" the sky.

The main problem with astrology is that there is no agreement about when Pisces ends and Aquarius begins. I've read that the Age of Aquarius began six hundred years ago and elsewhere that it doesn't start for another six hundred years, which averages out to now!

Just for kicks, according to the newspaper astrology column

model, we are moving out of an age that on the upside has been characterized by being imaginative and sensitive, compassionate and kind, selfless and unworldly, intuitive and sympathetic. The downside of the Piscean Age is that it has been escapist and delusional, at risk for alcohol and drug addiction, secretive and vague, weak-willed and easily led. We are presently moving into an age that on the positive side will be characterized by enhanced communication abilities and technologies, friendliness and humanitarianism, independence and intellectualism, originality and inventiveness, desirous of change, utopian, honest and loyal. The negative Aquarian character traits that may crop up to define the coming age are contrariness and tactlessness, perversity and unpredictability, excessively unemotional and unhealthy detachment.

THE SHIFTING AGES

"The shifting points between the ages is really critical and we can look at Western history and notice in the Old Testament period there was an obsession with the Age of Aries, in symbolism around the lamb. At the dawn of the Christian period, there became an obsession with fish symbolism that would signal our shift into the Age of Pisces. In the Western astrological tradition we are about to move out of the sign of Pisces, so there's great talk about the shifting of the age right now. We're at the cusp of the Age of Aquarius. This astrological doctrine has to do with the changing of our angular orientation to the larger cosmos."

—John Major Jenkins, On-Camera Interview in *2012: Science or Superstition*

THE MAYA WORLD AGES

This brief summary of the *Popol Vuh* is derived from the 1950 English translation of Adrián Recinos' 1947 translation of the Ximénez manuscript. The latter is an 18th century phonetic transliteration into the Spanish alphabet of a *K'iche'* Maya text.

> **First World:** In the darkness and in the night, it was decided by the trinity of gods to create human beings to keep them company. The gods' first attempts proved unsuccessful. The myriad animals they created were incapable of speech so they were cursed to be eaten and sacrificed.
>
> **Second World:** The gods then attempted to make man of mud, but this version of man could neither move nor speak and quickly dissolved in water.
>
> **Third World:** After destroying the mud men, they tried again by creating wooden creatures that could speak but these had no soul or blood and did not praise them.
>
> ---
>
> These were the first men who existed in great numbers on the face of the Earth. Immediately the wooden figures were annihilated, destroyed, broken up, and killed. A flood was brought about by the Heart of Heaven; a Great Flood was formed which fell on the heads of the wooden creatures.[55]
>
> ---
>
> The gods destroyed this first "recognizably human" race in a flood and any surviving wooden people were turned into monkeys.
>
> **Fourth World:** In their final attempt, the "True People" were constructed from maize. Their flesh was made of white and yellow corn. The arms and legs of the four men were made of corn meal. But apparently, the gods did *too* good of a job with this version of man. They had the gift of omniscience and expressed genuine gratitude towards their creators for all their god-given talents:

They were endowed with intelligence; they saw and instantly they could see far ... they succeeded in knowing all that there is in the world. When they looked, instantly they saw all around them, and they contemplated in turn the arch of Heaven and the **round face of the Earth.**

The things hidden [in the distance] they saw all, without first having to move; at once they saw the world ... Then they gave thanks to the Creator and the Maker ...

But the Creator and the Maker did not hear this with pleasure. "It is not well what our creatures, our works say; they know all ..." they said. And so the Forefathers held counsel again. "What shall we do with them now? Let their sight reach only to that which is near; let them see only a little of the face of the Earth!" ... "Let us check a little their desires ... Must they perchance be the equals of ourselves, their Makers, who can see afar, who know all and see all?" ... **Then the Heart of Heaven blew mist into their eyes, which clouded their sight as when a mirror is breathed upon. Their eyes were covered and they could see only what was close, only that was clear to them.**

In this way the wisdom and all the knowledge of the [first] four men the origin and beginning [of the K'iche' race], were destroyed.[56]

Generally, the Maya World Ages and the many similar Native American mythologies about successive versions of mankind and/or "worlds" express the sense that each new version of mankind is an improvement upon the previous version, quite the opposite from the World Age myths of Asia and Europe. However, in the *Popol Vuh*, we see that when the latest batch of *K'iche'* Maya turned out to be omniscient, the creator gods saw fit to "dumb them down." This is similar to the way Zeus intentionally created the Silver race to be "inferior in wisdom" to the previous Golden race, which we'll see in a moment. There are many similarities in detail between the Mediterranean World Age doctrines and the Maya version. The eeriest similarity between classical Greek and Mesoamerican accounts is that of the first "recognizably human" beings, who were in both cases fashioned out of wood—and intentionally destroyed by a Great Deluge. The gods giveth and the gods taketh away.

All previous iterations of man have ultimately displeased their capricious creator(s) who've cyclically sought to destroy humanity, in myths that are nearly identical and almost universal. Present-day humans are likewise doomed to suffer total or near-total destruction—by earthquakes, according to the *Popol Vuh* of the Maya and by the Armageddon of Judeo-Christianity—at least, we're hard-wired to believe so, by millennia of religious programming and perhaps by memories locked in our DNA of recurring astrophysical, geophysical and man-made cataclysms—and by the simple fact that we're all going to die, regardless of our Sun's expiration date and the "ultimate fate" of the universe, which we'll discuss further along ...

THE MESSAGE OF THE MAYA

"Could there have been a forgotten episode in human history? Could there have been a lost civilization, as many of the myths of the world speak? I began to find the evidence forcing me to look at a period of about twelve thousand years ago ... we have geological coordinates for this cataclysm, at the end of the last Ice Age ...

"The cataclysm that occurred then, in some way was going to come back. I found that my quest was not only for the beginning of human civilization but also for the end of human civilization. There seemed to be a curious way in which the period of twelve and a half thousand years ago was connected to our epoch today. And certainly in which the ancients seemed to be passing down some kind of warning or message, trying to find a way to speak to us across the ages.

"Taking into account that human civilization would change greatly, that cultures would change, that languages would be lost ... **If it's possible to encode your message by using the changing patterns of the stars, then you might hope that at some distant date, someone else might be able to read that message. And this is when I came across the ancient Maya.**"

—Graham Hancock, On-Camera Interview in *2012: Science or Superstition*

THE FIVE AGES OF ANCIENT GREECE

Hesiod, the ancient Greek poet who lived at the end of the 8th century BCE wrote the epic poem *Works and Days*, in which he makes the first recorded reference to the five successive "ages" or "races" of man in Western history. His account does not refer to the ages as being cyclical. It describes a mostly linear descent from mankind's original exalted, heavenly state, into successively degraded and debased versions of mankind. Here is an extremely brief summary of Hesiod's epic poem:

The Golden Age. Before the time of Zeus, his father Cronus reigned over the Golden Age, when men lived among the gods and there were no rules because everybody did the right thing.

It was always Spring. Peace and harmony prevailed and humans did not have to work to feed themselves; the Earth provided food in abundance. They lived to a very old age but with a youthful appearance and eventually they died peacefully, as if falling asleep. Their spirits were said to live on as "guardians" of the mortals.

The Silver Age. Zeus overthrew his father Cronus and ruled over the Silver Age and subsequent ages. Zeus created the Silver race of man to be inferior in appearance and wisdom to the last. He divided the year into four seasons. Man had to grow his food and seek shelter, but still, their childhoods were long and they could play for a hundred years before growing up. They lived only a short time as grown adults and spent most of that time in strife with one another, due to their childish foolishness. Zeus destroyed this race for refusing to worship the gods. Nonetheless, after death, the Silver race became "blessed spirits" of the Underworld.

The Bronze Age. Zeus created the "first recognizably human" Bronze race from the hardwood of ash trees. War and violence was the purpose and passion of the Bronze race. An odd detail about this race was that they did not "eat bread" (Hesiod doesn't say why). Their weapons, tools and even their homes were forged of bronze. Zeus destroyed this race of men with a Great Flood.

Hesiod says that the nameless spirits of this destroyed Bronze race dwell in the "dank house of Hades." A tiny handful of virtuous people survived, as recounted in the tale of Deucalion, where he and his wife Pyrrha survived the flood by following the instructions of his father, in a story that is basically the same as that of the biblical Noah and his Sumerian counterpart, Utnapishtim in the *Epic of Gilgamesh.*

The Heroic Age. This is the only age that improves upon the age that it follows and it is the only age that does not correspond with any metal. The demigods of this Age fought at Thebes and Troy. When they died, they went to the Elysian Fields, an area of the Underworld that was the final resting place of the virtuous. The Heroic Age frankly seems out of place in this scheme and is apparently a tribute to Homer's epic poem, *The Odyssey.*

The Iron Age. At the time of Hesiod's writing in the 700s BCE, the world was already in the throes of the Iron Age. Earthly existence was one of toil and misery. All manner of evils came into being during this age. Piety and other virtues disappeared and most of the gods who were still left on this Earth abandoned it. It was said that Zeus would destroy this (our) race some day. My favorite detail about the degradation of this age is that "babies will be born with gray hair." (!)

"THE GOLDEN AGE IS A STATE OF CONSCIOUSNESS"

"Beyond being a model of time in which the Golden Age was way back there in the past, we should see this as more of a state of consciousness. The Golden Age is the state of consciousness that can directly perceive the Primordial Tradition, or the Perennial Principles. It's really a question of opening up our consciousness to our true birthright, becoming fully human ... Allowing ourselves to develop into the eternal infinite beings that we are. In a sense, getting back in touch with that eternal source-consciousness that lies at the root of the world."

—John Major Jenkins, On-Camera Interview in *2012: Science or Superstition*

METALLIC AGES IN ROME, IN ARCHAEOLOGY & IN THE BIBLE

The 1st century BCE Roman poet Ovid describes a World Age doctrine that is virtually identical to the classical Greek version in his epic poem *Metamorphoses*, except that there are only four ages because he omits Hesiod's Heroic Age. Ovid's epic poem is a similarly forlorn history of the increasingly degenerated races of mankind, who are successively destroyed by the wrath of Jupiter, the Roman counterpart to Zeus.

If, as many scholars believe, most ancient myths are coded references to celestial events, there are many interesting interpretations one could make of these legends. Mythologist David Talbott takes the radical view that the Golden Age being ruled by Cronus (Saturn) literally means that in prehistoric times Earth was once a satellite of Saturn. Apparently, this myth recurs in many cultures. He has written a book about this subject and a film, *Remembering the End of the World*. A segment called "When Saturn Ruled the World" can be viewed on YouTube. Talbott follows the theories of Immanuel Velikovsky, author of *Worlds in Collision*, who himself raised the possibility that Saturn was Earth's previous "Sun," followed by Jupiter, when Zeus usurped his father's throne to initiate the Silver Age.[57] Not surprisingly, academics from several disciplines ranging from astrophysics to mythology have had a field day with the theories of Velikovsky—however, they sure are fun to think about!

In archaeological terms, the Bronze Age and Iron Age are part of a general timeline of technological development in (mostly) Mediterranean cultures. The Paleolithic, Mesolithic and Neolithic "Stone Ages" were followed by the Bronze and Iron Ages, as knowledge of smelting ores, forging metals and fashioning tools and weapons from these occurred around the same time, in that area. Some cultures outside of the Mediterranean basin developed differently. For example, Sub-Saharan Africa skipped the Bronze Age entirely, developing from stonecutting to working with iron.

In the stories of the Flood of Noah, Sodom and Gomorrah and in the destruction of the Tower of Babel, the Bible describes a God who can be just as "wrathful" as Zeus/Jupiter. The Bible also contains a reference to the four metallic World Ages in the Book of Daniel, where the prophet interprets a dream of Nebuchadnezzar, the King of Babylon, using the same four metals to describe the changing periods of history and the concomitant changing character of mankind during the four ages. The Book of Genesis describes the "Fall of Man" from a life that is carefree in the paradise of Eden into a life of toil and strife, compounded by God's special punishment of painful birth pangs for all future females.

THE GREAT FLOOD IN THE BOOK OF ENOCH

The Book of Enoch was lost to all but the Ethiopian Orthodox Christians until three copies of the Ethiopic (*Ge'ez*) text were brought to London by explorer James Bruce in the 18th century. It describes how a group of angels called the Watchers "begat" offspring with human women, creating a race of Nephilim or giants, who were 11,250 ft. in height, ate everything in sight and turned to cannibalism to sate their giant-sized hunger. The Book of Enoch is very strange, indeed; it's worth a read (free online). In addition to having babies with the Earth women, the Watchers also taught humans various arts and sciences:

Azazel taught men to make swords, and knives, and shields, and breastplates, and made known to them the metals of the Earth and the art of working them, and bracelets, and ornaments, and the use of antimony, and the beautifying of the eyelids, and all kinds of costly stones, and all coloring tinctures ... Semjaza taught enchantments, and root-cuttings, Armaros [taught] the resolving of enchantments, Baraqijal taught astrology, Kokabel the constellations,

Ezeqeel the knowledge of the clouds, Araqiel the signs of the Earth, Shamsiel the signs of the Sun, and Sariel the course of the Moon.[58]

—**The Book of Enoch**

For these deeds, in addition to "fornication," God ordered the Great Flood, where Noah and his family were saved and everyone else bit the big one. Again, like the Maya and Greek gods, the God of Abraham doesn't like it when average folks know too much, at least according to the Book of Enoch.

The idea of giants representing elder or "pre-Adamic" races of man also occurs in Greek mythology, as the Titans, in Celtic mythology, as the Fomorians and in many other cultures around the world, including the next two World Age doctrines that we will be exploring.

THE HINDU WORLD AGE DOCTRINE

The Hindu World Age doctrine shares some startling similarities to the Greek and Roman versions, with its account of man's descent into progressively degenerated levels of expression, sinking from the Age of Gold, to Silver, Bronze and finally, Iron, the same metallic correspondences. At least the Hindu version has a bright side, because it's cyclical and there will always be another Golden Age. It doesn't dead-end at the Iron Age, like the Mediterranean traditions. This is perhaps because Hinduism continues to be practiced in India, as the third largest religion in the world, whereas Greece and Italy converted to Christianity more than 1,500 years ago. Like all Abrahamic faiths, Christianity is not cyclical but linear, which we'll discuss further on.

The Hindu World Age doctrine is described in the sacred texts of the *Puranas* and is linked with a cosmology that is mathematically driven, with never-ending cycles of the creation and destruction of the universe. It is integrated into society by the human connection of incarnating avatars. The smallest creation cycle is called a *Maha Yuga*, equal to 4,320,000 human years and it is subdivided into four ages, whose lengths follow a ratio of 4:3:2:1.

> *Satya Yuga* also called *Krita Yuga* and known as the "Golden Age" or "Age of Truth" lasting 1,728,000 years. *Human beings average 32 ft. in height and have a minimum lifespan of 100,000 years, with death occurring only when willed.* It is an era when virtue reigns supreme.
>
> *Treta Yuga* Also known as the "Silver Age" and lasts 1,296,000 years. *Human beings average 21 ft. in height and they can live up to 10,000 years.* It is an era that is characterized as being three quarters virtue and one-quarter sin.
>
> *Dwapara Yuga* Also known as the "Bronze Age," lasting 864,000 years. *Human beings are over 10 ft. in stature and their life expectancy is 1,000 years.* This era is evenly divided between virtue and sin.
>
> *Kali Yuga* Also known as the "Iron Age," the "Age of Darkness" and the "Age of Vice." We're approximately 5,000 years into it, right now, and it is to last a total of 432,000 years. *Human stature averages 5 ft. 3 in. and the longest life expectancy is between 100 to 120 years.* This era is characterized as being one-quarter virtue and three-quarters sin.

The average height quoted for modern-day people might seem a bit short to many readers but a quick check online showed that globally, the current average height of men is 5 ft. 5 in. and that of women is 5 ft. 1 in., which averages 5 ft. 3 in.[59]—and I was blindly converting these heights from cubits!

THE SECRET DOCTRINE & THE "THREE INNER TANTRAS"

First published in 1888, the phone book-sized, two-part volume *The Secret Doctrine* is divided into *Cosmogenesis* and *Anthropogenesis*. Author H. P. Blavatsky, the co-founder of Theosophy, describes respectively the formation of the universe and the creation of successive versions of mankind in deep antiquity. Her information was allegedly based on the "Secret Doctrine" in an occult Tibetan Buddhist manuscript to which she claims she was given unprecedented access and which she referred to as the *Book of Dzyan*.

At the time of Blavatsky's writing, a standard for Tibetan transcription into the Latin alphabet had not yet been agreed upon. It was not until recently that it was established that the text she'd been referring to is what modern scholars write as *rGyud-sde*, which are the "Three Inner Tantras" of the Nyingma School of Tibetan Buddhism, the (1) *Mahayoga*; (2) *Anu* Yoga; and (3) *Ati* Yoga. The latter is more commonly known as *Dzogchen*, "the Great Perfection." Together they are described as "profound methods for awakening to buddhahood in one lifetime." [60] As the late Nyingma "Abbott," Khenpo Jigme Phuntsok Rinpoche said:

> Due to the degeneration of time, human beings' minds have become more complex and deluded in their attachment to the external world. So, this age of extreme confusion demands a teaching of comparably extreme power and clarity. [61]

It is unclear to me how Blavatsky's fantastical stories about the previous iterations of mankind could have anything to do with the most intense meditation practices for achieving spiritual enlightenment, but it is known that the Nyingma school of Buddhism has had a body of secret teachings ever since it was founded by Padma Sambhava, a.k.a., the "Second Buddha." The basics of *Anthropogen-*

esis practically mirror the Vedic World Age doctrine of the *Puranas*, which are no secret, at all.

One wonders if these legends were meant to be taken literally and if not, what did they symbolize? Is it possible that the physical size and density of human beings has actually changed, as the solar system has moved to areas in the Galaxy where matter becomes more compressed? Blavatsky's own interpretation of these stories appears to be very literal and she was someone who understood quite well about heavy use of symbolism in mythology. In the strictest Hindu/Buddhist sense and indeed, from the perspective of eternity, the phenomenal universe is *maya*, an illusion. To be "enlightened," according to East Asian beliefs and practices is to viscerally experience an awareness that the distinction between the self and the universe is a false dichotomy.

THE GIANTS OF HYPERBOREA, LEMURIA & ATLANTIS

Blavatsky has been called a fraud and much of her work has been called plagiarism but this has never been seriously substantiated. I would love to see the source materials she allegedly ripped off! The sheer volume, the granularity and the passion of her pronouncements, if at times cantankerous and oozing with despicable 19th century prejudices, don't totally detract from her accomplishments. She was definitely something more than a parlor trickster. I'll quote two respectable apologists, referring to her book, *The Voice of the Silence* about Buddhist practice, before getting into the wild and woolly ride of *Anthropogenesis*:

Zen Buddhism scholar Dr. Daisetz Teitaro Suzuki wrote: "Undoubtedly Madame Blavatsky had in some way been initiated into the deeper side of *Mahayana* teaching and then gave out what she deemed wise to the Western world ..." (*Eastern Buddhist*, old series, 5:377) He also commented: "Here is the real *Mahayana* Buddhism." (*The Middle Way*, August 1965, p. 90.)

H. H. the 14th Dalai Lama commented: "I believe that this book has strongly influenced many sincere seekers and aspirants to the wisdom and compassion of the Bodhisattva Path." [62]

Anthropogenesis focused on the history of the succeeding races of mankind over several millions of years, allegedly based on an esoteric Buddhist scroll, the *Book of Dzyan*. She referred to this body of information as being a part of "Esoteric Buddhism." The "root races" described by Blavatsky in *Anthropogenesis* share many similarities with the Traditional Hindu descriptions of the devolving races of humanity from the Golden Age to the present. She asserts that modern-day humans are the fifth version of the human race, akin to the words of the Greek epic poet, Hesiod.

Blavatsky goes on to say that the current race of mankind is the most solidified and dense in physical structure. The previous versions of mankind were more ethereal and voluminous. Each new version was successively less ethereal and more condensed, as the older versions shrank in size and as each became increasingly "degenerated." Similarly to the traditional Hindu descriptions of people who lived during the more virtuous ages, she says the elder races of mankind were giants. However, these Theosophical exemplars were even more gigantic than their *Puranic* counterparts.

First Race of Mankind on Earth, the "Hyperboreans," were incorporeal with ethereal bodies that, if we could see them would appear to be about *173 ft. in height*. This era occurred during the mid-Paleozoic era of geology, around 400 million years ago.

Second Race of Mankind were in a similarly diffuse but of a more dense state and approximately *120 ft. in height* at their tallest. This race began as androgynous and had separated into male and female towards their end of their cycle, which lasted millions of years.

Third Race of Mankind, the "Lemurians," were the first "recognizably human" race and of a more solidified structure, they arose 18 million years ago, in the Mesozoic era of geology. The Lemurians were *60 ft. tall*. They built empires all over what is now the Pacific Rim, though she notes that the landmasses were arranged very differently then. She said the last remnants of their civilization can still be seen in the cyclopean statues of Easter Island.

Fourth Race of Mankind, the "Atlanteans," *shrank from 30 to 15 ft. in stature*, over the course of their "degeneration," during several millions of years.

Fifth Race of Mankind corresponds to modern day *Homo sapiens*.

AFGHAN STATUES CARVED BY ATLANTEAN SURVIVORS OF THE DELUGE?

Blavatasky claimed that representatives of these previous gigantic human races had been carved by Atlantean survivors of the Great Flood, "for the instruction of future generations" [63] into to the cliffs of Bamiyan, in modern-day Afghanistan.

After a month of intensive bombardment in March of 2001, the Taliban finally succeeded in destroying the "Buddhas of Bamiyan." The UNESCO World Heritage Site was blown up in front of international television cameras, to the horror of the billions of viewers. Blavatsky claimed that Buddhist monks in the 1st century CE had refurbished these giant statues with Buddhist iconography but that they were actually far more ancient than is generally accepted by archaeology (or paleontology or modern science, in general).

Blavatsky claimed that the legends about giants appearing in cultures around the world were tales of actual ancient "fifth race" human encounters with the rare surviving members of these gigantic previous races of mankind.

THE DESTRUCTION OF ATLANTIS

"Plato's text tells us, the gods became angry and they decided that Atlantis had to be swept from the Earth because it had brought evil into the world.

"So they sent the flood and Atlantis was destroyed. Actually, this theme, implicating us and our own behavior in the disasters that the cosmos inflicts upon us is found in every single Flood story. All around the world. When I look at that body of tradition, I can't help feeling that in mythological terms, we look very much like the next lost civilization and that it would be wise of us to adjust our thinking and our behavior very rapidly. Because if ever there was a society that has fallen out of harmony with the universe, it is ours. And the message of history and pre-history is, you fall out of harmony with the universe at your peril."

—Graham Hancock, On-Camera Interview in *2012: Science or Superstition*

KALPA: ONE DAY OF BRAHMA

The founder of Buddhism was born a Hindu prince so the two religions share the cultural legacy of the Vedic scriptures and common beliefs about dharma, karma, and reincarnation, as well as a similar time philosophy of cosmic cycles called *kalpas, Maha Yugas* and *yugas*. Over the centuries, the interpretations of these time cycles have diverged somewhat between the two faiths. For the sake of brevity, I will summarize the cosmic time cycles of traditional Hinduism.

The Supreme Cosmic Spirit is called Brahman. It has three aspects: Brahma, "the Creator"; Vishnu, "the Preserver"; and Shiva, "the Destroyer." One day in the life of Brahma, whose physicality is represented by all of manifestation, is equal to one thousand *Maha Yugas,* which is called a *kalpa* and is equal to 4.32 billion years, which is about 20 million years less the estimated age of planet Earth, according to science.

Two of these 4.32 billion-year *kalpas* constitute a Day and a Night of Brahma. At the end of a Day of Brahma, all of creation in the physical and spiritual realms is dissolved. During the 4.32 billion-year Night of Brahma, nothing happens. This period of nothingness is called a *pralaya.* During the following Day of Brahma, the celestial bodies, planets and their inhabitants who were dissolved at the end of the previous Day can be reincarnated, when Brahma arises to renew creation. Even planets and stars get to reincarnate, in Hinduism!

THE "HINDU NOAH"

While Brahma sleeps and wakes, each *kalpa* is reigned by a succession of 14 *Manus* created by Brahma.

> Esoterically, every Manu, as an anthropomorphized patron of his special cycle ... each of the Manus, therefore [is] the special god, the creator and fashioner of all that appears during his own respective cycle of being or *Manvantara*.[64]

We are currently in the reign of the 7th Manu, a being who is referred to as the *Vaivasvata Manu* and who according to legend was incarnated as the King of Dravida, in the southeast of the Indian Subcontinent and is described as the "Hindu Noah."

As legend has it, Manu was engaged in devotions on the riverbank, a tiny fish swam up to him and begged him to save him from a bigger fish. Manu placed the little fish in a jar where, as it rapidly proceeded to grow larger and larger, the fish told Manu that a Great Flood was coming that would wash away all living things. As it kept growing, Manu put the fish into successively larger tanks, eventually into a lake and finally, in the ocean. While in the ocean, the fish instructed Manu to build a giant ark and to fill it up with the entire flora and fauna on the Earth. Manu did so and when the flood arrived, the fish, who turned out to be the god Vishnu in disguise, towed the ark to safety. Thus, *Vaivasvata Manu* became the forefather of post-diluvian mankind, otherwise known as "us."

WHAT THE *KALI YUGA* LOOKS LIKE

According to traditional Hinduism, humankind has been living in the *Kali Yuga*, the "Age of Vice," for around 5,000 years. It is interesting to look at what the ancient Vedic holy book, the *Mahabharata*, predicted would be in store for us during this time and how much of it is today considered to be just a part of normal, everyday modern life—or, at least, as it is depicted on TV. The implication, I guess is that when the *Mahabharata* was written, these things were practically inconceivable:

> Avarice and wrath will be common, men will openly display
> animosity towards each other ... Lust will be viewed as being
> socially acceptable. People will have thoughts of murder for no

justification, and they will see nothing wrong with that mind-set ... Family murders will also occur ... Husband and wife will find contempt in each other.

In *Kali Yuga*, even pre-teenage girls will get pregnant. The primary cause will be the social acceptance of sexual intercourse as being the central requirement of life ... People will take vows only to break them soon after ... People will without reason destroy trees and gardens ... There will be no respect for animals, and meat eating will start.

People will become addicted to intoxicating drinks. Men will find their jobs stressful and will go to retreats to escape their work ... [65]

PROOF: WE ARE CURRENTLY IN THE *KALI YUGA*

My favorite prophecies about what life would be like, as the *Kali Yuga* inexorably plunges humanity into unimaginable depths of debasement were made by the Hindu-born Buddhist holy man from the 8th century, Padma Sambhava, a.k.a., Lopon Rinpoche or the "Second Buddha." He noted trivial things that would indicate that humanity had definitely reached new lows: "people will eat standing up, and even running ... guides to enlightenment will be sold on street corners." [66]

I think that's pretty good evidence that we're fully in the *Kali Yuga*! I wonder what Sambhava would have to say about the five 24-hour drive-thru burger joints within a two-block radius of where I write this, in Los Angeles! The *Kali Yuga* will culminate in about 427,000 years during which time, according to another body of Hindu holy books, the *Puranas,* we can expect the following:

... increasing desertification and extremes of heat and cold. Gradually, plant life will become extinct, and animals will also die off, so that in the end of the *Kali Yuga*, humans will be reduced to cannibalism.

... finally, at the end of *Kali Yuga*, an avatar of Vishnu called Kalki will appear to destroy whoever is left. Then a new *Satya Yuga*, or Golden Age of spirituality will begin again.[67]

OUR 10,000-YEAR "MINI-GOLDEN AGE"

On the brighter side, for those of us who happen to be living in these days, *Forbidden Archaeology* author and Krishna Consciousness devotee Michael Cremo says that, as of the 16th century, we've been in a 10,000-year "mini-golden age" within the Dark Age of the *Kali Yuga*, as he explains:

The *Gaudiya Vaishnavas* believe that Krishna appeared in Gaudadesh (a name for Bengal) in the sixteenth century, taking the form of a devotee of Krishna. This avatar was known as *Chaitanya Mahaprabhu*. The appearance of *Chaitanya*, according to the *Gaudiya Vaishnavas*, marks the beginning of a ten thousand year golden era within the Age of *Kali*. Sometimes when winter is approaching, and the weather is getting colder, we experience a few warm days. So this golden era is something like that.[68]

THE NEW & "IMPROVED" HINDU YUGA CYCLE

In his book, *Holy Science*, published in 1894, Kriya Yoga master Sri Yukteswar makes the world-shattering statement that the Hindu almanacs and calendars, which correspond to the traditional *yuga* model of a 4,320,000-year *Maha Yuga*, are in error. He says this error crept in during the Dark Age of the *Kali Yuga* and got scholars confused, such that they misinterpreted the scriptures. Sri Yukteswar proposed to replace the traditional model with a 12,000-year *Maha Yuga*, which he claimed was supported by one of the oldest and most controversial of Vedic texts, *The Laws of Manu*, which also codifies the caste system and the different laws governing each caste (more of which in a moment). The new calendar was also based on his intriguing claim of our Sun's 24,000-year complete orbit around a companion star.

Not only did Sri Yukteswar propose to shorten the Hindu World Age cycle to 1/360th of its traditional length, he claimed that we were no longer in the *Kali Yuga*, as conventionally believed. He made the literally brazen claim that we'd already entered an upwardly-mobile, ascending cycle of the Bronze Age or *Dwapara Yuga*, rather than being saddled with another 400,000+ years within the *Age of Darkness*, per the traditionalist views.

In his book, *Galactic Alignment*, John Major Jenkins agrees with the premise and the structure of Sri Yukteswar's shortened calendar but not with Yukteswar's start date. Whereas, Yukteswar saw the scientific achievements of the West as evidence of an ascending Bronze Age, Jenkins disagrees, saying, "Technology has thrust us deeper into material dependency and spiritual darkness." [69]

So, Jenkins "corrects" Yukteswar's calendar by moving the start-date up by 701 years to have the *Kali Yuga* or "Age of Vice" begin in 10,800 BCE so that it cycles into an ascending Bronze Age in 2000 CE. Like Yukteswar, Jenkins believes that the "current" Bronze Age or *Dwapara Yuga* will last a total of 2,400 years after which time we'll move into the Silver Age or the *Treta Yuga*.

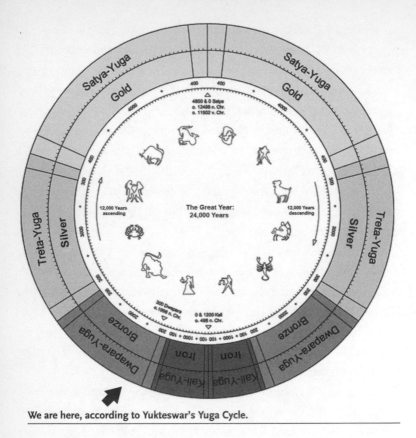

We are here, according to Yukteswar's Yuga Cycle.

INTERVIEW WITH *FORBIDDEN ARCHAEOLOGY*'S MICHAEL CREMO

In February 2009, I conducted an interview with Michael Cremo. As I mentioned previously, during his entire adult life he's been a devotee of Krishna Consciousness. ISKCON is a spiritual organization based on traditionalist Hindu practices that holds Krishna as the ultimate avatar or Supreme Lord, similar to the Christian view of Jesus Christ. Cremo is also a teacher of *Bhakti* Yoga, which is a Hindu term for the spiritual practice of "fostering loving devotion to God." This is part of our conversation:

BRUCE: Sri Yukteswar claimed there were "exaggerations and manipulations" in the traditional Hindu calendar. Mayanist John Major Jenkins has taken Sri Yukteswar's model and deduced that the most recent *Kali Yuga* ended in 2000 CE and that we're already into the ninth year of a 2,400-year *Dwapara Yuga* or an ascending "Bronze Age." Do you have any comments about Yukteswar's work and Jenkins' interpretation of it?

CREMO: I think Sri Yukteswar is representative of Hindu scholars who were overawed by Western science and theology, and were embarrassed by the truths revealed in the Hindu scriptures. To resolve their feelings of embarrassment they tried to artificially bring the Hindu truths within the range of the Western scientific and theological ideas of their time. One of the big problems with the Hindu texts is that they express the concepts of vast periods of historical time and equally vast times for human history. Sri Yukteswar solved the problem by proposing that originally the Hindu culture had short time periods. But I look at this as just a fanciful invention.

BRUCE: What is your opinion of Sri Yukteswar's updated *yuga* model [below] (as presented in John Major Jenkins' *Galactic Alignment*)?

NAME	DAWN	ERA	DUSK	TOTAL
Satya Yuga	400+	4,000	400	4,800
Treta Yuga	300+	3,000	300	3,600
Dwapara Yuga	200+	2,000	200	2,400
Kali Yuga	100+	1,000	100	1,200
MAHA YUGA				12,000

CREMO: My position is that it is not necessary to bring in the ascending and descending short *yugas* in order to incorporate the precesssion cycle into the traditional Vedic cosmological calculations.

As far as I can see, the idea of a short *yuga* cycle, with ascending and descending sequence of *yugas*, is unique to Sri Yukteswar and a couple of his contemporaries. I do not see any information that any of his predecessors in his line also taught this. My guru, Srila A. C. Bhaktivedanta Swami Prabhupada, and his predecessors in his line have taken the long *yuga* cycle as given by the *Puranas*, as have practically all the other gurus and lines that I know of in India itself ...

I suppose the difference between the two positions is that the long *yuga* idea, with *Satya* following *Kali*, is directly stated in the *Puranas*, and is supported pretty unanimously by the traditional Vedic teachers and astrologers, whereas the view of Sri Yukteswar began with him, in the early 20th century. The support for the short *yuga* cycle depends on his assertion that some earlier compilers of Vedic writings made a mistake or did some cheating that is reflected in the *Puranas*.

Having looked at the positions, I have decided to stick with what is there in the Sanskrit texts themselves, which are also followed by most gurus and Vedic astronomers. **Having looked into Sri Yukteswar's idea of the 24,000 year periods of the revolution of our Sun around another sun, and the relationship of that to the precession of the equinoxes, I think it might perhaps be possible to incorporate that cycle into the long *yuga* cycle, but using terminology other than that reserved for the long *yuga* cycle itself, i.e., don't use the** terms *Satya*, *Treta*, *Dwapara*, and *Kali* **to represent this other astronomical cycle.** In other words, you could say that there are 18 precession cycles of 24,000 years each in the 432,000 years of the *Kali Yuga* ...

But, **as I have said, the precession of the equinoxes is a fact. It is a fact acknowledged in the Vedic astronomical texts. And it can be incorporated into the traditional system of** *yugas*. **But this should be done without changing the traditional** *yuga* **cycles.**

Anyone who knows me and who is familiar with my work, knows that my practice is to simply set forth my views, without getting into criticizing others in the alternative history and alternative cosmology fields. People can read my books and read those of others, like Sri Yukteswar, and [Zechariah] Sitchin, and [Erich] von Däniken ... and make up their own minds. I do not go out of my way to criticize other researchers in alternative history and cosmology. But when I am directly asked, as in this case, to give my views on proposals different from my own, I feel obligated to give some honest reply.

(*We will return with more of our interview with Mr. Cremo later in this chapter.*)

"THE TOPOLOGY OF TIME": THE HYPERDIMENSIONAL SPHERE

Filmmaker Jay Weidner brings a very interesting alchemical perspective to the Vedic time philosophy. He sees the *Maha Yuga* cycle as analogous to the cyclical energy flow of a hypersphere, also known as a torus. He explains how alchemists believe that there is a hyperdimensional, luminous energy field around every living thing on Earth and, indeed surrounding every planet and star and that the entire 3D realm, itself, is the hardened, stepped-down energy expression or manifestation of its higher-dimensional aspects.

Weidner explains that a good example of how the workings of the energy dynamics of the hypersphere can be observed in nature is in the phenomena of tornadoes: As the winds descend from the upper atmosphere into the funnel of the vortex, the air particles spin with an increasing rate of speed and the particles become compressed. By the time the spinning air arrives at the tip of the vortex, it has "hardened" into a moving object that is as solid as iron and can have enough force to knock trains off their tracks and send cars flying, etc.

Weidner says that it is this "hardening" of higher-dimensional energies at the tip within a hypersphere (as with the spinning, condensed air particles in a tornado) that become manifest as the "solidity" of our three dimensional space. He says, "Each human, plant, animal and indeed every planet and star, alike are the *hardened tips* of hyperdimensional vortices." He continues,

It is well known in modern physics that the *four dimensional space, of which time is an aspect*, is in the shape of a hypersphere. This hypersphere appears similar to the shape of a donut, or a bagel. The energy, or the flow ... within this hypersphere works like this: ... the flow comes out of the bottom of the sphere, winds its way up around the outside edge, crosses the outside Equator of the torus sphere and moves towards the hole in the top of this torus. The energy flow then begins to fall through the top of the hole and begins to spin in a vortex. This energy flow continues until it comes out of the bottom side of the torus where the energy flow begins its outward expansion again. This flow is continuous and, in a sense, is infinite ... [70]

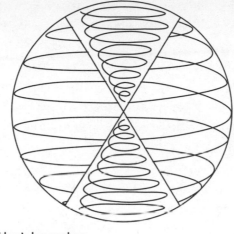

Sketch of Weidner's hypersphere.

Weidner uses this hypersphere analogy to explain the *yuga* cycles. He says the Golden Age begins at the null point in the center within the sphere and that as time flows downward through the "South Pole," it expands outwards around the Southern Hemisphere of the outer surface of the hypersphere. He says that from the point of view of those inside this field, time appears to "slow down," until it arrives at the "equator," which is the borderline between the Golden Age and the Silver Age. Once past the equator, the energy flow begins to contract, as it continues upwards towards the North Pole of the hypersphere.

The Silver Age continues, until the energy flows over the "top lip" of the hyperdimensional torus. The borderline between the Silver Age and the Bronze Age is at the North Pole, where the energy flow drops into the upper tetrahedral vortex. At two-thirds of the way into the upper vortex, the energy flow is spinning so fast that it becomes "as solid as iron," akin to the tip of a tornado. This area corresponds to the beginning of the *Kali Yuga*, or the Iron Age.

This spinning continues to gain density and compression and speed as it races towards the central null point in the very center of the sphere. As it approaches this null point the forces become unbelievably fast, violent and dense. It is only when these forces achieve maximum density and they can no longer compress any further that they begin to suddenly flip and ... [restart] the expansion of the flow [downward towards the South Pole]. This happens in an instant.

This is the shift from the Iron Age, or the *Kali Yuga* to the Golden Age ... The borderline between the Iron Age and the Golden Age is the most distinct border in this topographical illustration of hyperdimensional time. It is the most jarring and is instantaneous.[71]

THE ALCHEMICAL WORLD AGE DOCTRINE & THE *YUGAS*

Weidner agrees that we're in the *Kali Yuga* now and he agrees with the traditional Hindu precept that the cycle moves directly from the crushing density of the *Kali Yuga* into the expanded state of the Golden Age, without the ascending and descending *yugas* of Sri Yukteswar's model. However, Weidner tries to blend the alchemical World Age doctrine, which divides the precession of the equinoxes into four quadrants of 6,480 years each with the *yuga* cycle.

Because he has devoted years of his life to studying alchemy, Fulcanelli and the mysterious cross at Hendaye, France, and because he's friends with Alberto Villoldo, whose Peruvian shaman contacts are saying that the world is going to "turn over" in 2012, Weidner thinks that everything is pointing to our being headed for the null point in the hypersphere or the wormhole occurring in 2012 and that it will be "a paradise, especially to those who may have survived the passing through the wormhole ..."

Yes, that would be the catch! I keep thinking about the tornado analogy and it just seems to me that the "topology of time" is a giant meat grinder and the only things that could survive "passing through the wormhole" would be the finer, non-3D aspects of beings and things. "Surviving" this event would seem to me to require a "conscious death," which according to André Van Lysebeth is exactly what Tantra Yoga is all about.

"TO TANTRISTS ... DEATH IS THE ULTIMATE GURU"

The late André Van Lysebeth passed away in 2004. He was a yoga practitioner for 60 years and was the founder of numerous yoga associations in Europe. He was initiated into Tantra philosophy by the late *Nataraja* guru, and was considered the foremost European Tantra author and teacher of his day. In his 1988 book, *Tantra: The Cult of the Feminine*, which was translated to English in 1995, he explains,

> Tantrists do not wait until they come face to face, by chance, accidentally, with death to perceive the true meaning of life ... Their regular flirting with the fact of death and its meaning aims at the following objectives:
>
> • to reveal the true meaning of life which then conditions the right attitude toward oneself, others, and human values in general;
>
> • to discover the innermost secret of being;
>
> • to make it possible to prepare oneself to consciously experience one's own death;
>
> • to go beyond all fears, in other words to overcome the fear of death which is the substratum of all fears.

This is neither a morbid nor an obsessive attitude but rather a permanent awareness of the impermanent, precarious nature of life. Acceptance of the above dispels all anguish, but what counts is deriving practical lessons from this in order to live one's life, of course, but also to prepare for one's death.

The best way to prepare to die—seriously—is to do one's utmost to live as long [and as healthy; eating and breathing right, doing yoga, etc.] as possible.[72]

Van Lysebeth also claimed that the practice of "matrifocal" Tantra in the Indian Subcontinent preceded what he describes as the invasion of India by "barbaric Aryan tribes" who installed the patriarchal, oppressive caste system (based on skin color) over the darker-skinned indigenous *Shudras* (lowest caste), which pretty much sounds like a microcosm of the history of the whole world over the past millennium.

Indeed, another prediction of what the *Kali Yuga* would be like, in full bloom, according to the sacred text of the *Mahabharata* is that women will choose their own husbands (gasp!) and that the lowest caste will rise up in defiance of their lords:

... the Shudras will cease to wait upon and serve the Brahmins[73] ... Shudras [will] argue ... "Are we in any way inferior to you? A good Brahmin is he who knows the truth of God!" and defiantly glower at them.[74]

Well, the cheek! I have the utmost respect and love for Indian civilization, however I have no love for the caste system or Aryanism, which are bound up in a lot of the Vedic ideology we've been discussing in this section ...

THE *KALI YUGA* DOES NOT REFER TO THE GODDESS *KĀLĪ*

There are so many New Age accounts of the *Kali Yuga* as being the Age of the goddess *Kālī*, that I feel it necessary to set the record straight: "*Kali Yuga* is associated with the apocalypse demon Kali, not be confused with the goddess *Kālī*, as these are unrelated words in the Sanskrit language. The 'Kali' of *Kali Yuga* means 'strife, discord, quarrel, or contention.'"[75] Granted, it's an easy mistake to make because *Kālī* is a goddess associated with death and the battlefield. Still, it's annoying to see all these Westerners pontificating erroneously about this. I won't name names but at least now the reader will know who did their homework when they stumble upon doltish rants about the *Kali Yuga*, implicating the goddess.

Kālī is the Dark Mother, a goddess of wisdom. Her name literally means "black" but it has come to mean the "force of time (kala)" and she has in recent centuries, come to be considered the goddess of time and of change. In the Tantric approach to *Kālī*, the goal of the devotee is to become reconciled with death and to learn acceptance of the way things are. *Kālī* is often represented as the consort of Shiva, the Destroyer, on whose body she is classically seen standing, wearing a grisly necklace of decapitated heads.

Left: Kali, the demon of strife.   Right: Kālī, goddess of time & change.

In her most classic and popular depiction, *Kālī* is drunk on the blood of her victims on the battlefield, dancing with destructive frenzy upon the body of her husband, whom she tramples unknowingly. Shiva's cries finally get *Kālī*'s attention and calm her fury. As a sign of her shame, *Kālī* sticks out her tongue.

THE RAPTURE: LET THE END TIMES ROLL

The "2012 phenomenon" is to a large degree influenced by the "End Times" beliefs of modern-day Protestant fundamentalists. As of this writing, the biggest Google Ads buy and Google search result for the term "2012" was paid for by a splinter sect of Seventh-day Adventists, called The Church of God—PKG (Preparing for the Kingdom of God). This is what they say they believe, on their website, which is linked to their publishing brand, the-end.com:

> ... The Seventh Seal has now been opened and the world is being plunged into the final tribulation for mankind. Ronald Weinland, who is the pastor of God's Church on earth, has also been appointed by the God of Abraham to be His end-time prophet and one of the two end-time witnesses (and spokesman of both), preceding the return of Jesus Christ.[76]

The Adventists have a well-worn track record of "date-setting" Judgment Day and the Second Coming. When the church's founder, William Miller predicted the Second Coming of Christ on October 22, 1844—for the second time that year—and it *still* didn't occur, the fiasco was referred to as the "Great Disappointment" and he lost numerous followers.

The Jehovah's Witnesses Church has weathered a few similar crises. Since 1876, adherents have been told that they are living in the last days of the present world. In the years leading up to 1925 and

1975, Jehovah's Witnesses' publications expressed strong expectations that Armageddon would occur in those years, both times resulting in surges of membership and subsequent defections.

THE POWER OF APOCALYPTIC THINKING

Some modern-day fundamentalist religious groups today actively pray for the imminent "rapture" of the "true believers" in Christ. The "rapture" is the idea that believers will be literally caught up in the air and rescued by Christ, Himself, prior to the terrible Earth cataclysms that will be meted out as God's punishment for mankind's sinfulness. As evidenced by the unbelievable success of the 16 bestselling novels of the *Left Behind* series about the "rapture" by Tim LaHaye and Jerry B. Jenkins, with total sales surpassing 65 million copies,[77] this is clearly not a small, powerless fringe element in American society. The people who pray for this "rapture" may indeed welcome a massive nuclear exchange or any other extinction-level event, believing that they will find themselves safely in the arms of their Savior, while the Earth is scrubbed clean of all vile non-believers.

Of concern is that some people holding such beliefs are very politically ambitious and they may have succeeded in exerting an undue influence in U.S. policy. It is not inconceivable that there have been in the past or that there are currently U.S. governmental officials who believe in the "rapture" and that they may unconsciously or even intentionally base their geopolitical decisions on hastening the arrival of "Judgment Day." These people are driven by dangerous beliefs, bordering on mental illness; they pose a danger to themselves and to a global majority that does not agree with their profoundly disordered views. The majority would be wise to identify and vote out of government office all proponents of this demented fantasy called the "rapture"[78] and any agenda that helps to create the ideal conditions for this imaginary nightmare to become the reality.

THE SECOND COMING
· · · · · · · · · · · · · · · · · ·

"They're 2000-year periods, all leading to Armageddon. The Second Coming is in a linear progression of time, which has been modified I think by the Industrial Revolution as an uphill linear climb toward the End of the World."

—Dr. Anthony Aveni, On-Camera Interview in *2012: Science or Superstition*

THE SIXTH EXTINCTION & THE DEATH WISH DRIVE-THRU

Another World Age we can talk about is the "Sixth Extinction," the widespread, ongoing mass extinction of all species of life, an extinction event that is on a scale as high as any previous mass extinction (more of which in **Chapter 5**). This number is not too far-off from the mythical World Ages in traditions all over the world numbering either Four or Five.

Beyond religion and philosophies, the "end of the world" has been with us since the very beginning. 99% of Earth species that ever lived are now extinct and if the coincidental statistics presented in Annie Leonard's brilliant animated film, *The Story of Stuff* [79] are true, 99% of everything that Americans buy ends up in a landfill within six months of purchase. We all know that this is unsustainable behavior that is destroying the quality of life with its attendant environmental pollution, obesity and greed, all of it crystallized by the seemingly carefree, innocent, joyous act of buying a cheeseburger, fries and a shake at the drive-thru at 3 a.m. and then looking for a place to throw out all the accompanying masses of Styrofoam™, cardboard, paper and plastic ... unless you're the kind of pig who lets that stuff pile up in your gas-guzzling beater!

Western culture was encoded to self-destruct in the Good Book upon which it was founded, in eerie synchrony with the final 5,125-

year epoch of the Maya Long Count calendar. Equally eerie is the discovery made by correlating to the Gregorian calendar to the start-dates of the current epoch of the Maya Long Count and of the current Age in the traditional Hindu calendars: we find that the *Kali Yuga* began in 3102 BCE—exactly twelve years after the first year of the 13th *b'ak'tun,* that's about to end.

There are tussles among the experts about exact "end" dates in both Maya and Hindu cosmologies, but the fact remains that countless pre- and non-Western traditions sync up to the current general time period as a major turning point for the Earth's position in the cosmos and for the concomitant fate of its inhabitants.

CHICHÉN-ITZÁ: A "STAR CLOCK IN STONE"

"... the pyramid of *K'uk'ulkan* ... at Chichén-Itzá is much more than simply the shadow that appears on the equinox. There's a deeper encoded symbolism that involves the Sun and the Pleiades and the zenith, the exact center of the sky overhead. These different features line up only in the 21st century, so this pyramid is like a precessional star clock in stone, set to point to the End of the World Age, in the 21st century. It's really the greatest calendrical architectural achievement I think that any ancient culture has produced."

—John Major Jenkins, On-Camera Interview in *2012: Science or Superstition*

GEOLOGIC TIME & THE BIGGEST SECRET IN THE WORLD

Aside from everyday terms that are used to describe the periods and peoples from times distant and recent, such as "Paleolithic," "cave man," the "Enlightenment," the "Space Age," "Baby Boomers," "Generation X," etc., a scientifically accepted way to measure time over long periods is the "geologic time scale," which identifies time periods based on the distinct layers of rock on Earth's crust, starting from the beginning of the Earth's formation.

In geolochronological terms, the word "eon" represents a period of time of half a billion years or more. There have so far been only four geologic eons. An "era" is a period of several hundred million years and there have so far been twelve eras in Earth history. An "epoch" is a period of tens of millions of years and an "age" covers millions of years. We are currently living in the Phanerzoic eon, the Cenozoic era and the Holocene epoch, which began at the end of the last Ice Age, around 12,000 years ago, preceded by the Pleistocene epoch.

There are corresponding names for the succeeding layers of strata containing fossilized plants and animals of every kind, over the course of history and the succeeding depositions of lava flows and sediments from flooding, glaciers and up to 22,000 tons per year of cosmic dust that rains down on the planet's continents and oceans— but I'm not going to get into all of these, especially since there is debate as to whether we're currently in the Quaternary "period" or "sub-period." Generally, when an object is discovered buried in a certain layer, it is thought to date from the time period of that layer. For that reason, when miners during the Gold Rush in California found fossilized human remains and artifacts in Eocene layers that are over 50 million years old, the apple cart was turned over and the discovery became the basis for Michael Cremo's *Forbidden Archaeology*. I asked Michael to tell me more about these findings and the repercussions they had on established views.

INTERVIEW WITH MICHAEL CREMO: PART II

BRUCE: What is archaeology's "Biggest Secret"?

CREMO: I think the big secret is there is a huge amount of archaeo-logical evidence for extreme human antiquity.

BRUCE: Who do you think is hiding this information and why?

CREMO: The supporters of the evolutionary account of human origins are guilty of what I call knowledge filtration. I am not talking about some kind of satanic conspiracy to suppress truth. I am talking about something historians and philoso-phers of science have understood for a long time, namely that theoretical preconceptions often govern how evidence is treated in a discipline. I have simply tried to show how this process operates in the disciplines related to human origins, such as archaeology.

Those who are doing the knowledge filtering do not, for the most part, think they are suppressing true facts, which if known would cause people to disbelieve in their theories. Rather, they think something must be wrong with the alleged facts, which therefore do not deserve to be considered seriously. So in one sense, this kind of knowledge filtering is human nature ...

But there are also deeper reasons, which have to do with power. There are various kinds of power in the world—military power, political power, economic power. There is also intel-lectual power, which although subtle is very real. We see that those who have power do not like to give it up. For example, if one political party has a monopoly in the political life of a country, it does not like to give up its position. Or if one cor-poration has a monopoly in a certain sector of the economy, it does not like to give up its position. **For the past century or so, the evolutionists have held a government-enforced monopoly** in the education systems and scientific institutions of most nations. Only their ideas can be taught. Only their ideas are considered legitimate. So this is a powerful position to be in, and of course they do not want to give it up. To maintain their monopoly, they use governments to exclude alternative ideas from the education system.

BRUCE: What have been your own most important findings?

CREMO: I think the most significant thing is that the scientific literature of the past 150 years contains a vast number of cases of archaeological evidence for extreme human antiquity. But among these cases, I do have some favorites.

One case that has always fascinated me is the California gold mine discoveries. In the middle of the 19th century, gold was discovered in California, and miners went there from all over the world.

To get the gold, the miners were digging tunnels into the sides of mountains, through the solid rock. One of the mountains was Table Mountain, in the gold mining region of California. Sometimes, hundreds of meters inside these tunnels, the miners were finding skeletons of humans like us, not those of ape-men. There were also finding stone tools and weapons, hundreds of them, at many different locations in the gold mining region.

Now here is the most important point. These objects were found in layers of rock belonging to the lower part of the geological period called the Eocene, which means they would be about 50 million years old. A Vedic archaeologist would not be surprised to find evidence for humans existing 50 million years ago. Such an archaeologist might expect to find such evidence going back much further in time—perhaps as much as 2 billion years. But for ordinary archaeologists evidence for humans at 50 million years would be quite surprising. According to their way of thinking, that would be before the time of the first apes and monkeys.

THE ANATOMY OF A SCIENTIFIC WHITEWASH?

CREMO: The discoveries from the California gold mines were reported to the scientific world by Dr. J. D. Whitney, the state geologist of California. He wrote a massive book about these discoveries, which was published by Harvard University in the year 1880. But we do not hear much about these discoveries today. That is because of the process of knowledge filtration.

The scientist responsible for the knowledge filtering in this case was Dr. William B. Holmes. He was a very influential anthropologist working at the Smithsonian Institution in Washington, D.C. He said, "If Dr. Whitney had understood the theory of human evolution, as we understand it today, he would have hesitated to announce his conclusions, despite the imposing array of testimony with which he was confronted." In other words, if the facts did not fit the theory of human evolution, the facts had to be put aside, and the person who reported them had to be discredited. And that is exactly what happened.

(*The interview with Mr. Cremo continues in* **APPENDIX A**.)

THE 6,000-YEAR WALL

What all cosmologies and apocalypses have in common is how they demand that you accept totally illogical or otherwise unfathomable propositions. This is as true of the modern-day cosmology of accepted science as it is of the ancient cosmologies.

The human race is still digging itself out of the Stone Ages, when it comes to a functional understanding of the cosmos, let alone our "place" in it. According to the Judeo-Christian cosmology of the Bible, the Earth, Heavens and all creatures were created in six days. On the seventh day of this eventful week, our Lord took the day off. This was roughly 6,000 years ago. For over five thousand years, millions of people have lived and died, believing this to be the God's honest truth—and many still do.

The findings of modern science have introduced cognitive dissonance into the hearts and minds of the faithful. In a bid to keep the faith, some have taken a syncretic approach, where the "days" of Genesis are seen as symbolic of the Earth's geological ages. This line of thought is called "Day-Age Creationism" and it has many, many interpretations. However, most Westerners, including the religious, no longer consult the Bible to study physical cosmology.

Billions of people in Asia and elsewhere have totally different cosmologies, of course. We've been discussing Eastern cosmologies quite a bit throughout this chapter. Imagine what a difference in worldview there must be, between thinking in terms of 4,320,000-year cycles, rather than in terms of a linear story that is 6,000 years long—and just about to end?

One wonders whether the biblical 6,000-year time limit has influenced the way Westerners have conceived of time, whether this has culturally limited modern comprehension of cosmic cycles that are much longer than 6,000 years, such as the 26,000-year precession of the equinoxes, which were known to the Hindus and the

Greeks in ancient times and were only rediscovered in the West in the 18th century.

How does a 6,000-year oriented memory bank countenance the orbits of certain comets and asteroid clusters, which have cataclysmically impacted Earth in the past, in cycles of 26 million years? It's taking a while, but the 6,000-year wall is slowly crumbling. Over the past three decades, we have seen the official origin of modern humans get pushed back from 35,000 years ago to as far back as 400,000 years ago and if Michael Cremo and Hinduism have their way, we may see human origins pushed back a couple of billion years.

THE SHI'IA ARMAGEDDON

As noted previously, the Abrahamic traditions, particularly the Christian Protestant ones are much more focused on the End Times than with The Beginning. Millions of Christians, Jews and Muslims believe that we're living in the "End Times" right now, which is lending a lot of potency to the 2012 meme. In the version of Armageddon of Shi'ia Islam, Jesus descends from the sky to help the Mahdi, the "Guided One." Jesus helps the Mahdi kill the "False God," along with his armies of "unbelievers." They win, resulting in peace and brotherhood in the world. The Christians convert to Islam and Islam proceeds to "rule the world justly."[80] How have I never heard this story until today?

THE "GREAT ATTRACTOR" & "THE ULTIMATE FATE OF THE UNIVERSE"

According to modern astronomy, Earth's movement covers a daily distance of about 32,211,883 miles,[81] at a speed of about 390 miles per second towards the "Great Attractor," which is a gravitational anomaly that is collapsing into itself instead of expanding—like the rest of the universe is supposed to be doing. As if this makes any sense, which theoretically it does not, according to Einstein's special theory of relativity, because there is no non-moving frame of reference with which to compare the Galaxy's motion. Nonetheless, the "Great Attractor," which is located within the constellation of Centaurus, is pulling the Milky Way and our neighboring galaxies towards it from some 63 megaparsecs or 205,506,000,000 light-years away. (The Space Age began over 50 years ago and the UN is calling 2009 the "International Year of Astronomy,"[82] so I'm using "megaparsecs" in a sentence!)

Modern cosmology has its own Genesis, the "big bang," a theory which is taken as gospel in modern science but which makes about as much sense as "asking about the political affiliations of a tuna sandwich,"[83] to quote Columbia University's philosophy of physics director, David Albert (he was actually talking about the logical status of the position of a subatomic particle in a superposition—but it still fits). Modern cosmology also has its own Armageddon, i.e., the "ultimate fate of the universe," which has not been determined yet though there are numerous theories, including the "big freeze" and "heat death" (which are pretty self-descriptive), the "big crunch" (which is theorized to have preceded the "big bang"), the "big bounce," etc.

The names of these scientific theories for the creation and destruction of the universe sound as primordial if not more so than the name of the Maya deity, "Heart of Sky." Personally, I am partial to the never ending "multiverse" theory, which is just as sensible and fathomable as the 16.4-billion-year-units of time called *habla 'tuns* by the ancient Maya.

CHAPTER FIVE

The Science of Apocalypse

"We have the ability to make ourselves safe from cosmic extinction. If we cannot manage to meet this challenge, we will ... have failed to meet our evolutionary responsibility."[84]

—Rusty Schweickart, Apollo 9 astronaut,
Testimony to the U. S. House of Representatives

APOCALYPSE NOW

Nuclear annihilation and climate change are potential apocalypses that we've been living with for decades. What these scenarios have in common is that they'd be man-made and there's a sense that they're somewhat under human control. However, the extinction-level events associated with the 2012 meme are characterized by being *utterly beyond human control*. What is being expressed in pop culture is a feeling of powerlessness and fatalism, bolstered by modern scientific discoveries on one hand and by ancient prophesies on the other.

The hype about 2012 may have a bit to do with recent discoveries in Earth science and astrophysics. In his book *Apocalypse 2012*, veteran science writer Lawrence E. Joseph gives us a good sampling of the classic concerns that have come to be associated with the 2012 meme in his bullet-points of imminent planetary megadeath:

- We're a million years overdue for a mass extinction.

- The solar minimum is acting much worse than solar maximum, and one misdirected spewing of plasma could fry us in an instant.

- The magnetic field—which shields us from harmful radiation —is developing a mysterious crack.

- Our solar system is entering an energetically hostile part of the Galaxy.

- The Yellowstone supervolcano is getting ready to blow and if it does, we can look forward to nuclear winter and 90 percent annihilation.

- The Maya, the world's greatest timekeepers ever, say it's all going to stop on December 21, 2012.[85]

Joseph's book speaks to millennial fears about increasing instability within, on and around the Earth. His inflammatory headlines draw out the impotence and futility that people experience in the face of geophysical unknowns and astronomical statistics. He ends the list with a parting shot of angst over the lost wisdom of the indigenous peoples who've been invalidated, genocided or ultimately denatured by the relentless juggernaut of a dominator culture that has finally hit the wall and is staring into the maw of its own extinction.

Joseph's selection of apocalypses is interesting. Some are legitimate, others aren't. Some are overlooked. Let's take a deeper look at these statements, shall we?

ARE WE A MILLION YEARS OVERDUE FOR A MASS EXTINCTION?

Short answer: We are already in the Holocene extinction event also known as the Sixth Extinction.

What Joseph was suggesting is that we're a million years overdue for an extinction-level event, due to an impactor on a scale as massive as the most famous one, which exterminated the dinosaurs. Joseph cites a paper by Richard Muller and his graduate student, Robert Rohde, "Cycles in Fossil Diversity," published in *Nature* magazine in 2005, which says that there is a strong cycle of mass extinctions that regularly occurs every 62 million years, which Muller suggests is probably due to the periodic passage of the solar system through molecular clouds or galactic arms or an as-yet unknown structure (i.e., "Nemesis," our Sun's dark twin), which may periodically perturb the Oort cloud and trigger comet impacts on Earth.

If Muller is correct, that this 62-million-year cycle of mass extinctions is caused by major impact events, and if the most recent impact of such magnitude occurred 65 million years ago, well ... then we are indeed, overdue! Not one—*three million years overdue!*

But since we're already in the middle of an extinction event, on par with that of the great Cretaceous/Tertiary, on time for the 62 million-year cycle but without all the "bells and whistles" of a major cometary collision—can't we argue that impacts are *not* the main cause of mass extinctions? For its part, NASA is less than reassuring in its assessment of the threat posed by extraterrestrial impact:

> With so many of even the larger NEOs [Near-Earth Objects] remaining undiscovered, the most likely warning today would be zero—the first indication of a collision would be the flash of light and the shaking of the ground as it hit. In contrast, if the current surveys actually discover a NEO on a collision course, we would expect many decades of warning. Any NEO that is going to hit the Earth will swing near our planet many times before it hits, and it should be discovered by comprehensive sky searches like Spaceguard. In almost all cases, we will either have a long lead-time or none at all.[86]

Well, nobody can say that's not a full disclosure. They should put up a sign that says:

NASA WILL BE ABSOLVED AND HELD HARMLESS OF ANY
AND ALL LIABILITY AND/OR PROPERTY DAMAGE THAT MAY
ARISE FROM AN EXTINCTION-LEVEL EVENT.

THE LEGACY OF LUIS ALVAREZ

Dr. Richard Muller's work has been greatly influenced by his teacher, Nobel Laureate Dr. Luis Alvarez, who discovered the granddaddy of all cometary mass extinction events, the impact in the heart of what would 65 million years later become Maya country.

Ever since 1980, when Dr. Alvarez proposed his theory (soon verified by the discovery of the Chicxulub crater), the phrase "65 million years ago" has been branded into the minds of people everywhere. Prominent environmental scientist Norman Myers of the National Academy of Sciences had been saying since the 1980s that Earth is currently undergoing the "largest mass extinction in 65 million years," to much criticism at the time although that figure has since become widely accepted.

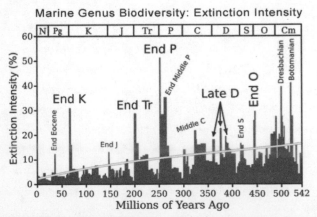

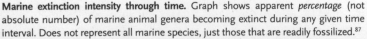

Marine extinction intensity through time. Graph shows apparent *percentage* (not absolute number) of marine animal genera becoming extinct during any given time interval. Does not represent all marine species, just those that are readily fossilized.[87]

However, a major study of the fossil record by University of Chicago's Dave Raup and Jack Sepkoski showed that the Cretaceous-Tertiary mass extinction caused by the Chicxulub impact was not an isolated event, but one of several mass extinctions that appear to occur on a regular cycle of 26–30 million years.

In 1983, Dr. Alvarez urged his student Richard Muller to come up with a theory to explain the findings of Raup and Sepkoksi. Muller came up with the "Nemesis theory" of an as-yet undiscovered dark companion star that caused disruptions in the Oort cloud, triggering comet impacts on Earth in a 26 million-year cycle. A similar conclusion had been simultaneously arrived at by astrophysicists John J. Matese and Daniel Whitmire, at the University of Louisiana.

As of yet, the dark twin has not been found but this may soon change with the November 2009 launch of NASA's WISE (Wide-field Infrared Survey Explorer), which should be able to detect our long-lost twin—if we have one—as well as many undiscovered Near-Earth Objects (and those not-so-near) that may be headed our way.[88]

If the theory of a companion for the Sun doesn't pan out, we can always go back to Dr. Michael Rampino's 1998 theory, "The Shiva Hypothesis: Impacts, Mass Extinctions, and the Galaxy," which was also based on the data aggregation of University of Chicago paleontologists Dave Raup and Jack Sepkoski[89] and the name for which was suggested by the late great Harvard professor, evolutionary biologist Stephen Jay Gould.

"THE SHIVA HYPOTHESIS": KILLER SPACE ROCKS

Presented in 1998 as a "unifying concept in Earth sciences," Michael Rampino, the long-time director of New York University's Earth & Environmental Science Program, in collaboration with NASA's Goddard Institute for Space Studies, proposed that every 26 to 30 million years, as the solar system orbits around the Milky Way Galaxy, it passes through a region packed with stars and clouds of interstellar gas and dust. Rampino says that work by astrophysicists John J. Matese, Daniel Whitmire and colleagues at the University of Louisiana has confirmed that **the alignment of just our Sun with the galactic center would cause enough of a pull on the combined mass of the material in the galactic disk to attract a hail of comets during our solar system's passage though the central galactic plane**, as it bobs up and down during its rotation through the dense, central portion of the Galaxy.

> Like Shiva, the Hindu Destroyer/Creator, the cyclic impacts bring an end to one world, and allow the beginning of a new one. With the Chicxulub impact 65 million years ago, the Mesozoic world, populated by giant dinosaurs and flying reptiles, gave way to the modern world of mammals and birds.[90]

THE APOPHIS APOCALYPSE

In 2029, it is predicted that a Near-Earth asteroid named Apophis will make another close encounter with Earth and that if it passes through a specific "gravitational keyhole," this will assure a terrestrial impact on April 13, 2036 and the release of an amount of energy estimated at 800 megatons of TNT or 13,000 times the yield of the atomic weapon that devastated Hiroshima in 1945. The path of risk runs in a sine curve, starting from Russia, heading north over Siberia and the northwest Pacific Ocean then heading south, along the Californian and Mexican Pacific coasts, then over land at Costa Rica, Nicaragua, Colombia and Venezuela, ending in the Atlantic, off the coast of western Africa.[91]

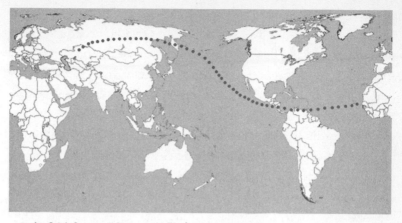

Path of risk for possible Apophis Earth impact in 2036.

In 2005, NASA set a schedule for handling the Apophis threat, suggesting a probe in 2019 and deflector by 2028. Also In 2005, China announced that as soon as they completed their Moon mission that the main focus of their space program would be to protect Earth from being hit by a comet or asteroid, with a method called "pasting," where a craft would be soft-landed on a comet or asteroid with an engine capable of pushing it off a collision course with Earth.[92] A 2007 study confirmed that China and the United States are the two nations most vulnerable to casualties from asteroids.[93]

IMPACTORZ 'N DA 'HOOD

Rampino's focus is on far-away impactors from the Oort cloud and the galactic plane but he overlooks the closer-to-home threats of the increasing number of discovered Near-Earth Objects that are found orbiting perilously close to us, every day. Besides the foreign objects that he cites in his paper, there are also the trails of ejecta from long-period comets like Swift-Tuttle, which has a 130-year orbit, and of short-period comets like Encke, which comes by every three years and has been breaking up over our heads for the past 20,000–30,000 years. Encke's trail of cosmic debris is called the Taurid complex, a stream of matter that is the largest in the inner solar system.[94] Oxford University astrophysicists Victor Clube and Bill Napier believe that most of the Holocene epoch impacts that have affected human history, have probably been related to the break-up of Encke from a much larger cometary body, as they discuss in their books, *Catastrophes and Comets: The Destroyers of Cosmic Faith*, *The Cosmic Winter* and *The Cosmic Serpent*.

Asteroid impacts from the Taurids peak every 2,500 to 3,000 years and the next peak will begin sometime between the years 2400–3000 CE, according to Napier and Clube.[95] So we're reasonably in the clear—for now—from these known objects.

In June 2002, the "Eastern Mediterranean event" demonstrated how a small impactor can be dangerous, even if it doesn't hit anything. This high-energy aerial explosion over the Mediterranean Sea between Libya, Crete and Greece was detected by satellites and seismographic stations, with a calculated yield of approximately double that of the Hiroshima bomb. At the time, two nuclear powers, India and Pakistan were on high alert, in a tense military standoff. It has been said that had the explosion occurred a couple of hundred miles to the east, it could possibly have been taken for an attack, potentially triggering a nuclear war between these countries. (The explosion event and Kashmir are on the same latitude.)

INTERDISCIPLINARY DATING

Napier and Clube's research is well supported by the completely independent research of Mike Baillie, professor of dendrochronology (dating by tree-rings) at Queen's University in Belfast. Baillie looked at the evidence of tree-rings and ice cores from Greenland and identified a series of natural catastrophes from 3195 BCE to the beginning of the 14th century, which were consistent with meteor strikes. These events had various effects on human civilization, including the Fall of Rome, which he documents in his two books, *New Light on the Black Death* and *Celtic Gods: Comets in Irish Mythology*.

With the Holocene Impact Working Group's recent underwater discoveries of several large impact craters from historic times and the proliferation of known Near-Earth Objects within the inner solar system, it is becoming increasingly accepted that there have been catastrophic impact events in Earth's past and that presumably, there will be more of these in the future. These are their current areas of interest:

The hypothesized oceanic/glacial impacts that are currently under study include the large comet impact over the Canadian ice shield some 13,000 years ago [a.k.a., the "Clovis comet"] that triggered the beginning of the Younger Dryas climatic ordeal at 12,900 BP [Before Present], the Burckle-Madagascar impact at around 4800–5000 BP, that may be associated with the Great (Noah's) Flood and the boundary change from middle to late Holocene around 4800 BP, the Gulf of Carpentaria impacts that are associated with "years without summers" climatic event 535–545 AD, and Mahuika crater just south of New Zealand that may be related to the beginning of the Little Ice Age at around 1450 AD. The focus of the current group activity is further search for physical, anthropological and archaeological evidence in support of these and other impact events.[96]

To better illustrate the relationship between extraterrestrial impacts within historical times—and their impacts on human history, I have assembled a table of those currently under study by this group of researchers and others (see next page).

HOLOCENE IMPACTS & GEOMYTHOLOGY

Los Alamos National Laboratory archaeologist Bruce Masse and Italian geologist Luigi Piccardi recently collaborated on "Myth and Geology" (*Geological Society of London—Special Publication* 273; 2007), the first professional textbook on the emerging sub-discipline of geomythology, which pairs geological evidence of catastrophic events and reports of such events encoded into the mythological lexicon of ancient societies.

Masse's analysis of astrological references in multiple myths from the Middle East, India and China—describing planetary conjunctions associated with the flood storm, whose actual times of occurrence can be reconstructed using contemporary astronomy software—leads him to conclude that the event happened on or about May 10, 2807 BC.

... they report massive rain, falling for days at a time. This turns out to be exactly what can be expected if a large comet plunged into the deep ocean—it would loft nearly ten times its mass of water into the upper atmosphere, where it would spread widely and then fall, taking days to empty the skies. A large impact in the ocean would also cause gigantic tsunamis, as many of the myths report. In India, for example, Tamil myths tell of the sea rushing 100 km inland, a hundred meters deep.[97]

IMPACT NAME	REGION	COUNTRY	CRATER SIZE (KM)	IMPACT DATE
Clovis Comet	Laurentide Shield	Canada	Airblast	10,900 BCE
Köfels	Austrian Alps	Austria	4	3123 BCE
Umm al Binni	SE Iraq	Iraq	3.5	< 3000 BCE
Luna	Gujarat	India	2.15	< 3000 BCE
Burckle	S. Indian Ocean	Madagascar	29	2807 BCE
Chiemgau	Bavaria	Germany	0.5	500 BCE
Sirente	Abruzzo Italy	Italy	0.14	317 CE
Kanmare	Gulf of Carpentaria	Australia	18	536 CE
Tabban	Gulf of Carpentaria	Australia	12	536 CE
Grendel	Norway	Norway	18	540 CE
Mahuika	S. Pacific	New Zealand	20	1440 CE
Tunguska	Siberia	Russia	Airblast	1908 CE
Quetzalcoatl	Gulf of Mexico	Mexico	10	under investigation
Kangaroo	Northeastern Coast	Australia	5	under investigation
Joey	Northeastern Coast	Australia	4	under investigation
Judge	Long Island Sound	New York	1	under investigation

Table of Holocene impacts.

When examining the locations, dates and diameters of these impact craters, old legends seem to come alive. That is part of what is driving some of this new research: the growing awareness that Earth history *is* human history—that Earth's astrophysical history is human history. The impact event that created the 5,000-year old Luna crater in Gujarat, India is speculated to be the inspiration for hymns in the *Rig Veda* about the demigod Indra hurling thunderbolts or *vajras* and metallic stones.[98]

As previously mentioned, according to aerospace engineers Alan Bond and Mark Hempsell at the University of Bristol, a written record related to what caused the Köfels landslide in Austria in 3123 BCE was recently discovered on a Sumerian tablet stored at the British Museum. The Aten-class asteroid, which entered Earth's atmosphere at a very low angle, scorched a large swathe of the Middle East before plowing into the Tyrolean Alps. This event has been proposed as the source of the "fire and brimstone" of biblical legend that was God's punishment of Sodom and Gomorrah.[99] "Brimstone" is an old English word for sulfur, which is frequently abundant in asteroids. Big meteors are notorious for their stench, due to the sulfur vapor that gets released, as they streak through the atmosphere.

This particular story, if accurate, has such an amazingly unifying subtext; that a massive landslide in the Austrian Alps, within hiking distance from where Ötzi the Iceman had expired about 200 years previously, was caused by an asteroid impact whose flaming passage was recorded on a Sumerian tablet and which has come down through the ages as one of the greatest infamies of biblical legend. Events in the sky and on Earth separated by several hundreds of miles, being witnessed and interpreted by humans in the Bronze Age and now, thousands of years later ... how cool is that?

The 500 BCE Chiemgau impact in Bavaria left a large debris field and formed Lake Tüttensee. The 1.1-km-diameter rock smashed into the ground with a force equivalent to 8,500 Hiroshima bombs. It has been linked with the legend of Phaëton of the Greeks and Romans, who is said to have lost control of the chariot of his father, Helios the Sun god, accidentally driving it into the ground. In the Greek version of the myth, Zeus intervened in Phaëton's destructive joyride by thrusting a thunderbolt at the chariot, knocking Phaëton into the river of Hades, to his death.

The 317 CE Sirente crater in Abruzzo, Italy is linked to a vision Constantine had before leading the battle that made him Emperor of Rome. A cluster of three large oceanic impacts in the mid-500s CE has been linked to crop failures, famines, the Fall of Rome and literally, the "Dark Ages."

The Fall of Phaëton by Rubens.

APOCALYPSE: MAN-MADE OR *AU NATUREL*?

Short Answer: Both?

According to a 1998 survey by the American Museum of Natural History, the present era may be the fastest extinction event of all time. Many other scientists, such as E. O. Wilson of Harvard University, Norman Myers of the National Academy of Sciences and others predict that humanity's destruction of the biosphere could cause the extinction of one-half of all species in the next 100 years.[100]

> Scientists forecast that up to five million species will be lost this century. "... There are about 10 million species on earth. If we carry on as we are, we could lose half of all those 10 million species," Myers said.[101]

I guess this is what poet T. S. Eliot meant by, "This is the way the world ends / Not with a bang but a whimper." Myers puts the responsibility for stopping this extinction trend squarely on humanity's shoulders and there is no doubt that the daily activities of mankind are relentlessly destructive to nature and that the industrialized lifestyle of human beings is the leading cause of these extinctions.

However, it is also true that the Holocene extinction event has been underway for the past 50,000 to 12,000 years, depending on whom you ask, though it became more obvious with the rapid decline of Pleistocene fauna, notably the gigantic mammals of the Americas, like the saber-toothed cats, giant beavers, giant sloths, mastodons and woolly mammoths which perished forever at the end of the last Ice Age.[102] It has been theorized that their annihilation was the result of a more recent meteor-related extinction-level event in another 2005 theory:

A team of researchers led by Richard Firestone, of the Lawrence Berkeley National Laboratory, in California, recently announced the discovery of evidence that one or two huge space rocks, each perhaps several kilometers across, exploded high above Canada 12,900 years ago. The detonation, they believe, caused widespread fires and dust clouds, and disrupted climate patterns so severely that it triggered a prolonged period of global cooling. Mammoths and other species might have been killed either by the impact itself or by starvation after their food supply was disrupted. These conclusions, though hotly disputed by other researchers, were based on extensive examinations of soil samples from across the continent; in strata from that era, scientists found widely distributed soot and also magnetic grains of iridium, an element that is rare on Earth but common in space.[103]

This event is sometimes referred to as the "Clovis comet" because it is thought to have triggered the demise of the prehistoric paleo-Indian Clovis culture that'd had no more than a 500-year foothold in North America, a demise that was simultaneous with that of the megafauna. The theory has drawn a lot of contention from the scientific establishment but the evidence is stacking up in its favor. At archaeological digs ranging from Alberta to the Carolinas, researchers have noted a black layer of carbon-rich sediment that was laid down around 13,000 years ago. Above this layer, Clovis artifacts are never found. This black layer usually lies between older strata that have lots of mammoth bones and the younger layers immediately above, of sediment containing no fossils.

A theory first published in January 2009 from the University of Bristol attempts to discredit Firestone's "Clovis comet" hypothesis by claiming that it was a period of global warming and drying, during which there were rampant wildfires throughout the Americas.[104] However, there are lots of intricate, microscopic meteorite ejecta comprised of exotic metals; tektites and "spherules containing rare hexagonal-shaped diamond crystals" in this blackened layer through much of the Northern Hemisphere, that stand in defense of the Firestone hypothesis:

Additional evidence supporting the impact hypothesis has been the discovery of a multitude of diamonds encased in carbon spherules in the sedimentary layer, which correlates with the time of the supposed impact(s). These diamonds have been found at over 30 sites stretching from Germany to California. Some of the diamonds within this layer are aligned in a hexagonal crystal structure instead of cubic. Such structures, which are formed at extraordinarily high temperatures and pressures, have previously been found only within impact craters and meteorites. It is noteworthy that Clovis artifacts have only been observed in layers preceding the diamond layer in time, and none after it.[105]

Resistance to the "Clovis comet" hypothesis may be due, in part to the strong uniformitarianism that has prevailed in the Earth sciences, which has long given preference to gradual, endogenous explanations for everything from global warming to mass extinctions, rather than catastrophic and/or extraterrestrial explanations, which we will get into later in this chapter.

Perhaps we can settle on there being extinction cycles within extinction cycles. The ancient Maya would probably go with that idea...

COULD THE SUN "FRY US IN AN INSTANT"?

Short Answer: Maybe. A history-making coronal mass ejection (CME) could conceivably fry our power grid, along with a slew of communications satellites, leading to societal and economic meltdown—and millions of deaths in the short term.

Many of us learned in grade school that our Sun will become a red giant in about 5 billion years and that Earth would eventually get dragged into the Sun by gravity. New data, however estimates that the Earth has less good years left than we'd thought:

> The increase in solar temperatures is such that already in about
> a billion years, the surface of the Earth will become too hot for
> liquid water to exist, ending all terrestrial life.[106]

A billion years may be less than 5 billion but when Larry Joseph says that the Sun is working itself up to "fry us in an instant"—he means now! He is referring to a particular freak coronal mass ejection on Jan. 20, 2005 that was so strange, it took NASA six months to release the data—as they could not believe what their instruments were telling them.

The CME sent several billion tons of protons to the Earth in about 28 minutes, which would normally take 48 hours. Since light takes 8 minutes to travel from the Sun to reach the Earth, this means that the protons struck sensors on Earth at a rate only 3.5 times slower than the speed of light. That is some fast-moving plasma, in our little solar system.

This is exactly the sort of "Critical phenomena ... typical of complex systems [that] may lead to sharp spatial or temporal features,"[107] that was predicted in 1942 by Swedish astronomer Hannes Alfvén when he proposed his controversial "plasmic model" of the universe, which we'll get into a bit later.

I haven't found any further reports of freakish, time-warp proton speeds in CMEs. However, the fact of our civilization's complete dependency on a functioning power grid does leave us totally vulnerable, should that grid suffer a protracted failure. In a NASA-funded report produced by the National Academies of Science Space Studies Board in 2008, "Severe Space Weather Events—Understanding Societal and Economic Impacts Workshop Report,"[108] the prospect of an extended power outage due to cascading failures is real and quite dire. The report says that if an incursion of plasma from a storm as big as the Carrington event in 1859 (the largest ever measured) were to induce currents in the long wires of our power grids, it could lead to runaway currents that would melt a lot of hardware at several power stations, which could take months to repair around the world. With no alternate energy supplies in existence, this could conceivably lead to millions of deaths. We would fare far worse than the people of the mid-19th century because virtually all of our infrastructure, from food production to water pumps and treatment, from fuel pumps to food refrigeration— the entire lifeline of our civilization is mediated at so many points along the way by electric power, supplied by a centralized grid.

But the people most vulnerable to getting physically hit with no warning are the astronauts—and as it happens, NASA is currently gearing up to train more astronauts for its new Moon mission, a.k.a., "Apollo on Steroids," for which it plans to build a reusable 18-foot diameter capsule to conduct four-person Moon expeditions.[109]

The sun-lit side of the Moon is totally exposed to solar flares. It has no atmosphere or magnetic field to deflect radiation. Protons rushing at the Moon simply hit the ground or whoever might be walking around outside. An astronaut on the Moon, caught outdoors on Jan. 20, would have had almost no time to dash for shelter, and would have become sick. At first, he'd feel fine, but a few days later, symptoms of radiation sickness would appear: vomiting, fatigue, low blood counts. These symptoms might persist for days ... This January storm came fast and "hard," with proton energies exceeding 100 million electron volts. These are the kind of high-energy particles that can do damage to human cells and tissue.[110]

Should these time-warping solar plasma ejections become the norm and not an unusual, freak event, exposure to these energy fields could indeed become a very serious concern for those of us on the face of the Earth—and those of us flying the paranoid skies of commercial aviation ... especially as we're losing the protection of our magnetosphere ...

IS OUR MAGNETOSPHERE CRACKING UP?

Short Answer: Yes—and so is the heliosphere (the magnetic field around the Sun), which itself protects Earth from 90% of cosmic rays.

A breach was discovered in Earth's magnetic field "ten times larger than anything previously thought to exist," according to data recorded on June 3, 2007 by NASA's five new THEMIS spacecraft, which had been launched in February 2007 to explore the magneto-sphere, the bubble of magnetism that surrounds Earth and protects us from the most harmful radiation in the solar wind.

"The opening was huge—four times wider than Earth itself," says Wenhui Li, a space physicist at the University of New Hampshire who has been analyzing the data. Li's colleague Jimmy Raeder, also of New Hampshire, says "1027 particles per second were flowing into the magnetosphere ... This kind of influx is an order of magnitude greater than what we thought was possible ... The entire day-side of the magnetosphere was open to the solar wind." [111]

Besides the large size of the coronal mass ejection, the event was especially unusual because our magnetosphere behaved in a way that was totally abnormal. Normally, CMEs that are polarized to the north reinforce Earth's magnetic shielding, because Earth's magnetosphere is polarized in the same direction—but this blast had the total opposite effect. We were informed that our magnetosphere had become so loaded up with plasma and that we could look forward to "stronger geomagnetic storms than we have seen in many years." [112]

As of this writing, this event happened two years ago and I don't recall hearing about any auroral activity that's been particularly out of the ordinary. Still, the upcoming 2012 solar maximum is expected to be the "strongest since 1958 in which the Northern Lights could be seen as far south as Rome." [113]

What is unquestionable, based on tons of geological data, is that Earth's magnetic field has been declining for millions of years. This could be related to a geomagnetic reversal of Earth's polarity, which appears to have been taking place over a prolonged period and would go far in explaining why the magnetosphere is "cracking," as discussed above.

IS THERE A GEOMAGNETIC POLE SHIFT UNDER WAY?

Short Answer: Yes.

Geomagnetic reversals have happened several times before and the process has been very erratic and unpredictable in the history of this planet, usually taking thousands of years to complete:

> NASA's website features a map showing the gradual northward migration of the North Magnetic Pole in the past century and a half. Since more than double the time interval has elapsed since the last reversal, compared to the time lapse between the previous two pole reversals, some believe we may be overdue for the next north-south flip. However, though the interval between reversals of the Earth's magnetic field can be as short as 5,000 years, it can also be as long as 50 million years. There does not seem to be any logic or rule governing the planet's behavior.[114]

Although it is not known what the physical effects of a geomagnetic reversal might be for those of us living on the Earth while it takes place, I asked top geophysicist Bernhard Steinberger (more of him up ahead in this chapter) to guess what the potential effects might be and his response was, "During a reversal, energetic charged particles can more easily hit the Earth, and this may indeed lead to an increased occurrence of genetic mutations, but I don't think the effect is very dramatic. In any case, life has gone through many reversals, and it doesn't seem much dramatic has happened during those."[115]

IS THE EARTH LOSING ITS MOJO?

Short Answer: Yes.

A very interesting observation by Canadian science writer Mary-Sue Haliburton confirmed my own intuitions about the extinction of the North American megafauna and how the surviving animals were often smaller versions of the ones that didn't make it past the end of the last Ice Age.

It is not only the direction but also the strength of this magnetic field that is a concern. In the time of dinosaurs, at an estimated 2.5 gauss, it was eighty percent stronger than it is now. This may have been one of the reasons such gigantic life forms thrived. It is now accepted that a catastrophic event ended the reign of giant reptiles. However, they did not re-evolve to equivalent dimensions. And the disappearance of mammalian megafauna in more recent times is still considered to be a mystery. The mastodons and mammoths would have towered over modern elephants. Why are there so few large terrestrial animals today?

The smaller average size of modern animals may be due to the gradual decline of Earth's ... magnetism. Thousands of years ago the Chinese, with their astute discovery of bioelectrical energy flows known as "meridians," learned that magnetism promotes vigor in biological life. They used magnetic rocks in medical treatment. In the past century there has been a further decline of earth's magnetic field by another five percent down to only 0.5 gauss ... [116]

It isn't known exactly what would happen if Earth's magnetic field were to drop to zero gauss. It is guessed that electronic devices and satellites might cease functioning, that migrating animals might lose their sense of direction, that the atmosphere might expand and become thinner, causing altitude sickness at sea level and that deadly cosmic rays could eventually kill all life on Earth's surface. Some life-loving folks have been building underground bunkers, believing that this is the only way that they will survive. Anyone who wants to be completely paranoid and assured of some form of survival should have access to a comfortably outfitted underground bunker, with all the MREs and TP and other necessities to last at least eleven years. It may be of some comfort, or not, depending on your point of view, to know that the Svalbard Global Seed Vault, a secure seedbank located on the Norwegian island of Spitsbergen, contains a wide variety of plant seeds from locations worldwide in an underground cavern to provide a safety net against accidental loss of diversity in the event of a major regional or global catastrophe.[117]

WOULD A GEOMAGNETIC REVERSAL BE CATASTROPHIC?

Short Answer: No.

The general scientific consensus is that the magnetosphere will not entirely disappear and that humans will survive geomagnetic reversal, even if communications may become patchy for a while.

In the 2002 paper by UC Berkeley's Dr. Richard Muller, "Avalanches at the core-mantle boundary," he says evidence suggests that the Nördlinger Ries impact event, which occurred around 15 million years ago in what is now Germany, caused a geomagnetic reversal immediately following the impact that also left behind a 24-km crater. In the same 2002 paper, Muller states that the region between the core of the Earth and its surrounding mantle, once thought to be homogeneous, has now been found to vary greatly in viscosity and to have areas of "turbidity," suggesting that the core-mantle boundary could easily become destabilized,[118] lending credence to statements made by Graham Hancock during his on-camera interview for *2012: Science or Superstition*.

THE DAY THE EARTH CAPSIZED

"Do I give credence to pole shift theories? Yes I do, actually. What happened at the end of the Ice Age, to my mind has never been satisfactorily explained by mainstream science. It was truly a cataclysmic event. We had ice sheets that were two to three miles thick, sitting on top of northern Europe and North America, covering enormous areas of land and in a very short period of time, all of this ice melted down and returned to the oceans, raising sea level by 400 feet, all around the world, submerging ten million square miles of land.

"This was not the gradual drip-drip-drip of global warming, this was a dramatic and sudden change that took place on the Earth. I think that [there is a] possibility of some kind of capsizing of the Earth in space, some kind of pole shift, whether it was a shift of the outer crust or mantle of the Earth or whether it was actually a pole flip. And we know the magnetic poles have flipped repeatedly in the past.

"Magnetic North and South Poles are connected in some way that we don't fully understand, to the rotation of the planet. There is information to suggest that something very dramatic and very cataclysmic may have happened at the end of the Ice Age and that it may have involved a shifting of the poles, perhaps not a 180-degree shift, but a change of polar positions. This is all highly speculative. It can't be proved, but I don't see enough in conventional explanations of the end of the last Ice Age to explain the sudden dramatic and cataclysmic nature of the change that occurred.

"**My sense is this planet has at its heart a ball of molten iron with enormous mass and weight, which is also spinning inside the Earth itself. Is it possible that there is some interruption in this spin, perhaps to do with magnetism, perhaps to do with solar magnetism, which literally capsizes the Earth?** I wouldn't rule it out entirely. And there's much that's come down to us from the past to suggest that. I went into this in great depth in *Fingerprints of the Gods.*

—Graham Hancock, On-Camera Interview in *2012: Science or Superstition*

THE LAST OFFICIAL POLE SHIFT

According to accepted geology, "The last reversal was the Brunhes-Matuyama ... approximately 780,000 years ago." [119] It has not been established that a geomagnetic reversal occurred anytime afterwards, such as between 13,000 BP and 9000 BP, as Hancock and many others suggest. Officially, though it does remain rather unsettled and obscure as to what, exactly happened at the end of the last Ice Age.

Dr. Anthony Aveni is a professor of astronomy and anthropology at Colgate University. In his interview for the film *2012: Science or Superstition*, he does not see past and future magnetic pole shifts as having cataclysmic effects, in and of themselves.

Rendering of Earth's molten core.

GEOMAGNETIC REVERSAL: "NOT CATACLYSMIC"

"I don't think it's known whether the consequence will be calamitous, disastrous. It certainly won't be sudden ... What you have inside the Earth is a semi-molten mass of matter, magma that carries electrical charge. Now, when it comes to these reversals, the explanation of the "dynamo effect" [would] predict when these overturnings of magmatic matter take place [but] we don't know enough about that because the flow of material inside the Earth, as we understand it, is too random.

"We know less about what's going on a thousand miles under our feet than we do a thousand light-years away on a bright star like Rigel! That's kind of unsettling, isn't it? But we do know from archaeo-magnetism, from the study of magnetic records preserved in materials, that these changes have occurred.

"They don't coincide with the demise of dinosaurs, as far as we know. They don't coincide with an overflowing of the sea. They happen. And they must have had their effect. I have a sense that that effect would be short term and not cataclysmic."

—Dr. Anthony Aveni, On-Camera Interview in *2012: Science or Superstition*

SHOULD WE WORRY ABOUT EARTH CRUSTAL DISPLACEMENT?

Short Answer: No, according to accepted geophysics. Yes, if you don't trust the scientific establishment. (See the alternative view of this topic in **Chapter 3**).

The theory of Earth crustal displacement was superseded in the 1960s by plate tectonics, which posits that Earth's crust consists of eight major continental plates and several minor ones, with new crust upwelling from ocean ridges and old crust getting recycled at subduction zones. However, Earth crustal displacement was still in play in the early 1900s and a concise description of the theory appears in a book by one of its chief proponents, Charles Hapgood, in its foreword written by none other than Albert Einstein:

> In a polar region there is a continual deposition of ice, which is not symmetrically distributed about the pole. The Earth's rotation acts on these unsymmetrically deposited masses [of ice], and produces centrifugal momentum that is transmitted to the rigid crust of the Earth. The constantly increasing centrifugal momentum produced in this way will, when it has reached a certain point, produce a movement of the Earth's crust over the rest of the Earth's body, and this will displace the polar regions toward the equator.[120]

There is geological evidence that Earth's rotational axis was higher than 54° for as long as 2 billion years,[121] making the present-day equator the coldest part of the planet and the current polar areas the "paleo-tropics." Lots of tropical fossils have been found at extremely high latitudes in both the Arctic[122] and Antarctic, in geological layers from the Carboniferous period, 300–350 million years ago. This was at a time when all Earth's continents were still part of the Pangaea Supercontinent, before they began separating into Gondwana and Laurasia and spreading out into the continents that we know today. There hasn't been any evidence that has been officially accepted by modern science of a sudden, massive crustal shift occurring 12,000 years ago, at the end of the last Ice Age, as alleged by Hapgood or at any time in the past several hundred million years.

Many myths from all over the world refer to strange times, with reports that the Sun didn't rise—or didn't set (depending on the culture's location) for days and of other unusual movements of the Sun, which could be apt descriptions of what it was like to be on Earth if Earth's rotational axis were to shift or if the crust itself were to shift in a matter of days. But according to the scientists who are certified to read our planet's mineral entrails, these events physically happened hundreds of millions of years ago, over the course of millions of years—not days. If one is to believe the experts, these legends can't be taken literally, even if they do express a mysterious knowledge of Earth's Paleozoic contortions. Perhaps these legends were derived from shamanic visions ... ? The view of Allan and De-lair, the Flem-Aths and others, that both Earth's rotational axis and its crust shifted at the end of the last Ice Age, are irreconcilable with the official view.

TRUE POLAR WANDER: 1° PER MILLION YEARS

I looked up one of the top research scientists in the study of Earth's changing axial tilt, Dr. Berhard Steinberger, a German geophysicist with numerous university fellowships, and he was kind enough to give me the most accepted views on a variety of geophysical phenomena.

BRUCE: What causes the Earth's rotational axis to change?

STEINBERGER: Generally, the rotational axis always orients itself such that it moves excess masses towards the equator. Since the Earth isn't a perfect ellipsoid (flattened sphere) and even the ocean surface has humps and dents (the actual shape being called the "geoid") the rotation axis "tries" to orient itself to move the "humps" towards the equator.

The question, "what causes the rotational axis to change?" then essentially becomes, "what causes those humps and dents (i.e., the geoid) to change?"

This is something that is not addressed in our published paper, but we are right now working on another paper addressing this issue. Essentially, we think the biggest contribution to geoid changes are changes in the distribution of subduction—that is, where and how much tectonic plates converge and (as so-called subducted "slabs") sink towards the Earth interior. Based on what we know, when a slab sinks into the Earth, it first (as long as it is [more or less] in the upper half of the mantle) causes a hump in the geoid, which then would tend to move towards the equator, and when it gets to the lower part of the mantle it causes a dent, which then would tend to move to the pole.

Our [previous] article[123] essentially proposes a way to distinguish between (1) motions of plates relative to the underlying mantle and (2) a re-orientation of the entire Earth (i.e., the plates AND the underlying mantle) relative to its rotation axis.

I think an important aspect of our (as well as others') work is that the second mechanism works fairly slowly; my estimate is that it won't be much faster than one degree per million years. So it certainly cannot lead to substantial shifts of the crust (and underlying mantle) relative to the poles over historic times, as some proponents of crustal displacement theory would suggest.

I am ... aware of the book by Hapgood with the foreword by Einstein, but in order for a dramatic shift of the crust within a short time to happen it would have to be globally underlain by a low-viscosity (likely liquid) layer, and there is no evidence for that, and there isn't any evidence documenting such rapid shifts either.

BRUCE: Did these incidents coincide with the beginning of the split between North America, South America and Africa?

STEINBERGER: According to the model we are using the split between North America and Africa began at 175 million years ago (which would be during the clockwise movement) and the split between South America and Africa at 132 million years ago.

BRUCE: Do these movements relate to the early 20th century discovery of tropical fossils in Carboniferous layers in the Arctic of Spitsbergen, Norway?

STEINBERGER: We also point out in our paper that, superposed on these clockwise and counterclockwise movements, there is a general northward trend in the motion of continents, such that, for example, Spitsbergen was in the tropics during the Carboniferous. We argue in the paper that this general northward motion is likely not true polar wander but represents a motion of the continent relative to the mantle.

BRUCE: Do you agree with Williams, Kasting & Frakes, in the December 1998 *Nature* article, "Low-latitude glaciation and rapid changes in the Earth's obliquity explained by obliquity-oblateness feedback," where they propose that about 2.4–2.2 billion years ago and then again, about 820–550 million years ago, the Earth experienced low latitude glaciation and that the Earth's rotational axis was higher than 54° for a 2 billion-year period, that "Earth's obliquity may have been greater than 54° during most of its history, which would have made the equator the coldest part of the planet."?

STEINBERGER: Yes, I suppose it is possible that the obliquity has changed, and I presume they have done their math right to infer that the equator would be coldest with a 54-degree obliquity.

These changes in obliquity are concerned with changes of the Earth's rotation axis in space, whereas true polar wander is a change of the rotation axis relative to the Earth, so those two mechanisms can operate independently. However, as the paper you cite points out, there can be feedbacks between changes in obliquity and the internal dynamics of the Earth, which can change its oblateness and also can cause true polar wander.

(I would like to thank Dr. Berhard Steinberger for the time and care he put into his responses.)

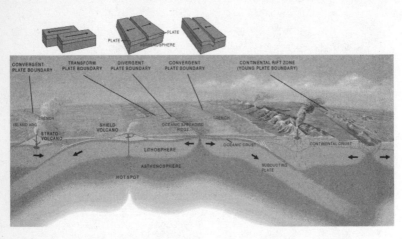

Tectonic plate boundaries and the full gamut of tectonic activity.

PLATE TECTONICS: BUSTING THE MYTH OF ABRUPT CRUSTAL SHIFT?

Hewing to the uniformitarianist line, Steinberger busts the myth of abrupt crustal shift. Not only is Earth crustal displacement theory incongruent with the accepted geological timeline, with its claims of massive cataclysmic movements of Earth's crust occurring 12,000 years ago, it also assumes Earth's asthenosphere, which is directly beneath Earth's crust to be much more liquid than it actually is. The idea that the asthenosphere would allow for the movement of the entire "shell" of Earth's entire crust to spin around Earth's mantle as a single unit, at neck-breaking, tree-snapping speeds—is "not even wrong," according to plate tectonics, which holds that the asthenosphere is essentially solid rock, albeit viscous enough to behave as a liquid over geological time scales, allowing for continental drift and subduction.

Evidence of continental drift are readily apparent at two "hotspot" locations of the planet, the Yellowstone caldera and the Hawaiian Islands. At Yellowstone, the North American plate has moved over 400 miles

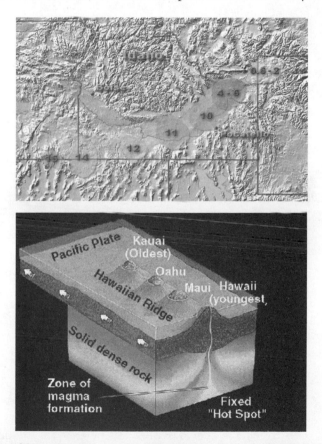

Images of the southwesterly continental drift of the North American plate from the Yellowstone caldera and the northwesterly drift of the Pacific plate, forming the Hawaiian Islands.

in a southwesterly direction from the caldera's hotspot over the past 15 million years and in Hawaii, the Pacific plate is drifting in a northwesterly direction with respect to its hotspot, forming a chain of islands, at a rate of about 32 mi. (51 km) per million years.

ARE WE ENTERING AN ENERGETICALLY HOSTILE PART OF THE GALAXY?

Short Answer: Maybe physically. Some say the effects are spiritually beneficial (See **Chapter 7**).

Russian geophysicist Dr. Alexey N. Dmitriev, author of the 1997 scientific paper "The Planeto-physical State of Earth and Life," claims that the solar system is entering an area of space with a high concentration of plasma, which is leading to irreversible changes in the basic energy states to which we are accustomed, here on Earth:

> Effects here on Earth are to be found in the acceleration of the magnetic pole shift, in the vertical and horizontal ozone content distribution, and in the increased frequency and magnitude of significant catastrophic climatic events. There is growing probability that we are moving into a rapid temperature instability period similar to the one that took place 10,000 years ago. The adaptive responses of the biosphere, and humanity, to these new conditions may lead to a total global revision of the range of species and life on Earth. It is only through a deep understanding of the fundamental changes taking place in the natural environment surrounding us that politicians, and citizens alike, will be able to achieve balance with the renewing flow of "Planeto-Physical" states and processes.[124]

In this 1997 paper, Dmitriev describes an increase in the kind of effects we have been discussing throughout this chapter, such as increased quantity of matter and energy radiating from the solar wind (which Dmitriev suggests is the major cause of global warming), the increased velocity of CMEs and geomagnetic field reversal. Dmitriev notes that these changes are being felt throughout the solar system, with polar ice caps melting on Mars, increasing atmosphere on both Mars and the Moon and the increased luminosity and magnetic storm activity in our solar system's gas giants.

Dmitriev states that the causes of Earth's changing geomagnetic and atmospheric conditions originate from external, interstellar, cosmic space and that they're an outgrowth of the "continuous creation that has shaped, and continues to evolve our universe." **He says the present excited state of the Sun is present within the whole organism that makes up the solar system; including all of its planets, moons, Near-Earth Objects, as well as the plasmas, and/or electromagnetic mediums and structures, of interplanetary space.** We will continue to see unprecedented energetic processes and formations on all of the planets and between their moons, and between the planets and the Sun.

According to Dmitriev, Earth is in the process of a dramatic transformation due to the geomagnetic shift, which will effect compositional changes in the ozone, and hydrogen, saturation levels of its gas-plasma envelopes. He says that this is part of the transition into a new state and quality of Space-Earth relationship.

> ... vast historical and statistical material has showed that Solar activity acts as an accelerator and moderator upon the whole biosphere, which manifests in the frequency and quantity of: births, deaths, harvests, epidemics, heart attacks, emergencies, bank crashes, catastrophes, suicides, population growths and decreases, etc.

> All of this places humanity, and each one of us, squarely in front of a very difficult and topical problem; the creation of a revolutionary advancement in knowledge which will require a transformation of

our thinking and being equal to this never-before-seen ... There is no other path to the future than a profound internal experiential perception and knowledge of the events now underway in the natural environment that surrounds us. It is only through this understanding that humanity will achieve balance with the renewing flow ... [125]

The official view of accepted science, at least according to NOOA (National Oceanic and Atmospheric Administration), the U.S. federal agency that monitors the conditions of the oceans and the atmosphere, is that, while it is clearly established that sunspots and CMEs have a direct effect on geomagnetic storm activity on Earth, the jury is still out on whether these can (or do) affect the Earth's climate (or crime rates, etc.).

Astronomers generally agree that the solar system has been passing through an interstellar cloud that is known as the "Local Fluff," for 44,000 to 150,000 years and that we will continue to traverse it for another 10,000–20,000 years. There are numerous reports from reliable sources about climate change occurring on individual planets in the solar system but I haven't found any Anglo-American scientific sources referring to these phenomena as "solar system-wide" (though they clearly are) and I've seen no major source attributing the *cause* of solar system warming to a rough patch we seem to be hitting in the Local Interstellar Cloud. It will be interesting to see how this story develops.

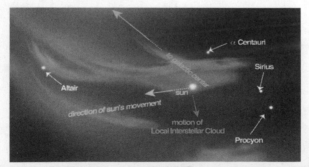

The Local Interstellar Cloud, a.k.a., the "Local Fluff."

THE ELECTRIC UNIVERSE

Many statements in Dmitriev's paper sound a lot like those proposed in the "electric model" of the universe, also known as plasma cosmology. As with all alternatives to the big bang model, it is referred to as a "non-standard cosmology."

> The two major pillars of modern cosmology are based on the theory of relativity and quantum theory and yet, as Einstein himself noted, the two are incompatible.
>
> And that may be because the two theories deal with matter, as if its only consequence is the bending of space. The Electric Universe, on the other hand, deals with the electrical structure of matter at the subatomic level, and works its way up, through living systems, if you like, planets, stars, galaxies and the entire universe and it shows that it is the electrical structure of matter that forms these amazing shapes we see in deep space ... Magnetic fields are threaded through space in all dimensions, through the solar system, on the surface of the Sun, between stars, within galaxies and even between galaxies.[126]

This alternative cosmology is presented in a documentary film called *Thunderbolts of the Gods*, viewable online for free as of this writing. The fundamental assertion of Hannes Alfvén, one of the theory's main proponents, is that *electromagnetic forces are equal in importance with gravitation on the largest scales*. This view is considered to be heretical by the mainstream, though Alfvén received a Nobel Prize for his work on this in 1970. Alfvén's biography, posted on the Los Alamos National Laboratory website, says that many of his ideas have played a central role in the development of several modern fields of physics and astrophysics, yet they were "dismissed or treated with condescension" for most of his career because they were so ahead of their time. "Alfvén's theories in astrophysics and plasma physics have usually gained acceptance only two or three decades after their publication." [127]

THE CORONAL HEATING PROBLEM

Contrary to what one might imagine, sunspots are the coldest features of the Sun. An unsolved problem in classical physics is an explanation of why the Sun's surface temperature is 6,000 K, yet high above the surface in the corona, the temperatures range around 2,000,000 K, seemingly in violation of the second law of thermodynamics. Such a radical deviation from this law requires an equally radical explanation.

The plasmic model holds that the Sun is electrically connected to the rest of the Galaxy and that it receives its energy from the Galaxy, acting as a focus for that energy.

> The question has been, "How do we get the energy from the center of the Sun, somehow past that surface to heat the upper atmosphere of the Sun to millions of degrees?"

> In the Electric Model, we don't have that problem, because if we have the energy arriving outside of the Sun, the first place you'd expect to see that energy expressed is above the Sun and its tenuous atmosphere. That is the place where particle acceleration occurs and the apparent temperature is very high, indeed, up into the millions of degrees ... [128]

I find this way of looking at the planetary bodies' relationship to each other to be quite fascinating and I encourage all of those likewise interested to check out this documentary and the related websites.[129]

THE THREAT FROM GAMMA RAY BURSTS

Paul LaViolette asserts that gamma ray bursts emanate cyclically from the galactic center every 10,000 years—and that the next such major impact event could occur "within a decade or so." However, he says that there are also less catastrophic events that occur more frequently, the most recent one around 700 years ago.

> While these low intensity events could have passed unnoticed in earlier centuries, today they could be extremely hazardous. The electromagnetic radiation pulse accompanying such a superwave would be far more intense than any gamma ray pulse we have experienced in modern times. **It could knock out electrical power grids and communication networks on a global scale and possibly even inadvertently trigger nuclear missile launchings. Consequently, study of this phenomenon deserves a very high priority.**[130]

It just so happens that Earth has lately been buffeted by the largest gamma ray bursts ever measured, coming from different exotic stars near the center of the Milky Way Galaxy. A giant flare from the magnetar, SGR 1806-20 was so intense it measurably affected Earth's upper atmosphere from 30,000 light-years away. Paul LaViolette claims that this explosion's massive gravity wave, traveling faster than the speed of light, triggered the cataclysmic 2004 Indonesian Earthquake/Tsunami, which killed 300,000 people and despoiled millions of acres of land.

Another soft-gamma-ray repeater 50,000 light-years away named SGR J1550-5418 has been erupting for months, logging 68 outbursts in the last week of January 2009 alone, drenching Earth in record levels of radiation.

It remains to be seen how these energies will affect us: gene mutation, cancers or complete global cataclysm, depending on the power of the energies that get blasted our way.

IS THE YELLOWSTONE SUPERVOLCANO IS GETTING READY TO BLOW?

Short Answer: No.

The most recent eruptions of Yellowstone were 150,000, 110,000 and 70,000 years ago, respectively at 40,000-year intervals from each other. Based on these numbers, we're 30,000 years overdue for an eruption of lava, which is what these three previous eruptions consisted of.

None of these three eruptions came close to the last caldera explosion which occurred roughly 600,000 years ago, when 240 cubic miles of Lava Creek Tuff were spewed around the rim, pyroclastic flows rushed across the countryside at over one hundred miles per hour, vaporizing everything in their path, huge 1,800 °F plumes of ash jetted into the stratosphere, scattered by the winds around the world, blanketing tens of thousands of sq. mi. in volcanic dust and leaving behind a gaping caldera 45 miles wide and 28 miles long.

During the first week of 2009, there was a swarm of hundreds of small earthquakes in Yellowstone, prompting wannabe hero, Christopher C. Sanders to post a YouTube video and the following web announcement, complete with a United States Geological Survey logo that week:

> I am advising all state officials around Yellowstone National Park for a potential State of Emergency. In the last week over 252 earthquakes have been observed by the USGS. We have a 3D view on the movement of magma rising underground. We have all of the pre warning signs of a major eruption from a supervolcano. I want everyone to leave Yellowstone National Park and for 200 miles around the volcano caldera.[131]

To the contrary, according to the USGS and officials at the park, their ongoing geophysical studies show that the conditions for an eruption, let alone a supervolcanic eruption, are simply not in place, though they do anticipate more lava flows in the foreseeable future.[132] The

USGS was considering taking legal action against Sanders for using their logo in the bogus warning that he posted.

UNIFORMITARIANISM VS. CATASTROPHISM

One of the world's leading catastrophists cited previously in this chapter, Victor Clube, retired dean of the astrophysics department at Oxford and former professional astronomer at the Royal Observatory, has had his lifework largely ignored by the scientific establishment and he is fully cognizant of the reasons why. He contends that uniformitarianism became dominant during the formative period of modern science, as a reaction against the rabid "fire and brimstone" worldview of Puritanism, which had been imposed upon the English people during the fitful, military rule of Oliver Cromwell in the mid-17th century. Cromwell became a man so despised that he was posthumously executed by an angry mob and his severed head was displayed on a pole outside Westminster Hall for over 25 years. As Clube explains:

> It was the pragmatic English decision to get rid of all the angels and demons, invisible sky gods, and a once visible heaven. It was the decision to stop worrying about the evidence of fireballs and the supposed behavior of comets. It was a decision to reconstruct the cosmos without heaven in the solar system and put it in the ether or outside the cosmos altogether of infinity, à la Bruno. It was the decision to create a purified, less frightening cosmos in much the same way as Aristotle did after Plato. On both occasions we shifted from astrology to physics, and from a sky of foreboding to a sky of inspiration, from prison and terror to freedom and hope. Indeed, **the cry of the revolutionary periods of 1640 to 1680 and 1760 to 1800, the time of the American War of Independence, was the cry of freedom from heavenly oppression, demons, and fireballs.**[133]

CHAPTER SIX

The History of the 2012 Meme

"We [are] not a sideshow, or an epiphenomenon, or an ancillary something-or-other on the edge of nowhere."[134]

—Terence McKenna, author, ethnobotanist, speaker

TERENCE McKENNA & *TIMEWAVE ZERO*

Before "2012" became a souvenir T-shirt for the "End of the World," it was a hipster reference—at least, that's how it came down to me, through Terence McKenna's brilliant books and spellbinding lectures, of which I was a fan in the mid-1990s.

The concept of *Timewave Zero* was initially presented in the 1975 book, *The Invisible Landscape: Mind, Hallucinogens, and the I Ching*, written by Terence McKenna and his brother Dennis, where they developed a theory that a wave-pattern of "novelty" was an inherent quality of time, which was dubbed the "timewave."

> ... what I noticed was that running through reality is the ebb
> and flow of novelty. And some days, and some years, and some
> centuries are very novel indeed—and some ain't. And they come
> and go on all scales differently, interweaving, resonating. And
> this is what time seems to be. And science has overlooked this,

this most salient of facts about nature: that nature is a novelty-conserving engine.[135]

McKenna arrived at his initial timewave pattern by graphing the progression of 64 hexagrams in the King Wen sequence of the *I Ching*, which means the *Book of Changes* and is among the most ancient of Chinese texts, dating as far back as 2800 BCE. The *I Ching* is a philosophy based on the dynamic balance of opposites, the unfolding of events and the inevitability of change. It is also a system of symbols used to find order in random events. McKenna had an insight that this progression may have been derived from an even more ancient Neolithic Chinese lunar calendar in which the 64 six-line hexagrams—384 lines in all—had represented the 384 days in a thirteen-month lunar year.[136]

The King Wen Sequence of the *I Ching*.

In order to correspond his timewave to actual historical events, he needed to peg the end-date of his graph. McKenna experimented with a few dates and eventually settled on the 2012 winter solstice, which is also the epochal end-date in the Mayan Long Count calendar. At the time, this date was an obscure factoid, virtually unknown in the West.

In 1994, an English-language MS-DOS version of his *Timewave Zero* software was released and became popular among a young generation of fans. Interest in the Maya calendar and in the significance of 2012 grew steadily during the mid-1990s through the activities of this ultra charismatic, subversive philosopher and self-described "ethnobotanist," who proudly chronicled his psychonautic journeys on "heroic doses" of hallucinogens, in his quest to solve the mysteries of the universe, all the while encouraging others to do the same.

The graph below is a screenshot of one of the older versions of his software, which depicts the four-year interval leading up to December 21, 2012. The downward movements indicate time periods of heightened novelty.

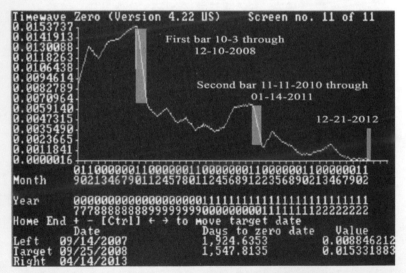

Screenshot of *Timewave Zero* software of the time period between September 2007 through December 21, 2012.

The first highlighted bar represents the period between October 3, 2008 and December 10, 2008. As it happens, these 9½ weeks correspond to a time period that billions of people would consider to have been tumultuous. It was during this time that it became evident that the global financial system was in a complete meltdown. Centuries'-old institutions folded and governments around the world used their treasuries to bail out the world's biggest banks. At the midpoint of this precipitous period of upheaval was the November 4, 2008 U.S. presidential election—resulting in the historic and novel election of the nation's first black president, Barack Obama.

The next two periods of major novelty predicted on this graph occur between November 11, 2010 and January 14, 2011, followed by the "last" event on December 21, 2012 when novelty is predicted to progress towards infinity and when any number of events that are currently unimaginable can be expected to occur.

An important feature of McKenna's *Timewave Zero* graph is its fractal nature, meaning that the same wave pattern can be seen when zoomed out, for a view of billions of years of Earth history, as can be seen when zoomed in to view a period within a phase of just a few months or days. In McKenna's words, in 1995:

> Hemlines are rising and falling, in a rhythm based on the rise and fall of empires millennia ago and these things are as causally linked as the orbit of the Earth is linked to the Sun, you see, because we are being drawn towards the attractor through shorter and shorter epochs ... there's a final 6-day period when all of these things are compressed again. So, you see what's happening? The spiral is tightening, as it goes faster and faster. The resonances are impinging. The thing is getting nuttier and nuttier and nuttier, as computers link all cultures together, all informational barriers dissolve. Everything is becoming connected to everything else, not only everything in the present moment

but all past moments, as well are being drawn, compressed, squeezed into the transcendental object at the end of time.[137]

THE "END OF TIME"

McKenna envisioned a spiritual/cosmic "singularity of novelty," where runaway newness would hit critical mass on December 21, 2012, entropy would cease to exist and humans would transcend the physical dimension of 3D, which is a recurrent theme of the 2012 mythos. (As an aside, I might note that it is common for people to report the experience of 3D reality as a preposterously pretentious, fake façade of a much deeper reality while tripping one's brains out).

McKenna's singularity is not to be confused with the "technological singularity" touted by inventor, author and futurist Ray Kurzweil, where "sometime within the next three decades" (which means it's already a fact), artificial intelligence will outstrip human beings in every way that intelligence can be measured and that computers would begin to improve upon their own designs, leading to a sudden, exponential growth of intelligence. Kurzweil also predicts that humans will enhance themselves with cybernetic implants to supercharge their intellectual and physical abilities and that within 50 years, medicine will have advanced to the point where aging is curable and human beings will technically be able to live forever. Kurzweil's hardcore materialist values are in plain evidence in his desire to resurrect his father:

> In a soft voice, he explains how the resurrection will work. "We can find some of his DNA around his grave site—that's a lot of information right there," he says. "The AI [Artificial Intelligence] will send down some nanobots and get some bone or teeth and extract some DNA and put it all together. Then they'll get some information from my brain and anyone else who still remembers him.[138]

One guesses that this process would be a test-run for his own eventual self-reconstitution, should he not live long enough to avail himself of future age- and death-eliminating medical advances. (Has he ever heard of *Frankenstein*?) McKenna's "singularity" is the complete opposite of Kurzweil's:

> History is ending because the dominator culture has led the human species into a blind alley ... what we need is a new myth ... [a] new true story that tells us where we're going in the universe and that true story is that **the ego is a product of pathology, and when psilocybin is regularly part of the human experience the ego is suppressed and the suppression of the ego means the defeat of the dominators, the materialists, the product peddlers.**
>
> **And as we break out of the silly myths of science, and the infantile obsessions of the marketplace ...** getting it all reconnected means putting aside the idea of separateness and self-definition through "thing-fetish." ... **[It] means tapping into the Gaian mind, and the Gaian mind is what we're calling the psychedelic experience ... And without that experience we wander in a desert of bogus ideologies ... This is what we have to do, to make the forward escape into hyperspace ...** the *dénouement* of human history is about to occur and is about to be revealed as a universal process of compressing and expressing novelty that is now going to become so intensified, that it is going to flow over into another dimension ... **The language-forming capacity in our species is propelling itself forward, as though it were going to shed the monkey body and leap into some extra-surreal space that surrounds us, but that we cannot currently see.**
>
> Even the people who run the planet, the World Bank, the IMF, you name it, they know that history is ending. They know by

the reports, which cross their desks: the disappearance of the ozone layer, the toxification of the oceans, the clearing of the rain forests. **What this means is that the womb of the planet has reached its finite limits, and that the human species has now, without choice, begun the descent down the birth canal of collective transformation toward something right around the corner and nearly completely unimaginable.**[139]

PSILOCYBIN & GALACTIC INSIGHT

"Modern shamans and explorers are utilizing sacred plants, like sacred mushrooms and I believe that there's an expanded state of consciousness that can be achieved ... it's a state of consciousness that has great unity ...

"Terence McKenna, for example, might be characterized as a modern shaman who utilized these substances. In his model, *Timewave Zero*, he pointed to December 21, 2012 as a sudden change, a rupture of plane.

"The Maya perspective that was pioneered and achieved over 2,000 years ago seems to have been fueled by the consciousness-expansion that can occur through the use of these psychedelic plants. It was a profound, integrative vision of reality that utilizes precession and the galactic alignment in this incredible model that is really galactic in scope."

—John Major Jenkins, On-Camera Interview in *2012: Science or Superstition*

SCIENTIFIC EVIDENCE FOR AN APPROACHING "END OF TIME"?!

Maybe all those mushrooms did help McKenna to perceive an approaching "end of time," after all! According to University of Salamanca Professors José Senovilla, Marc Mars and Raül Vera, time itself could cease to be and everything will grind to a halt—but billions of years from now—not in 2012:

> Scientists have come up with the radical suggestion that the universe's end may come not with a bang but a standstill—that time could be literally running out and could, one day, stop altogether ...

> The motivation for this radical end to time itself is to provide an alternative explanation for "dark energy"—the mysterious anti-gravitational force that has been suggested to explain a cosmic phenomenon that has baffled scientists ...

> The problem is that no one has any idea what dark energy is or where it comes from, and theoreticians around the world have been scrambling to find out what it is, or get rid of it ... [140]

Contrary to the New Age refrain that "time is speeding up," this theory suggests that time is actually slowing down:

> ... according to this new suggestion, our solitary time dimension is slowly turning into a new space dimension ... the far-distant, ancient stars seen by cosmologists would therefore, from our perspective, look as though they were accelerating ...

> In some number of billions of years, time would cease to be time altogether—and everything will stop.

> "Then everything will be frozen, like a snapshot of one instant, forever," Prof. Senovilla tells *New Scientist* magazine. "Our planet will be long gone by then."

... While the theory is outlandish, it is not without support. Prof. Gary Gibbons, a cosmologist at Cambridge University, believes the idea has merit. "We believe that time emerged during the Big Bang, and if time can emerge, it can also disappear—that's just the reverse effect," he says.[141]

EARTH ASCENDING & THE INVISIBLE LANDSCAPE

Talk about synchronicity. Working independently of Terence McKenna during roughly the same time period, author-academic José Argüelles also wrote a book that described correspondences between the Maya calendar and the *I Ching*.

In *Earth Ascending: An Illustrated Treatise on Law Governing Whole Systems*, Argüelles cites the work of German philosopher Martin Schönberger, *The Hidden Key to Life*, in which the sixty-four hexagrams of the *I Ching* are equated with the sixty-four DNA codons of the genetic code. Argüelles states that the two sets are exactly the same when written in binary order and he notes, "... the binary code not only underlies the code of life—the genetic code—but all electrical, electromagnetic and neurological functions as well." Argüelles predicts that the binary model will eventually be shown to govern the operations of all systems in the universe, "from the atomic to the galactic."

José Argüelles also discusses the theory of University of Pittsburgh physicist Oliver Reiser about the "psi field," which is related to what French philosopher Pierre Teilhard de Chardin had called the "noösphere," or "the sphere of human thought." Theosophists and New Agers refer to something similar called the Akashic Record, which is viewed to be a non-physical, etheric record of all human knowledge and actions. However, Reiser describes the psi field as an actual physical energy field and he related it to two major scientific discoveries that had occurred in 1953:

THE HISTORY OF THE 2012 MEME

Both the genetic code and the [Van Allen] radiation belts were "discovered" in 1953. What Reiser did was posit the noösphere or psi field as functioning in conjunction with the radiation belts and, like DNA, operating in a double-helix manner ... Pointing further to the actuality of a *planet mind*, with the obvious implication that humanity comprises a single organism ... [142]

Argüelles refers to this planetary mind as the "psi bank," of which the human element is just one component and he describes it as a creatively evolving information storage and retrieval system. He states that the psi bank is "giving *at this point in time* an actual *conscious* direction and purpose to the evolution of the planet." [Emphases by Argüelles.]

An unnerving development of late is that Argüelles has begun referring to himself as "Valum Votan," the reincarnation of the great Maya king of Palenque (who himself claimed to be an avatar of *K'ulk'ulkan*, a.k.a., Quetzalcoatl). He's alternately referred to himself as "the true heir of Pacal Votan and the instrument of his prophecy, Telektonon." [143] (Perhaps Argüelles discovered this by consulting the psi bank ... ?)

It's a bit of a shame, really, how Argüelles has continuously undermined a wider acceptance of his groundbreaking work with claims that are as strident as they are strange. We will come back to the concepts of the noösphere/psi bank/Akashic Record in **Chapter 7**, as these may well be germane to the next phase of the evolution of human consciousness.

JOSÉ ARGÜELLES & THE HARMONIC CONVERGENCE

The "end of history" in relation to the Maya calendar was first introduced to a broad public during a New Age event in 1987 called the "Harmonic Convergence," which was organized in part by José Argüelles and staged worldwide. It was held on the dates August

16–17, during a rare alignment within the inner solar system when Mercury, Venus, Earth and Mars lined up perfectly with the Sun.

There were those who speculated that this alignment would cause gravitational instability between the planets, that it might cause earthquakes and other catastrophes—but none occurred.

Less than a year before the Harmonic Convergence event, Mayanist scholars had released a mother lode of deciphered glyphs to the public. The Harmonic Convergence piggybacked on the novelty of this important archaeological and epigraphical breakthrough, which was very big news to the public at large, at the time:

> According to Argüelles and others, the Harmonic Convergence also began the final 26-year countdown to the end of the Mayan Long Count in 2012, which would be the "end of history" and the beginning of a new 5,125-year cycle. All the evils of the modern world—war, materialism, violence, abuses, injustice, governmental abuses of power, etc.—would end with the birth of the 6th Sun ... on December 21, 2012.[144]

Thus began the drip, drip, drip of a kinder, gentler countdown to Armageddon. The 2012 meme wafted in the background, like so much incense and panpipe music at a New Age book store until suddenly, as if cued by Terence McKenna's *Timewave Zero* program—the 2012 meme leapt from the bosom of the New Age community, where it had slumbered for over 20 years, to become the viral pop cultural phenomenon *du jour*.

JOHN MAJOR JENKINS' PARTICIPATORY COSMOLOGY

Jenkins has devoted decades to studying ancient Maya civilization and he has probably done more than anyone to raise awareness about Maya culture in recent decades. He is at his best when sharing his euphoric wonder at the genius of the ancient Maya and when he is inspiring us to seize the opportunity presented by visionary shamans 2,000 years ago to transform ourselves and our world; to restore our relationship to the Divine Immanence that's all around us and within us.

Jenkins is downright evangelistic in his promotion of "the great sophistication of the ancient Maya." More than anyone, he recognizes the many potentially transformational opportunities that are presented by the fact of the ending of the 13-*b'ak'tun* cycle at this juncture in human and Earth history. He stresses the importance of our *participation* in this pivotal moment, which he sees as a grand opportunity for humanity to take stock of its ways and to make responsible decisions for our future. As Jenkins sees it, the Apocalypse stops here.

> ... the 2012 date ... has its own special power based on the Mayan 13-*b'ak'tun* cycle calculation, which by now many millions of people are aware of ... **humanity's participatory expectation or collective belief is as much a determinant on transformation as anything else we have looked at. In fact, without the human element of participation, a desire for transformation, nothing will happen. In this sense, 2012 may be our best hope as a trigger point for creating a new world.**[145]

In his book, *Maya Cosmogenesis 2012*, Jenkins puts a lot of stock in the idea that the December 21, 2012 date is related to a purportedly rare astronomical alignment of the solstice meridian with the galactic equator that would occur on that date. He later admitted that this might already have occurred 15 years prior to 2012, while at the same time debating whether such an alignment could really be nailed down to a single day (the main problem people had with his original claim). In a subsequent book he asserted that the "window" of our "alignment" with the vast center of our Galaxy has been "open" since the 1980s and that this window will be "closed" around 2017 or 2018. So, why all this emphasis on "alignment in 2012," when from both an anthropological and scientific standpoint what's more solid is the *correlation* of the end-date of the 13th *b'ak'tun* with the winter solstice in December 21, 2012? Is this not amazing enough?

Alonso Mendez is of Maya heritage and he has studied and worked at the Palenque site for several years, creating a map of the site and helping to decipher the stele, following clues from archaeo-astronomy. Mendez objects to Jenkins' assertion that the 2012 end-date signified a "galactic alignment," in the minds of the ancient Maya, calling it a "mistake."

MAYA OPINION
• • • • • • • • • • •

"The Maya's perspective probably did not incorporate a view that saw the center of the Galaxy as a 'Dark Rift in the Milky Way.' We see much more strength in the philosophies of the Earth as the primary axis point for observations and for humanity, in general.

"It's a mistake, I think to make a great leap like that and impose upon a people a point of view that does not correspond to the time and place of the Maya people."

—Alonso Mendez, On-camera interview for *2012: Science or Superstition*

ANTHONY AVENI: GROUNDED IN SCIENCE

Dr. Anthony Aveni, professor of astronomy and anthropology at Colgate University, is the prolific author of mountains of academic papers and books about Native American civilizations and about archaeo-astronomy, including *People and The Sky: Our Ancestors and The Cosmos*, *The First Americans: Where They Came From and Who They Became*,

Foundations of New World Cultural Astronomy, Stairways to the Stars, Skywatchers, Conversing With the Planets: How Science and Myth Invented the Cosmos, Uncommon Sense: Understanding Nature's Truths Across Time and Culture, The Madrid Codex: New Approaches to Understanding an Ancient Maya Manuscript—and many, many more. He is the extremely rare, bona fide academic who is willing to speak on the subject of 2012, primarily because of what he sees as the "psychological damage" that the meme is wreaking upon children and other people:

> I must say that I worry seriously about the psychological damage that can be done by those expositors of bizarre theories and I won't name them, but there are many, many books about the cataclysm and the apocalypse and I do have an interest in bringing words out of academe to a broader public, I think it's very important that we scientific investigators play a role in educating the public, giving our side of things.[146]

Aveni is in agreement with the views of Mexican archaeologist Alonso Mendez, noted above, and he has strong scientific arguments against Jenkins' claims about the ancient Maya being aware of a "galactic alignment," let alone the Galaxy or whether they were really aware of the full cycle of the precession of the equinoxes.

AVENI: ANCIENT MAYA WERE NOT AWARE OF MILKY WAY GALAXY; GALACTIC PLANE DISCOVERED BY RADIO ASTRONOMERS IN THE 1950s

"... [it wasn't] until the 18th century that an understanding of the Milky Way Galaxy as a large unit that's super-ordinate to our solar system in the local system of stars. That is not to say that any other culture [around] the world could not have seen it that way. But the Maya were not terribly concerned with these super-ordinances. To them, for most non-Western cultures before the Enlightenment ... things are geocentric. In fact I'll go further than that, I'll say they're 'lococentric' ...

"The galactic plane, as a fine line is not visible to the naked eye. Look and see for yourself ... This plane was defined by radio astronomers in the 1950s. It is the plane where the density of hydrogen in the Galaxy is the strongest, that hydrogen being determined by radio astronomical observations.

"... the galactic plane, *per se* and what I've seen diagrammed in most [2012-themed] books and articles, comes right off of a computer. It's the plane of neutral hydrogen determined by radio astronomical observations, [it's] not visible."

—**Dr. Anthony Aveni, On-Camera Interview in *2012: Science or Superstition***

Dr. Aveni agrees that there is great appeal in the ancient Maya vision of succeeding World Ages, which consistently improve upon one another, as well as in their view of a cosmology that is participatory, of which he said,

Maybe we can learn something from them and I'm all for it. I think there could be a positive outcome from the 2012 "hype and mania," as I've characterized it.

Perhaps it'll make us take our cosmology a bit more seriously, look into it a bit more and think a little bit more about collective human consciousness and think a little bit more about what we can do to make the world a better place.[147]

As to any claims that the Long Count's 13-*b'ak'tun* end-date was timed for anything besides a winter solstice, Aveni sees these as doubtful. It might also be worthwhile to point out here that Aveni fully admits that he has never had any "shamanic" experiences. One might therefore suspect that despite all of his impressive technical knowledge, Aveni does not have a very deep understanding of the intensely shamanistic aspect of ancient Maya culture. One would wonder whether academics without a direct experience of this sensibility and worldview could be very well-qualified to fully appreciate the subjects of their study? Such scholars can be helpful in assembling statistics and performing statistical analyses—which is important work, as well—but if their mentalities do not comprehend the shamanic realms, which were and continue to be so central to the Maya way of life, one wonders if can they truly claim to be experts on this culture?

DARTMOUTH ACADEMIC BASHES JENKINS

Not all academics are as charitable as Dr. Aveni. Nowhere is Jenkins' work as derisively bashed as it is in an undated article, "The Astronomical Insignificance of Maya Date 13.0.0.0.," posted online by Vincent H. Malmström, Professor Emeritus of Geography at Dartmouth College and author of the 1997 book, *The Calendar in Mesoamerican Civilization,* now out of print but viewable on his personal website.[148]

> More recently, a writer with far less impressive academic credentials ... has at last given us the answer: according to John Major Jenkins, the Maya fixed the termination of their Long Count to mark the coincidence of the winter solstice with the "galactic center of the universe." ... He assures us furthermore that it was a relatively simple matter for the Maya to identify the galactic center of the universe because it lies in the middle of the Milky Way, which they visualized as "the birth canal of the Mother Goddess", "a source-point, or creation place." What this has to do with the winter solstice, or

how the latter, which can be easily marked by horizon-based astronomy *during the day*, can be shown to coincide with the center of the
Milky Way, which can *only be seen at night*, he doesn't inform us ...
our brash new savant has credited a people who had no knowledge
that the Earth was even round, much less that it wobbled on its
axis, with more than supernatural powers. In the process, however,
it would seem that Jenkins has advanced our understanding of the
Maya from the sublime to the ridiculous.

But, before rejecting this imaginative hypothesis altogether, I decided to test it to see if, in fact, the Maya themselves would have been
able to view this momentous "event" as it takes place on December
21, 2012. For this purpose, I used the Voyager computer program
as my "planetarium" and I chose the Mayas' major astronomical
center of Edzná in the Yucatán as my viewing point. (Actually, it
makes no difference which viewing point is selected within the Maya
realm, for the results are the same everywhere in Mesoamerica.) As
dawn approaches on that critical day, the Galactic Center, imbedded
as it is in the Milky Way, would "appear" above the horizon just as
the Sun itself does about 6 degrees farther to the north. Of course,
the only problem is that, with the Milky Way gone as a point of
reference, the Galactic Center is also invisible, and it remains so as
long as the Sun is above the horizon. Expectantly I looked forward to
the sunset, hoping to regain my critical reference point once the sky
again darkened. But no such luck. I found that the Galactic Center
slipped below the horizon at 4:57 p.m. that afternoon, exactly half
an hour before the Sun itself sets some seven degrees farther to the
south. So, so much for "much ado about nothing." [149]

Jenkins' main position is defensible if one accepts his assertion that the
pre-telescopic Maya priest-kings were in possession of such powerful
shamanic vision, aided by the use of psychedelics, that they would un-

derstand that the Earth was part of the Milky Way Galaxy. Jenkins has thus found himself the unlikely champion of psychedelics, which he expounds upon at length, in a manner that is so stilted and scholarly, it truly borders on the comical! Jenkins puts a lot of stock in the powers of shamanism and psychedelics—and apparently, there are plenty of alternative thinkers who agree with his views, such that he continues to maintain his standing as an independent scholar with a loyal following.

THE DREAMSPELL & TOAD VENOM

My first presentation with what I thought was the Maya calendar was during the heady days of the Internet bubble around 1997, while I was working at the film-production division at New York online video pioneer (long since defunct) Pseudo.com, who's former CEO recently announced that it was a "fake company." [150] Well, Internet history was made in a fake company with 10,000 sq. ft. of prime SoHo office space and where more online radio and TV programming was produced and "Quakecasts" were held than at any company prior to the tech crash in 2000.

I'd stayed in the office late into the evening, writing a business plan with my boss and along came his new friend with a cosmic-sounding moniker that he had given to himself.

For the sake of his privacy, I'll call him "Starshine." He was a wild-eyed, grizzled longhair who'd been rudely awakened in the early dawn when his property was raided by the DEA. He'd been ranching *bufo* toads in his basement and selling the psychedelic powdered venom to happy customers, like my boss. Starshine was out on bail and a federal court hearing loomed the following month. Starshine was unflapped. In fact, he was absolutely confident that he would emerge victorious, by dint of his supernatural powers—which he'd acquired through the incessant use of toad venom.

I never discovered Starshine's legal fate but I'll never forget how excited he was about the "Mayan calendar," which he showed to me. He ranted about how our Gregorian calendar was off-kilter "on purpose, to keep us off-balance" and he raved that if all human beings were to follow the "Mayan calendar," the whole planet would be healed of its woes, as we took our rightful place in the universe, in cosmic attunement. Starshine's messianic fervor to convert the planet to the "Mayan calendar" was intense—and it even made some sense—until he started to explain it to me ...

Why would memorizing a calendar with whimsical year-names like "Red Electric Dragon" and "White Planetary Wizard" put me in sync with the cosmos? I found these designations to be quite frankly, what New Yorkers like to call "super-cheese" or just plain "cheese." My impatience with this motor-mouthed, toaded-out federal defendant grew as his litany became increasingly interspersed with his desperate pleas for me to have sex with him.

What I didn't know until I started researching for this book was that Starshine had been giving me a presentation of José Argüelles' *The Dreamspell* calendar and that his hysterical zealotry was somewhat representative of that of many members of the international movement/business that Argüelles had founded. Starshine was a fanatical convert to *The Dreamspell*—he was not teaching me the Maya calendar.

Argüelles has had scuffles with Mayanists and supposedly with a couple of Maya priests, as well. As John Major Jenkins recounts,

... in 1992 I published a review of the calendar game-system created by José Argüelles called *The Dreamspell*. The system was very different in structure, operation, and placement in real time from the surviving 260-day calendar in Guatemala. Yet it identified itself as "the Mayan calendar." It was over 50 days out of synchronization with the authentic day-count and also skipped counting February 29th—something Maya calendar-priests would never do.

My critique of these and other issues with *The Dreamspell* are well-documented; between 1992 and 1996 I responded to hundreds of letters, often handling venomous attacks from those who had joined the *Dreamspell* clique and saw my truth-telling as threatening.[151]

Argüelles is undeniably brilliant, if a bit self-aggrandizing, with his diva-like deportment and vehement convictions. Here's an extract from a 1987 interview with Tami Simon:

The code upon which the Mayan calendar is based, and upon which Great Cycle [of 5,125 years] is based, is something like the periodic table of elements, only it's a periodic table of galactic frequencies ... that govern the manifestation of all phenomena at many different dimensions. It's the universal code. It's a phenomenal, mind-boggling code ...

We're precisely at a point in time where the difference between a considerable number of us waking up and taking command, and not waking up is the difference between the planet going into self-destruction and the planet continuing on its evolutionary path ...

From the point of view of the code, being awake means being means opening up receivers. **This can only be done by having a genuine change of heart about what is happening in our lives, about what is happening on our planet, and realizing that if we are to continue, we must open up our receivers so that we can begin to receive the information and know what to do next ...**

... the Great Cycle is only a sub-factor of a larger cycle ... that we're dealing with [of] approximately 26,000 years, this cycle roughly encompasses the evolutionary stage of *Homo sapiens.*

The peak of the last Ice Age was in 24,000 BC. This was when what we call "modern humanity" emerged. So, this 26,000-year cycle actually encompasses five Great Cycles. We're in the fifth and last of a set of Great Cycles that began in 24,000 BC. It's on this basis that we're looking at 2012 as being a very, very critical juncture. It's what I refer to as "galactic synchronization," and it also is a major evolutionary shift ...

There are other dimensions of reality, and there are more evolved stages of being and intelligence than ours. The universe is be-nign and compassionate. No one's out to destroy us.[152]

MAYANISM: A NEW AGE CREED

Argüelles is a quintessential exponent of Mayanism, the syncretism of New Age beliefs and pre-Columbian Maya mythology. Some other well-known proponents of related ideas include Erich von Däniken, Barbara Hand Clow, Drunvalo Melchizedek and Carl Johan Calleman.

The extraordinarily charismatic writers noted above have produced a large body of well-written, compelling books, whose ideas deviate sub-stantially from mainstream worldviews. I guess one could say that some of these authors are shifted so far out of the "old paradigm," that their pronouncements are marooned within the context of the mainstream.

CARL JOHAN CALLEMAN'S NINE HELLS

The Swede Carl Johan Calleman comes from a scientific background, with a degree in toxicology from the University of Stockholm. Con-trary to his pointed avowal of not bringing a "New Age" approach to his study of the Maya calendar, I think most people would agree that his approach is among the most New Agey out there. In essence, he believes that the Maya Long Count calendar points to a radical shift in the human species whereby duality consciousness will be replaced by a "unitive" field of enlightened consciousness. The reason why the Maya calendar is "ending" is because the dualistic mindset that "needs" time will no longer exist and "all limiting thoughts will disappear."[153] Well, I could certainly see that happening if the Earth exploded and everybody died!

Calleman says that his childhood interest in the subject of the Maya[154] was suddenly crystallized during his attendance at a ceremony for that seminal global New Age event, the 1987 Harmonic Convergence, while he was living on the West Coast of the United States. He freely admits that his full-time devotion to the Maya calendar began shortly afterwards. I guess we can infer that he became a devotee of Argüelles' movement and that he must have been very honored to co-author *The Mayan Calendar and the Transformation of Consciousness*, with the demigod, "Valum Votan," himself.

UNDER-WORLD	SPIRITUAL COSMIC TIME	PHYSICAL EARTH TIME	INITIATING PHENOMENA	SCIENTIFIC DATING OF INITIATING PHENOMENA
Universal	13 x 20 *k'ins*	260 days	?	2011 CE
Galactic	13 x 20^0 *tuns*	4,680 days	?	1999 CE
Planetary	13 x 20^1 *tuns*	256 years	Industrialism	1769 CE
National	13 x 20^2 *tuns*	5,125 years	Writing	3100 BCE
Regional	13 x 20^3 *tuns*	102,000 years	Speech	100,000 BCE
Tribal	13 x 20^4 *tuns*	2 million yrs	First Humans	2 million BP
Familial	13 x 20^5 *tuns*	41 million yrs	First Primates	40 million BP
Mammalian	13 x 20^7 *tuns*	16.4 billion yrs	Matter: Big Bang	16 billion BP

Figure: The durations of the Nine Underworlds in both spiritual and physical time and some of their initiating phenomena.[155]

Calleman's main divergence from the mainstream view can be seen in the alterations he's made to the most widely accepted correlation of the Maya and Gregorian calendars, with his version ending on October 28, 2011. Obviously, this caused John Major Jenkins to set out after him, like an attack dog. Jenkins' position is that the correlation question was fully and finally resolved in 1950, "after decades of research." [156] Jenkins meticulously refutes Calleman's model in his "Review-Essay Critique of Carl Johan Calleman's 'Solving the Greatest Mystery of Our Time: The Mayan Calendar'":

[Calleman] neglects to state clearly that 2012 is not a fanciful creation of New Age writers, but is based on a century of academic trial and tribulation, reconstructing the correlation of the Maya calendar with our own Gregorian calendar. This work involved correlating the base date of the 13-*b'ak'tun* cycle of the Long Count calendar with a Julian Day number corresponding to a Gregorian date. The work was accomplished through many decades of interdisciplinary effort, comparing evidence from astronomy, surviving Maya codices, ethnography, hieroglyphic statements on Creation Monuments, and iconography. [157]

Calleman's main disagreement with the prevailing December 21, 2012 end-date correlation of the Maya and Gregorian calendars revolves around the "Nine Hells" of Maya prophecy, during the current and final *b'ak'tun* of the Maya Long Count calendar. While Calleman says that, "it is not possible to gain detailed understanding of the origins of these [Maya] Underworlds," he confidently states that, "we may surmise that they are sequentially activated frames of consciousness mediated by Earth's inner core." [158] That is some woo-woo stuff! The lynchpin of Calleman's theory is this:

Each of the Nine Underworlds of Mesoamerican mythology is a different "creation" generated by a cycle 20 times shorter than the one upon which it was built ...

As of this writing (2003), we have come to the third day of the creation of the Eighth Underworld. There are now only two more Underworlds to go—the Galactic (12.8 years) and the Universal (260 days)—until we reach the highest level of creation. In this hierarchical structure, the different frames of consciousness do not replace each other, nor do they follow one another. Instead they add to each other, so that the creation of all the Underworlds, and thus the climb of the nine-story cosmic pyramid, will be completed at the same time, October 28, 2011, in the Gregorian calendar ... [159]

New Age author/publisher Barbara Hand Clow not only embraces Calleman's view, her latest book on 2012, *The Mayan Code: Time Acceleration & Awakening the World Mind* is largely an endorsement and an explication of Calleman's system.

GREGG BRADEN'S *FRACTAL TIME*

Gregg Braden is a former computer scientist who has been a leading author and lecturer in the New Age sector of the self-improvement industry since the late 1990s. His latest book, *Fractal Time: The Secret of 2012 and the New World Age* melds Terence McKenna's timewave concept with the theory championed by John Major Jenkins, that the ancient Maya purposefully timed their current World Age cycle to end during the "rare astronomical configuration":

... it's what the Maya knew about Earth's journey through the Heavens that makes their story even more astounding.

Specifically, they knew that during a zone of time before and after the 2012 winter solstice, **Earth and our entire solar system would move into a position that is extraordinary by any standards. It's during this time that we pass an imaginary line that defines the two halves of our disk-shaped Galaxy** ... As the planets of our solar system line up with one another and our Sun, our crossing of the conditions that it creates signal the completion of the great cycle, as indicated by the Mayan calendar.[160]

Braden takes great care to support Jenkins' scientifically tenuous assertion that the ancient Maya timed their *b'ak'tuns* to culminate during a "galactic alignment," that the Maya ancients were ever so aware of the Galaxy and the Sun's "alignment" with the galactic equator. However, Braden is wise to state, "Because of the size and relative distances of heavenly bodies to us here on Earth this alignment appears as a slow, gradual shift over a period of time."

The centerpiece of Braden's book is the interactive "time code calculator," based on the 5,125-year, 13-*b'ak'tun* cycle of the Maya Long Count calendar, an automated version of which is on his website, along with instructions on how to use it.

Just as such gifted seers can identify the events that are probable at a given time, the Time Code Calculator shows us when we can expect the conditions of the past to play out again as our present or our future.[161]

Braden offers the time code calculator as a useful aid in self-empowerment, revealing cycles in our personal lives and giving us the opportunity to act differently the next times certain situations arise, calling these revealed moments "choice points." Ironically, this is the name of a large and often controversial data-mining company that provides private intelligence services to the U.S. government and to corporations. Maybe this nomenclature is a nod to Braden's previous career as a senior software programmer for a U.S. defense agency, which he freely admits to in the introduction of *Fractal Time*.

Braden describes his system, which incorporates McKenna's timewave; Jenkins' "galactic alignment"; the Golden Ratio, also known as *phi* (approximately 1.6180339887); and the 1950s many-worlds interpretation of quantum mechanics—as nothing less than a "new path of self-discovery." [162]

To him, 2012 represents a mass "choice point" for human beings and he encourages his readers to "choose" which universe they want to live in. He also claims, in so many words, that the solar system has been moving through the apsis (furthest distance) in its elliptical orbit around the galactic center of the Milky Way, resulting in a Dark Age, where:

> ... we would forget who we are—our connectedness to one another and the Earth ... It's precisely this disconnected feeling that seems to be the consequence of the cyclic journey that carries us to the far end of our galactic orbit. It's also the fear that is spawned by such feelings that has led to the chaos of war, and destruction at the end of cycles past. [163]

Fair enough, but I haven't found any scientific evidence to support Braden's claim that our solar system's orbit is elliptical and now returning towards a closer pass of the galactic center, after a long period of estrangement. Actually, I found something completely different: Teams from the Universities of Massachusetts and Virginia using a supercomputer sorted through half a billion stars to create a new star map, suggesting that the solar system—whose movement around the Galaxy is described as nearly circular, contrary to Braden's assertion—may not even have been orbiting around the Milky Way Galaxy for very long. They claim that the solar system did not originate in the Milky Way Galaxy; rather it was pulled out of the Sagittarius Dwarf Galaxy by the stronger gravitational force of the former:

> ... our own Milky Way is consuming one of its neighbors in a dramatic display of ongoing galactic cannibalism ... [and] it has been postulated that this is the real reason for both global warming ... [and] higher temperatures ... on virtually all the planets in our system ... since higher energy levels of the Milky Way are almost certain to cause our Sun to burn hotter and emit higher energies.[164]

Braden anticipated criticism that *Fractal Time* is packed with pseudo-science in his book's introduction: "This book is *not* a science publication ... This book is *not* a peer-reviewed research paper ... **It has been written in a reader-friendly way that describes the experiments, case studies, historical records, and personal experiences that support an empowering way to think of ourselves in the world.**"[165] Gregg Braden's audience likes feeling empowered and he delivers. But although Braden used to be a scientist, if you're looking for hard science in his books, he himself warns that you're searching in the wrong place.

2012 & ACADEMIC MYSTIFICATION

Despite their impressive academic credentials and their important achievements in the field, members of academe who specialize in the Maya civilization are not immune to a bit of mystification of their own. In a recent CNN article, a very respected academic, David Stuart, director of the Mesoamerica Center at the University of Texas at Austin, repeated the academe-approved mantra on the subject:

"There is no serious scholar who puts any stock in the idea that the Maya said anything meaningful about 2012." [166]

Stuart is correct to suggest that most academics in his field despise the 2012 hype machine and the whole "Galactic Maya" business, the parade of Johnny-Come-Latelies and Know-Nothings, the profusion of wacky books and shows being released that distort or otherwise ignore the Maya.

If you'd devoted your whole life to digging up and decoding Mayan artifacts, as Stuart has done, you wouldn't want to give any juice to the exponents of New Age Mayanism. Most Ivory Tower folks won't touch 2012 with a 10-foot pole. Academics appear to stand united in a wholesale pooh-poohing of the 2012 phenomenon. If so, it's an unfortunate, missed opportunity to promote greater awareness of the very culture that they are so passionate about and an opportunity to drive more bequeathments towards their Mesoamerican centers. If nothing else, 2012 is an opening for all of us to gain a better understanding of Mesoamerican peoples and to acknowledge their innumerable contributions to civilization, both past and present— and who better to disabuse us of the misconceptions being sold in the 2012 bonanza and to enlighten us about the real wisdom of the Maya than the experts—besides the Maya, themselves, of course ...

Stuart claims that the ancient Maya "never said anything meaningful about 2012," inasmuch as they obviously never said a thing about the Gregorian calendar ... Somebody, talk me down: Stuart's statement is otherwise a total mystification, on a level more egregious than the balderdash of a carnie who wants to sell you that Crystal Skull. Note the emphasis: "... no serious scholar ... puts any stock in the idea ..."

Well, what about the ancient Maya, who *created* the Long Count calendar? Did they "put any stock" in their dates, which they meticulously set, according to cycles within cycles, to begin some 2,000 years in their own past and to end 1,000 in their own future?

Given their predilection for prophecy, I can only guess that this World Age cycle and its eventual end must have been "meaningful" to the ancient Maya. It's odd to observe such a "facts-be-damned" attitude in such a serious academic as Dr. Stuart, someone who was part of the group who decoded much of the Maya script in the 1980s and who is the youngest-ever recipient of a MacArthur Fellowship "Genius Grant" at the age of 18.

If so few relics remain that refer to the end-date, then you can thank the 16th century Spaniards for destroying almost everything. Else, chalk it up to the Maya for not obsessing about an "end time" that was 1,000 years in the future—and, as it turns out, one that punctuated five centuries of oppression and genocide at the hands of the Spaniards and succeeding military governments and corporations, like the United Fruit Company.

Stuart and fellow academic Dr. Aveni wring their hands and bellyache about the misrepresentation of the Maya throughout that CNN article and elsewhere, yet if it weren't for the "2012 phenomenon," neither of them would have signed book deals to "set the record straight." I very much look forward to their books, hopefully on a clear day post-2012, when all is fine and dandy with the world.

WHAT THE HELL IS "PLANET X"?

At the opposite end of the credibility spectrum, there's the urban legend that's been circulating since the mid-1990s about "Planet X," which has recently come to be associated with 2012. Planet X was a term that was originally used over the centuries to describe undiscovered objects that were predicted to be found orbiting the Sun beyond Neptune, of which several have been discovered and given proper names by astronomers, such as Pluto. In the past decade, there have been many new discoveries of such trans-Neptunian objects, including Eris, which is 27% bigger than Pluto, Sedna, Makemake, Orcus, Haumea and others.[167]

In recent years, the significance of the term "Planet X" has morphed into a bogeyman of contemporary New Age legend, threatening to knock all the local planets, comets and asteroids out of their orbits and headed on a fatal collision course with Earth.

ZECHARIA SITCHIN, NIBIRU & THE ANNUNAKI

The Planet X meme has its roots in the works of Zecharia Sitchin, author of thirteen books released between 1976 and 2009 that concern an as-yet undiscovered 12th Planet, which the ancient Sumerians called "Nibiru," that allegedly has a very elliptical, 3,600-year orbit around the Sun.

Sitchin claims that this unlikely celestial body is the home planet of the highly advanced "Annunaki," the extraterrestrial genetic engineers of *Homo sapiens* and the founders of the Sumerian civilization. Sitchin translates "Annunaki" from Sumerian into Hebrew as the "Nephilim" of the Bible, which was translated into the English of the King James Bible as "giants." The Sumerian word *shem*, which is translated into "renown" in the King James Bible, Sitchin translates as "the rocketship":

There were giants [Annunaki] in the earth in those days; and also after that, when the sons of God came in unto the daughters of men, and they bare children to them, the same became mighty men, which were of old, men of renown [the rocketship].

—Genesis 6:1–4 (KJV)

Sitchin's volumes expound at length on the "real" meanings of the Sumerian cuneiform tablets, whose legends are often older versions of many biblical and classical myths. He also claims that the Annunaki "engaged in genetic engineering to fashion 'The Adam'— the Earthling—by upgrading the wild *Homo erectus* found in southeast Africa to become *Homo sapiens* [you and me]."[168] A mutiny by Annunaki workers in their gold mines on Earth created a need for a new labor pool; by hybridizing *Homo erectus* with their own genetics, the Annunaki created *Homo sapiens* to be their slaves.

Sitchin maintains that the human civilization in Sumer was created under the guidance of the Annunaki and that an aristocracy was also created as a custodial caste, to intermediate between mankind (the slaves) and the Annunaki. It's a fascinating yarn that has captured the imagination of a loyal following, despite being thoroughly discredited, eight ways till Sunday, by several different kinds of scientists. Shockingly, Sitchin says that the Vatican has given his interpretations its seal of approval!

SITCHIN RECEIVES THE *IMPRIMATUR* OF THE VATICAN

In what must be a historic first, a high official of the Vatican and a Hebrew scholar discussed the issue of Extraterrestrials and the Creation of Man, and though different from each other in upbringing, background, religion and methodology, nevertheless arrived at common conclusions:

- Yes, Extraterrestrials can and do exist on other planets
- Yes, they can be more advanced than us
- Yes, materially, Man could have been fashioned from a pre-existing sentient being.

The Participants

The high Vatican official was Monsignor Corrado Balducci, a Catholic theologian with impressive credentials: A member of the Curia of the Roman Catholic Church, a Prelate of the Congregation for the Evangelization of Peoples and the Propagation of the Faith, leading exorcist of the Archdiocese of Rome, a member of the Vatican's Beatification Committee, an expert on Demonology and the author of several books. Appointed in the Vatican to deal with the issue of UFOs and Extraterrestrials, he has made in recent years pronouncements indicating a tolerance of the subjects; but he has never before met and had a dialogue with a Hebrew scholar, and gone beyond prescribed formulations to include the touchy issue of the Creation of Man.

The Hebrew scholar was me—Zecharia Sitchin: A researcher of ancient civilizations, a biblical archaeologist, a descendant of Abraham ... We ended the dialogue as friends, determined to stay in touch and continue.[169]

"PLANET X" HAS GOT LEGS!

In 1995 Nancy Lieder, a self-described contactee of extraterrestrials from Zeta Reticuli, started a popular website, ZetaTalk.com, as her mission to warn mankind about "Planet X," which she equated with the "Nibiru" of the Sitchin books that she was "told":

> ... would sweep through the solar system in May 2003, causing a pole shift that would destroy most of humanity. The ... magnetic disruption of the Earth's core and subsequent displacement of the crust of the Earth is said to correspond with the event Christians refer to as the biblical Armageddon.

Sitchin disagrees with Lieder's claim of impending global
catastrophe ... in 2007, partly in response to Lieder's claims, he
published a book, *The End of Days*, which set the time for the last
passing of Nibiru by Earth at roughly 600 BC, which would mean
it would be unlikely to return in less than 1, 000 years.[170]

Lieder's meme of an "imminent" terrestrial conflagration with an in-
terloping planetoid is so strong that it spurred the 2007 publication
of *Planet X Forecast and 2012 Survival Guide*—despite the failure of
Lieder's "Planet X" to materialize on the heavily-promoted May 15,
2003 forecast date—or by Zecharia Sitchin's strong public denials of
Nibiru's imminent return.

CARLOS BARRIOS: "A FUSION OF POLARITIES"

The reader may have noticed a conspicuous dearth of Maya voices in
the history of the 2012 meme. The following is from a press release
posted on the Manataka American Indian Council website about the
2012 hype machine, written by Carlos Barrios, a Guatemalan author
who trained for 25 years with Maya shamans to become a ceremonial
priest and spiritual guide:

Anthropologists visit the temple sites and read the steles and
inscriptions and make up stories about the Maya, but they do
not read the signs correctly. It's just their imagination ...

Other people write about prophecy in the name of the Maya.
They say that the world will end in December 2012. The Mayan
elders are angry with this. The world will not end. It will be transformed. The indigenous have the calendars, and know how to
accurately interpret it, not others.[171]

In other interviews, Barrios has explained how the few surviving Maya-written documents, such as the Dresden Codex, have been misinterpreted by Western epigraphers because of the latter's failure to grasp the obsession of the ancient Maya with the planet Venus and its importance in ancient Maya cosmology. For example, the first pages of the *Popol Vuh* describe how during the previous age the male deity called *Wukub Kaquix* (Venus) tried to "take over the place of the Father Sun" and the conflagration culminated in the destruction of the last world, of the "men of wood" in a rain of "resin."

Some ancient Maya legends are strikingly reminiscent of the claims of the extremely-controversial independent scholar Immanuel Velikovsky. As related by Barrios:

> ... the oral tradition of the Elders describes to us: "millions of years ago Venus suffered the crash of another celestial body that provoked the destruction of the latter (perhaps an asteroid?), at the same time taking Venus out of its orbit. This provoked a series of cataclysms and readjustments in the planetary system, on the way to its current orbit and due to its proximity to the terrestrial orbit. It changed the rectitude of the Mother Earth (the terrestrial axis?). It also tried to take over the Sun's position, since it seemed bigger than any other celestial body in the skies and it outshone the Sun and the Moon [such that] they were no longer visible, and its pride and vanity grew to a point that it demanded the humanity of that time to worship it and pay tribute to its children, who could raise the mountains in one night (Zipacna) and destroy them on the next day (Cabracan) ... [eventually], the Great Father Sun got its power back and the Moon [again] appeared at night. Now when Venus is seen it is only announcing that the Father Sun is coming and its power had been reduced to being the first star to be seen at night." In few words, this is the story of Venus told in the year 1987 by Don Pascual, who was one of the

highest Wise men of the Eagle Clan of the MAM nation, the most ancient next to Qanjobal in the great Mayan civilization.[172]

Barrios says that the four traditional elements of earth, air, fire and water have ruled the preceding epochs of the past but that the Fifth Sun will be ruled by the element of ether saying, **"Within the context of ether there can be a fusion of the polarities. No more darkness or light in the people, but an uplifted fusion."**

> We live in a world of energy. An important task at this time is to learn to sense or see the energy of everyone and everything: people, plants, animals. This becomes increasingly important as we draw close to the World of the Fifth Sun, for it is associated with the element ether—the realm where energy lives and weaves.[173]

Barrios' latest offering, *The Book of Destiny*, was not yet released at the time of this writing but according to the publisher's description it was written at the request of a council of Maya elders, to accurately and poetically enunciate the scientific legacy of the Maya people, which has been preserved and transmitted over the centuries through their oral tradition and surviving written texts.

DANIEL PINCHBECK: *HOW THE SNAKE SHEDS ITS SKIN*

Daniel Pinchbeck has added his erudite and personal take on the 2012 phenomenon, in his book *2012: The Return of Quetzalcoatl*. He studied shamanism and participated in rituals with different indigenous groups in Africa and South America where psychedelic substances are used as a sacrament. The book journals Pinchbeck's transformation from a dyed-in-the-wool atheist into a man convinced that the shamanic and mystical views of reality are valid. Moreover, he opines that the modern world has become overly materialistic and has lost touch with an aspect of consciousness germane to the human experience.

While visiting the Brazilian Amazon in 2004, Pinchbeck participated in a Santo Daime ceremony, which involved the use of psychedelic ayahuasca tea. During this psychedelic ceremony, he experienced what he was convinced was the voice of the Mesoamerican deity Quetzalcoatl speaking to him, which he described on-camera, during the filming of *2012: Science or Superstition*. An excerpt of the interview with *2012* producer Gary Baddeley appears below.

2012: THE RETURN OF QUETZALCOATL INTERVIEW WITH DANIEL PINCHBECK

BADDELEY: Do you think the messages you received were external?

PINCHBECK: I began to receive a sort of prophetic transmission that seemed to come through this archetype or entity, Quetzalcoatl. And, you asked me whether this was that an external phenomenon or an internal phenomenon? Well, trying to take a non-dual perspective, it's kind of both.

What it really felt like to me—or it could be a bunch of nonsense? I had done a lot of intellectual and philosophical work to put together this paradigm that really took over. I couldn't sleep and when I dreamed I would pick up philosophical fragments and I was reading all the time, from Carl Jung and Jean Gebser and Rudolf Steiner and so on. This paradigm was sort of self-organizing. And when I was in that ceremony in Brazil, it was like this other form of consciousness kind of touched down and introduced a different frequency or level of information or resonance, which I tried to transduce into that transmission.

BADDELEY: How would you summarize the message you received, and does it have a practical application?

PINCHBECK: It was kind of like a fierce electric current of possibility and according to this transmission, we are in an apocalyptic period and part of the message was, "Get ready, prepare the vehicle of your higher self because this is the time to do that."

The message would be to abandon the lesser concerns and goals of the ego and in this critical time, figure out how you are best able to contribute to the transformation process of humanity. And there were some pretty stern messages for people who were not using their energy and creativity in the service of emancipating human consciousness.

BADDELEY: Do you see 2012 as the apocalypse or as a renewal?

PINCHBECK: There's a debate between people who see 2012 in a destructive, apocalyptic in a negative sense and people who see it as regeneration, renewal, new possibility. You've suggested that I'm more on the side of renewal. There may be a lot of destructive manifestations of this process. It's very much like a birth process, which is a very violent process with, vomit and shit and blood flying all over the place.

And then new energy or new life comes into being. I think there's potential for accessing these deeper potentialities in the psyche, and that that could really lead to hyper-accelerated evolution of humanity. What that would exactly look like, I'm not totally sure.

One thing I write a lot about is the Burning Man festival in Nevada, which is a temporary autonomous zone, where a huge amount of creativity is unleashed, and people are allowed to reinvent themselves, reconfigure their identities, play with identity, play with sexuality, and so on. That seems to be one little indication of some kind of future state.

What I see and what I'm trying to write about in the new book is that we could really break down the boundaries, the barriers that are now restricting us from positive evolution. You know, so at the moment we have an ego-based materialist culture based on separation and there might be a whole different potentiality for the human species.

If you look at the history of political evolution, every time there's a really profound new media technology it leads to a different form of social organization. You couldn't have had mass democracy before the printing press and maybe the Internet and social networks are pointing toward a much more deeply-democratic form of organization where there's a scaffolding based on trust and resource sharing.

And it may be that we have to go through this shattering of the vessel, of the material world in order to really embrace each other and work together and move from the third to the fourth *chakra*. That's another way a lot of people look at this 2012 thing. Humanity is kind of in the third *chakra*, which is the belly, which is, you know, eating, appetite, you know, desire. Then to move into the heart *chakra*, which would be compassion, giving, generosity, sharing.

I think that that we could really get to that place. And it looks very unlikely if you look at billions of people forced into slums around the world, and the ocean almost empty of fish and the water running out and the oil running out, everyone getting poised, with their weapons bristling to go after each other. **But on the other hand, it feels really close and I think we can see there's really a lot of phenomena that point towards the potential for tremendous liberation of the human spirit, something like the fall of the Berlin wall in 1989.**

If you look at our political think tanks, highly paid analysts, government geniuses or whatever they're called—nobody had predicted that the wall could just be taken down by people and there wouldn't be massive bloodshed. So what caused that wall to come down? On a subliminal level, people just couldn't have that wall in their world anymore. They were done with it.

There may be other walls, which are going to fall, as surprising and precipitously, including Wall Street. The origin of Wall Street was that the Dutch settlers built a wall to keep out the indigenous people, right? And what separated the Europeans and the indigenous people? One thing that separated them was a different economic paradigm. Indigenous culture was built on a gift economy. We have structured everything according to a market economy. So, maybe that's a wall that comes down and either we go back to a gift economy, or we integrate market and gift.

BADDELEY: As we approach 2012, have people related to you things they plan to do differently?

PINCHBECK: You'd have to consult with José Argüelles, but it seems possible that he has taken off to the farthest place he could possibly go, New Zealand, because of his sense that there is going to be cataclysm in the U.S. and he just didn't want to be around for the mess. I guess, I'm seeing there are people who are making changes right now, in how they invest their resources and psychic energy.

And **it's a kind of a person-by-person, incremental process. I have some friends who are starting sustainable communities, or, buying land. It seems that there's something about this process, which is just still kind of outside of our conceptual grasp. And I think that, definitely relocating, building a strong community is probably really a powerful thing to do right now.**

I also feel that it's kind of outside of our capacity to really, fully understand how this change is going to be unleashed. In England there's a model called "Transition Town." Have you heard about that? Basically, 40 cities and towns through-out England, they've got groups meeting together and really looking at the effects of peak oil and climate change and then thinking about how, as a community they can begin to prepare for these kind of things.

And at a certain point, when they get a nucleus together they bring in local government officials so it's not like an either/ or thing. They're trying to really make an integrated *gestalt*. In some cases they're creating local currencies that support local businesses, local agriculture, but they're even thinking about things like okay, well if they re-localize food supply, then what happens to the African country where they're now bringing in a lot of their food from? How do they work with them? It's like in the '60s, it's the local and global thinking have to work together at this point.

BADDELEY: Do you think there'll be an obvious change in 2012?

PINCHBECK: Will we magically, in 2012 feel that we're in a different reality? It's possible. It could be, like nanotechnology kicks in and we're suddenly able to grow tentacles on our head or something—we're able to access psychic energy in a more profound way that just becomes something demonstrable. So that's a possibility. I don't feel that I know. I also think that we're already in a change situation, we're changing constantly.

I think technology is reformatting the human psyche and at the same time, the devastation that's happening to the biosphere is affecting more and more people all the time, and it's making people at least subliminally, and I think largely consciously aware, that all bets are off at this point. When San Diego goes up in flames, when New Orleans disappears, when half of England is underwater, when huge amounts of Mexico are now underwater, when the polar ice caps are melting exponentially faster than scientists said they would, a few years ago.

When 90% of the large fish in the ocean are gone, when the agriculture tables are all changing because of climate change, so that wheat is much more expensive than it was a few years ago, all bets are off. We're in a very different reality. **We have a system that is frozen in inertia, on a global level. We've created these slow-moving representative democracies that are beholden to corporate interests and that's probably not going to be a sustainable model, at the level of transformation that we're moving into.**

It seems quite plausible that we will see a kind of crumbling of the current systemic infrastructure and we're going to have to be very creative and innovative and see what else can emerge there. Maybe some kind of global, direct, responsive democracy can emerge through the Internet.

PINCHBECK ON CROP CIRCLES & "GALACTIC INTELLIGENCE"

PINCHBECK: A lot of [my] 2012 book is discussing these incredibly complex patterns that appear in England, the crop circles. I studied them for several years and spent time in England and talked to lots of scientists and researchers and thinkers and hoaxers also, I ended up pretty convinced that—not that some of them aren't human-made, but **the phenomenon, as a whole is not a human-made phenomenon.** There are good reasons to think that some or a lot of the patterns are made by non-human intelligence.

There are biophysicists who've published peer-reviewed science journal papers on the molecular changes in the plant samples taken from these patterns. And when I got into this study of these patterns, I was writing about it for *Wired* magazine, and then one of the researchers told me that he'd been studying them for years, and he was convinced they were predicting or projecting a kind of dimensional shift that was currently underway in our world, and was going to complete itself in the year 2012.

I think there's a bunch of evidence that more and more of them have used Aztec and Mayan imagery, and even had dates encoded in them. So, there are some very sophisticated things happening with these patterns. To me, they suggest that there is some kind of galactic intelligence, or maybe different levels or layers of galactic intelligence that is trying to communicate with us. I've ended up seeing the whole phenomenon as a teaching on the nature of consciousness and on the nature of reality.

Part of what it suggests is that personal intention and setting is absolutely connected with anything that can happen. That you're only allowed to get the reality that you're ready to receive. So I watched people go into these phenomena and what kind of setting they had was kind of what got reflected and magnified back at them.

So it could be that we're going to go through some kind of threshold experience with other forms of being that have developed in other dimensions or extraterrestrial civilizations. So, maybe 2012 is the threshold for that, too. It's almost like if we can get through this constriction period potentially a huge amount of avenues open up for us to evolve and make it really, really good.

—Daniel Pinchbeck, On-Camera Interview in *2012: Science or Superstition*

CHAPTER SEVEN

Revelation, Survival, Ascension or ... ?

"... we are in the middle of a transitional period ... the old world hangs on, still all-powerful, still dominating the ordinary consciousness, while the new one is slipping in, still very modest ... growing until the day that it will be strong enough to assert itself visibly."
—**Sri Aurobindo,** *The Human Cycle: Ideal of Human Unity, War and Self Determination*[174]

MAYA RENAISSANCE

By far, the best news to come out of the 2012 hubbub is the Maya Renaissance now blossoming in the communities of Southern Mexico and Central America. On February 22, 2009, a group of community leaders from all over Maya country gathered at the sacred site of Iximché in the Guatemala highlands to pray, to atone, to make offerings and to welcome in the New Year 5125, the "Year of the Wind" or the "Breath of Life." These gatherings had been prohibited for centuries and had been driven underground, but this time the community leaders officially scheduled the gathering with the authorities and even invited the president of Guatemala—who was a no-show—and the U.S. ambassador, Stephen McFarland, who reportedly did attend. According to the Guatemalan news organization *Prensa Libre,* "Many tourists in attendance were emotionally moved to be present at a Maya religious ceremony." [175]

IS 2009 THE "REAL" 2012?

What I find most interesting about this *Prensa Libre* report is that, in the early days of the year 2009 CE, a group of modern-day Maya leaders declared their solar calendar year to be "5125," also known as the all-important FINAL year of the 13-*b'ak'tun* cycle in the ancient Maya Long Count calendar, a date which has been ballyhooed in places very far away from the Maya communities of the Guatemala highlands.

As discussed earlier in this book, the Long Count was developed in Mesoamerica ca. 200 BCE for the purpose of tracking linear time, as well as for marking epochal events, which remain as yet mysterious to us. The cyclical calendars mainly used by the Maya prior to its creation didn't express the concept of a linear progression of time. 20th century scholars busted their asses for decades figuring out the correlation between the Long Count and the linear Western calendar. Today, most agree that 5125 corresponds to 2012.

Along comes this group of elders in Guatemala, claiming that the Maya solar year 5125 began in February 2009, presumably ending 365 days later, in February 2010. Was this very public ceremony, with invitations to heads of state, the elders' way of telling the rest of the world that their own calculations differ from those of Western scholars? Are they saying that the 13-*b'ak'tun* cycle is ending more than two years sooner than the date argued for by academics—and that the "next age" begins around February 2010?

There are no references made in this article or elsewhere that I could find as to any epochal significance of this year 5125. However, given the forecasts of Alex Kochkin and the Web Bots, it appears that "2012" may have actually already begun ...

ALEX KOCHKIN & *GLOBAL AWAKENING*

According to the geopolitical, financial and metaphysical predictions of Alex Kochkin of the *Global Awakening Press*, as well as in the April 2009 Web Bot forecast of his friend Clif High of HalfPastHuman. com, the years 2009 through 2011 will see many dramatic changes.

Alex Kochkin has dedicated the past three decades of his life to studying the capacity and the will of humanity to evolve a new way of being. He is the founder of Positive Future Consulting and of the Fund for Global Awakening, which commissioned a three-year, million-dollar study of 1,600 U.S. households in the late 1990s, analyzing the values and beliefs that are prevalent in the U.S. population. This research uncovered previously undistinguished commonalities among seemingly disparate communities across America. Kochkin proposed that these commonalities could be used to help stimulate positive social change. He published the results in his book, *A New America* [176] and noted that, "... a significant portion of the American population places a high value on spirituality, service, and the interconnectedness of all life—values not yet well-recognized by our leadership or popular culture." Kochkin is also a founder of the New Earth Summit, a public online forum for people who are actively engaged in personal and planetary transformation.

NEW EARTH SUMMIT: PREDICTIONS & ADVICE

The predictions from the April 2009 issue of *Global Awakening*, which were posted on this public online forum—some of them rather alarming—were based on a "composite of personal intuitive insights and analyses from various sources."

> **If you can, buy now and stockpile.** Form local co-operatives—not just for foods but for other necessities. Where is there a local machine shop and weldery? Where does all the toilet paper come from (an important health and sanitation improvement over the medieval days)? First Aid items? Important prescriptions? Spare socks and galoshes?
>
> The global economic crisis will continue to worsen in terms of the effects on the lives of billions of ordinary humans. There will be no "recovery" ... those **who are most focused on finding a right way of living and new way of being with one another need to get about making this happen. There is no one and nothing to wait for. Make it happen with those in your personal network and geographic community.**[177]

There will be those who persevere with new cooperative modes of social and economic life ... Some cooperatives will find ways to take over certain manufacturing and transportation. There is much potential for communities of people to create transitional social economies.

> ... the guiding principles we articulated can help in the transition: trust, caring, service in a large context of connection to our true nature as spiritual beings. Whatever the choices and actions people engage in, **there is so much more to existence than re-organizing the means of production and distribution for greater social and environmental benefit. It is the larger context of our higher spiritual nature that is beckoning for our reconnection to our greater self** ...[178]

To what extent will people recognize the falsehoods they have been living under and create new ways of being with one another and this planet? That is a big question and an immense challenge for enough of humanity to continue on and learn to evolve and grow as embodied spiritual beings—or not. **For those who do not need to comprehend all this, it is directly a matter of detaching oneself from reaction and fear and a matter of connecting to one's higher self and Source.** [179]

"RADICAL LINGUISTICS" & THE WEB BOT PROJECT

The Web Bot project claims to have repeatedly demonstrated that human beings are "precognitive at a preconscious level." The bots are software applications that run automated tasks over the Internet, sweeping chat boards, blogs and other areas rich in posted language. The Web Bot project has been producing ALTA (Asymmetric Language Trend Analysis) reports since 1994, publicly since 2004.

What they have found, over and over again, is that major events show up at the archetypal level of consciousness before they physically occur in 3D reality. This is expressed by changes in everyday language, which precede major events in mass consciousness. The larger the emotional impact of an event, the more advance-notice that the bots seem to give. Words expressing emotional reactions to particular events begin to show up all over the Internet in synchronous clusters, twelve to five weeks prior to their actual physical manifestation—*as if these events had already occurred in the past.*

> We employ a technique based on radical linguistics to reduce extracts from readings of dynamic postings on the Internet into an archetypical database. With this database of archetypical language, we calculate the rate of change of the language. The forecasts of the future are derived from these calculations. Our

calculations are based on a system of associations between words and numeric values for emotional responses from those words. These 'emotional impact indicators' are also of our own devising. They are attached to a database of over three hundred thousand words. This database of linked words/phrases and emotions is our lexicon from which the future forecasting is derived.[180]

The reports also produce a lot of useless "noise" but they claim to have accurately predicted, among other events, 9/11 (which showed up as a "life-changing tipping point"), the 2003 Northeastern U.S. Mass Power Outage, the December 26, 2004 Indonesian Earthquake/Tsunami and the October 2008 global financial meltdown.

Clif is the first person to call what he does "crap," saying, "The ALTA reports are definitely derived from the 'voo-doo, and hoo-doo, and woo-woo' school of future viewing. As such, most humans will wisely refrain from subscribing to an ALTA series."[181]

WEB BOT FORECAST

This book you are holding in your hands began with an idea from ancient Maya prophecy that the current time period represents the end of an era and the birth of the new, so I thought it would be interesting to know what some future viewers of the present day have to say. Between 2008 and 2012, the Web Bots predicted "vast changes in the planetary social order."[182]

The timeline suggests that the 2012 date—**anything from Oct. 2011 through to 2013—is felt by the Powers That Be as being the point of maximum risk for them,** *which I believe relates from the condition of our solar system and where it is in universe.* This is to say that if we're approaching some form of a nexus in awareness or increase of the consciousness field, you would probably not have to do anything at all and may still find that over the period of time, from 2011 through 2013, you experienced this to a heightened degree.[183]

The Web Bots predict that by the end of 2009 a large number of people will be "economically dislocated" or will otherwise find themselves living in significantly altered circumstances, as a direct result of the macro-level events that were predicted to occur during the year, such as the continued increase in unemployment and to what was being called "dollar death." By the September equinox of 2009, the mainstream press will have lost whatever credibility it has left. A "trigger event" on October 26, 2009 will take ten days to simmer before exploding on November 5th as a "cause for war." Specifically:

In the predictive linguistics work from HalfPastHuman.com there's language around October 26th that goes to the idea of Israel attacking Iran and that, in turn, sets a clock of about 4 weeks, or so, to an attack by North Korea on South Korea using a nuke or two.[184]

- War compounds the disaster of the collapsed dollar, which could become globally repudiated as a reserve currency and "rejected by all." The housing and debt bubbles continue their collapse, along with the collapse of service industries. In short, the end of 2009 will spell the "end of the 'comfortable high tech/high consumption' lifestyle and an involuntary return to lifestyle of previous generations."[185]

- Expect several unemployed staffers from places like NASA and the Bush regime to become whistleblowers. After all, they have to "put food on their families," to quote the former U.S. president.

- A mysterious "global coastal event" with no further details sticks out in the Web Bot report. It could mean anything from a disruption of shipping corridors to an abrupt rise in sea levels.

- A strong anti-press sentiment prevails throughout 2010, as they simply have no good news to report. Alternative groups doing alternative things, including the construction of "free energy" vehicles will make a mockery of the competence and the relevance of corporations, government and the mainstream news media.

- **Anybody having any success will be doing so "out of the box and away from the corporate fascist world."** [186] **These success stories will become the models for an emerging paradigm because the corporate model is on its way out.**

Well, so much for that—remember that Web Bot creator Clif High says it's crap—but it clearly does reflect an extremely pessimistic view of the future that is part of the zeitgeist as this book goes to press in 2009. Personally, I have found that those who feel the most pessimistic are those who are the most attached to and invested in the values and the systems of the old economic model and to everything that goes with it, from the kind of energy used to the means of production to the product consumed ...

MASSIVE INFLUX OF NEW ENERGIES COMING OUR WAY

In an online radio interview,[187] High explained how the solar system is currently moving through a "magnetic ribbon" in the middle of the Milky Way Galaxy and that everything in our solar system is being "dampened down." The Web Bot's language for these magnetic-plasma effects is the "big squeeze."

There has been very little in the media about this but I did find a story published by NASA late in 2008 that describes this phenomenon as "a puzzling surplus of high-energy electrons bombarding Earth from space, [of] unknown" origin.[188] There has also been a sharp increase in gamma ray bursts from stars close to the galactic center, as discussed previously in **Chapters 3** and **5** of this book. Our solar system is suddenly awash with all kinds of new cosmic radiation.

Due to these energetic fluctuations, in conjunction with Earth's unstable geomagnetic field, there could be mass navigation problems and an overall sense of "surreality," as these changing magnetic fields affect human beings both physically and mentally. Animals that rely on Earth's magnetic field for navigation, such as whales and many bird species could have a rough go and we may see increased beachings and species extinctions from these ranks. Movement around the country and around the world could become curtailed for a host of reasons, not the least of which may be episodes of people flying commercial aircraft in areas of high radiation (due to the loss of Earth's protective magnetosphere) and suffering physical damage. "It will only take one or two of those before a lot of the impetus to fly will be removed,"[189] says Clif.

GAMMA RAY BURSTS & COSMIC RAYS

The weakening of both Earth's and the Sun's magnetic shield coincides with a time of a abrupt increase in gamma ray bursts from relatively close stars. The Earth is receiving 1,000% more cosmic radiation than at any time ever recorded, much of which we don't know anything about. There are those who view this massive influx of new energies to be spiritually beneficial while also keeping the "powers that be" off-guard.

The big question has nothing to do with "survival." Survival for what? **Spiritual evolution is key.** Not a low level species-centric survival for its own sake, **unless humans are to only regard themselves as genetic imperatives to breed and die and make monkey-mind things and believe that buying and selling is their social imperative.**[190]

PERUVIAN PROPHECIES ABOUT 2012

"The Inca prophecies speak about a time of tremendous turmoil on the Earth today. They refer to it as the *Pachacuti* ... '*Pacha*' means 'Earth' or 'time' and '*cuti*' means 'to turn over or to step outside of.' They speak about a time of a 'culling of humanity,' of 'a harvesting of souls' and the decimation of large parts of the human race ... the prophecies speak about this time of great up-heaval and the beginning of a millennium of gold, of tremendous opportunity. They're very optimistic. They're very hopeful for the planet—they're not that optimistic for humanity, at large ...

"These people did not know where the United States was. They did not know about China or the Middle East. Yet, they were able to read the turmoil that would be occurring in these various places. For the United States, they said that our country was at war but that the war was 'happening within.' They were referring to the breakdown of the moral fiber of the United States, which was once a great country that was known for its compassion ... the breakdown of those values that made this a great country, that is now at war with its own people. We're talking about the poverty, the poisoning of the environment, the terrorists that are already within the United States that are seeking the destruction of this country. So, that was one scenario.

"The other one was that the United States had the possibility of being the Elder Brother that would provide the leadership and the energy and the power to bring the world into balance—and remember, that it's up to us to make those true. They're not written in stone. They're possibilities, probabilities.

"They also brought a message about optimism. And they brought the processes. Even more important than the prophecies are the processes. How do we 'quantum leap' into this new form of humanity? That was the most important message of these shamans was of the processes; what you and I can do to create new bodies, to dream the world into being differently? So it wasn't just bad news. It was the bringing of technologies that we can use to 'quantum leap,' to dream a new world into being.

"The best preparation for this coming change which is happening today: You need to drink clean water, eat clean food, keep your system in as clear and un-toxic a state as you possibly can because you cannot grow a new body if you're eating poison. On junk food, you cannot grow a new body."

—Alberto Villoldo, On-Camera Interview in *2012: Science or Superstition*

Alberto Villoldo with Peruvian Shaman Don Francisco.

"HOMO LUMINOUS"

Villoldo has been studying with the indigenous peoples of South America for over 20 years; in particular, he's been studying the sha-manistic mind. He explains that the shamans are people of the *percept*, of perceptual traditions, whereas Westerners are people of the *precept*. Western thought is based on precepts, theories, laws and rules:

> We get the Ten Commandments, elect legislators and lawmakers that make more rules. When the shamans want to change the world, they work at the level of the essential to bring about a shift in perception. By shifting perception, we dream the new world into being and the world changes. That is our task, to dream with our eyes open.[191]

Based on the prophecies that he's been documenting from tribes all across the Americas, Villoldo believes that a new kind of human is emerging on Earth that he calls *"Homo luminous,"* which has the ability to interact with the electromagnetic vibrations and forces that make up the physical world from a much higher level. Villoldo be-lieves that we can become *Homo luminous* in our lifetimes and when we choose truth, when we choose life, we transform the world. "It is for us to take that quantum leap into who we are becoming."

IN A NUTSHELL: ASCENSION

How to countenance this "Variety Pak" of distressing factors that would demolish the jet-setting, shopaholic way of life that is the lodestone of Western aspirations? It looks like there's nowhere to go but up: Time to ascend! Alex Kochkin, along with his writing partner on this subject, John Crawford, identifies the main variations of the ascension process:

- **Basic Ascension,** a conscious shift of the human personality out of the old human body into a higher vibrational body, leaving the old physical body behind.

- **Descension of higher self into the human body,** having first developed the abilities of enhanced light capacity in order to physically house these subtle and physical bodies of the higher self. This is a more challenging feat than the basic form of ascension, above, and those who choose this path may be able to provide valuable assistance to people who are on the verge of awakening. Though there are tales of those who have perfected their 3D body and "walked out of this reality with no trace," this state usually cannot be maintained for too long before one either becomes re-attached to 3D reality or ascends the basic way.

Somehow, I don't get the feeling that there is anything easy about ascension or descension! Here are some more details about what is involved in the process:

> ... We as individuated souls inhabit seven distinct levels within this Creation Structure ... The goal of ascension is to have all seven bodies or aspects complete the ascension process within its individual level. When this happens each of our seven selves on the seven levels moves upward or ascends within the dimensional structures.

> We have individuated bodies on each of the seven levels ... These seven levels are an out-picturing or projection of our soul just as our seven *chakras* are an out-picturing or projection of our place at this level. Our *chakras* are also a direct connection to the two aspects below and the four aspects above us ...

One of the difficulties of the movement through the levels towards the ascension is that it has been a gradual process. **This process can be speeded up through the aligning of the seven bodies and their purpose. Also what is needed is to get all seven bodies vibrating at the same frequency at the same time as well as beginning the process of aligning these bodies with the frequency of the greater soul self. There are techniques available for this requiring focused intent to bring it about. You are in a unique place to help this happen, as you are on the third density level, comparable to the third *chakra*, the level of power.**

You can develop the ability to bring your other aspects or energy bodies into harmony and supply the power necessary for the connection to take place. This leads to freeing oneself from the life-to-life, level-to-level requirement that has characterized ascension.[192]

SRI AUROBINDO, MIRRA ALFASSA & THE "SUPERMIND"

In the mid-20th century, Sri Aurobindo and his partner Mirra Alfassa worked on their radical process of spiritual transformation, with the intent of grounding higher energies within the 3D realm, to help bring about the ascension of the entire planet. Contrary to the *kundalini* meditation of classic yoga, in which seekers visualize their consciousness energy flowing upwards along the spine, upwards through their interdimensional energy centers, or *chakras*, the technique developed by Aurobindo and Mirra sought to start at the top; to visualize and draw down into their physical bodies the energies from the highest, subtlest realms.

Such is the Secret. It is here, everywhere, at the heart of the world. It is the "well of honey under a rock," the "childlike laughter of the Infinite" that we are, the womb of the luminous Future that impels our past. Evolution is not over; it is not an absurd merry-go-round, not a fall, not a vanity fair, it is *the adventure of consciousness and joy.*" [193]

When asked to describe by what signs a person would know that they established contact with the "supermind," Mirra replied,

[There] are two things that can ONLY come with the supramental consciousness; without it, one cannot possess them—no yogic effort, no discipline, no *tapasya* [austerity] can give them to you, while they come almost automatically with the supramental consciousness.

The first sign is perfect equality, as Sri Aurobindo has described … in *The Synthesis of Yoga* … this equality (which is not "equanimity") is a particular STATE where one relates to all things, outer and inner, and to each individual thing, in the same way. That is truly perfect equality: vibrations from things, from people, from contacts have no power to alter that state …

The second sign is a sense of ABSOLUTENESS in knowledge … It's … not a "certainty," … The feeling it gives is altogether unique—far beyond certainty … it is … a kind of **absoluteness in knowledge springing from identity**—one *is* the thing one knows and experiences: one is it. **One knows it because one is it**.

… **when a person possesses both, then you can be sure he has been in contact with the Supermind** … it's what Sri Aurobindo says: you step into another world, you leave this entire hemisphere behind and enter another one. That's the feeling. The day it's established, it will be good. [194]

Sri Aurobindo and Mirra Alfassa established a community at Auroville, a city in south India that grew out of Aurobindo's ashram. Auroville is the only internationally-endorsed[195] ongoing experiment in human unity and transformation of consciousness and is also engaged in practical research into sustainable living and in anticipating the future cultural, environmental, social and spiritual needs of mankind. In 1966, it was unanimously commended by UNESCO as a project of importance to the future of humanity.

For those interested in learning more about ascension and descension, the books of Sri Aurobindo including *The Life Divine*, *The Synthesis of Yoga* and *The Human Cycle* are recommended. Also particularly instructive is the work described in Mirra's 13-part book, *Mother's Agenda*, which is posted online and viewable at the Auroville.org website.

Mirra's book covers the period of time during which she focused on physically transforming her body, with the goal of finding the secret passage to the "next species," in become among the first of what she envisioned as a "new type of human individual." Through (drug-free) purifications and deep meditation, she accessed what Aurobindo termed "supramental truth consciousness," or the "supermind," which corresponds to the highest levels of the "Gaia mind," "noösphere/psi bank" discussed by José Argüelles, Daniel Pinchbeck and many others.

THE DYNAMICS OF TRANSFORMATION

In his essay "Birthing of a New World," systems theorist Ervin László says that we have arrived at a "chaos point." Life as we know it will change dramatically, either in the form of global collapse or by our seizing this opportunity for worldwide renewal; we can either choose a more sustainable world or to sit back and watch our civilization and ecological systems break down. László notes:

In remarkable—and *perhaps* not entirely fortuitous agreement with the date predicted by the Mayan civilization—the chaos point is likely to be reached on or around the year 2012 ... The year 2012 is indeed a gateway to a different world, but whether to a better world or to a disastrous one is yet to be decided.[196]

László refers to the unclassified 2000 report by the U.S. National Intelligence Council, *Global Trends 2015: A Dialogue About the Future with Nongovernmental Experts* which says that the conditions on Earth in 2015 will be determined by the unfolding of several key trends and key drivers, namely demographics, natural resources, environment, science, technology, the global economy and globalization; a future of "regional competition," in other words, "a post-polar world." In the "optimistic scenario," 2015 will be much like things were back in 2000, except that a shrinking minority will be better off and a growing majority will be less well off.

Needless to say, these predictions by the U.S. National Intelligence Council had already been proved true in half the time expected, leaving us to wonder about the remaining seven years. László agrees that this kind of trend-based forecasting is limited by its inability to account for the breakdown of trends that gives rise to new ones.

This is where the application of chaos theory can be useful: "Because of the unsustainability of many aspects of today's world, the dynamics of development that will apply to the future is not the linear dynamics of classical extrapolation, but the nonlinear chaos dynamics of complex-system evolution."[197]

CHAOS DYNAMICS IN SOCIETY

László states that the world has arrived at a supersensitive decision-window, where small fluctuations create large-scale effects. This is what he calls the the "chaos point," where the system is critically unstable, the status quo is no longer sustainable and the system's evolution will tip in either one direction or the other: towards breakdown or towards breakthrough. He describes this as a "window of unprecedented freedom to decide our destiny ... If we are aware of the power in our hands, and if we have the will to make use of it."

If our personal values and our institutions are too rigid to adapt or if they move to too slowly in making the necessary changes, the growing social inequalities, combined with a degraded environment could lead to our society's descent into violence and world anarchy. Alternatively, we could show ourselves to be adaptable and to formally establish our adapted values, worldviews and ethics. "People and institutions master the stresses that arose in the wake of the preceding generation's pursuit of wealth and power." Thus, the economic, political and ecological dimensions of society may stabilize in a non-warlike and sustainable mode.

The most important component in the creation of the next age "is not more technology but the rise of new thinking—new values, perceptions and priorities—in a critical mass of the people who make up the bulk of society." [198]

Conclusion

"Those civilizations of antiquity and those tribal shamans today have a huge amount to teach us and we can only recover the better part of ourselves if we are willing to listen to what they have to say."
—Graham Hancock, On-Camera interview in *2012: Science or Superstition*

THE MOMENT OF TRUTH

Modern-day speculation that a global cataclysm could accompany the ending of the 5,125-year 13-*b'ak'tun* cycle has been widely dismissed as a New Age urban legend that started in the mid-1980s. In this book, we've charted the propagation of this and associated memes, such as "the end of time," by such charismatic psycho-activists as José Argüelles and Terence McKenna. We've also noted a surprising factoid: that the first 20th century linkage between 2012 and Armageddon was made in the 1966 book *The Maya*, written by one of the most respected Mayanists in the world, Michael Coe, professor emeritus of anthropology at Yale University and curator emeritus of the anthropology collection in the Peabody Museum of Natural History.

We have talked about how the ancient Maya had a tradition of World Ages similar to those of the ancient Hindus, Greeks and Romans, involving the gods' creation and destruction of successive versions of humankind. By definition, World Ages both emerge from and expire during major Earth cataclysms. We've looked at cyclical mass extinctions of varying degrees of intensity in Earth's geological record and surmised that large-scale cosmic cycles are likely at the root of ancient mythologies relating to World Ages, the same way that much of ancient mythology has been shown to be a coded priestly language for celestial and astrophysical events. We've also noted the astuteness of ancient Maya astronomical observations and wondered whether they were onto something of which we are as yet unaware—and whether this knowledge may not be encoded in the end-date of their Long Count calendar?

Although we may never know whether the ending of the 13-*b'ak'tun* cycle was in any way significant to the ancient Maya, as so much of the written legacy of the Maya was expunged by Spanish colonists, we point to a defaced carving on Monument 6 at the archaeological site at Tortuguero in Mexico, which contains a partially decoded reference to the 2012 end-date in conjunction with the deity called *Bolon Yokte K'u*, who is associated with war, conflict and the Maya "Underworlds" of night-time and death.

Bolon Yokte is also present during the creation of new worlds and of new versions of humankind in Maya mythology. We could deduce from this stele that the ancient Maya may possibly have envisioned the year 2012 as a time of creation—or of a recreation of the world, likely during a time of war, conflict and death.

2012 IS NOT ABOUT THE MAYA CALENDAR

What has become clear is that the 2012 meme has evolved beyond any debates about the relevance of the Maya Long Count calendar to the lives of contemporary human beings. 2012 is about us on planet Earth at this time. It expresses the inexorable unwinding of our nihilistic civilization and it offers a hint of what may lie beyond the end of this era. 2012 encapsulates the growing sense of urgency about the unsustainability of our current way of life on many levels, not the least of which are the psychological and the spiritual.

It has been said by the wisest among us that global transformation begins with each person discovering their **profound inner connection to each other and to the Earth**, with every one of us awakening to the immanence that's all around us and within us, by simply recognizing the sacredness of our beautiful planet and of life, itself.

JEAN GEBSER'S *EVER-PRESENT ORIGIN*

Jean Gebser's *Ever-Present Origin* masterfully reveals how something like the 2012 meme presses all of the buttons of human consciousness at every level, from the most animalistic, instinctual plane of survival, to the magical sway held over us by numbers, to the power of myth, to our quasi-religious faith that the scientific method can explain away and put all of these symbols and signifiers in their place.

Originally published in German in 1947, Gebser's book analyzes the history of culture and of the different predominating modes of consciousness of each era. In his model, the previous dominant structures are superseded and yet retained in a subordinate fashion in the process of the "unfoldment of structures" in human consciousness. To view this process as "evolutionary" would be linear and retrogressive, ignoring the fundamentally non-linear and non-local character of reality revealed by quantum physics over a century ago.

> ... The immense processes of transformation like those taking place today, and the far- and deep-reaching mutations that have been occurring for generations and extending into the present, are neither accidental, nor explicable in ontological, existential

or sociological terms. They are latent in origin; they are always back-leaps, so to speak, into the *already (ever)-present future*. This is the way in which origin, budding and unfolding in space and time, emerges on earth and in our daily lives. The divine spiritual source and future of that which appears to us as an event ought never be forgotten when attempts are made at mere explanation. And origin, from which every moment of our lives draws its sustenance, is by nature divine and spiritual. Anyone who denies this, denies himself, and there is a considerable number today who do.

Those who do not deny but rather affirm it in their open-mindedness and simplicity are already the co-creators of ... the Integral consciousness structure. This is founded on the emergent consciousness and on the transparency of the whole ...

What does all of this have to do with daily life? ... it is [not] the number of those who realize and live the new that is decisive; decisive is the intensity with which individuals live the new.[199]

According to Gebser, we are currently experiencing a transition from the Mental structure into what he calls the Integral structure of consciousness. The latter is next to impossible to describe using the terminology of the Mental structure and his book is loaded with neologisms for the purpose of avoiding the language of the old paradigm. *The Ever-Present Origin* can be a tough read and it isn't for everybody but I personally think it is the most important book I have ever run across.

The following is an extremely abbreviated rendition of Gebser's model of the structures of human consciousness:

1. **The Archaic structure** is described as a non-perspectival world characterized by non-differentiation and no sense of separation from the environment. Very instinctive and primitive, it could be

described as the state of mind of the animal kingdom, as it also recalls humanity's animalistic aspects.

2. **The Magical structure** is characterized by a degree of separateness and could be described as a pre-perspectival state of timelessness and spacelessness. It has been likened to a state of sleep. Humans operating primarily within the Magical structure feel secure only within a local group, tribe or clan. The magical is very tribal and heavy on participatory rituals.

Gebser notes that music and mathematics arise from this Magical structure. It is interesting how fixated people can become on a "magic number," such as 2012. He notes how mathematicians are often big fans of music and vice versa. One of my favorite details in Gebser's observations related to the Magical structure of consciousness is the marked impatience he often encountered in the personalities of musicians and mathematicians, alike.

3. **The Mythical structure** of consciousness has been likened to a dream state. Imagination and attunement with the cyclical rhythms of nature became important factors in human life.

We can see how ancient Maya culture was very centered in this Mythical structure of consciousness, with their cyclical time, etc. and how they also maintained strong aspects of the Magical, as well, with their elaborate mathematics and their units of time.

4. **The Mental structure** of consciousness is a three-dimensional, perspectival world that has been described as "wakefulness." It is linear and distinguished by the analytical separation of duality and opposition. In its latter phase, rational thinking has become primary and it is highly skeptical of all the other structures of consciousness.

Modern civilization has been mostly centered in the Mental struc-ture of consciousness, which is clearly distinguished by the conten-tiousness and debates it wages against everything it perceives to be "wrong," a phenomenon that we have witnessed in the expressions of many people in this book, myself included!

We can perhaps look forward to an easing of the argumentative litigiousness that has been so endemic to our Mental way of life, as the Mental structure yields to the final mutation in Gebser's model. What will the consciousness of the next age be like? Here are some possible clues:

5. **The Integral structure** of consciousness is described as a four-dimensional, aperspectival world of transparency, where we see through things and perceive their true nature. For Gebser, this structure integrates those that have come before and enables the human mind to transcend the limitations of three-dimensionality. Relationships between things may sometimes be even more important than the things, themselves and how the relationships develop over time takes precedence to the mere fact that the rela-tionships exist. Gebser proposes that this way of looking at things would enable human beings to overcome the dualism of the Men-tal structure and to actually participate in the transparency of self and of life. This is a time-free, space-free, subject- and object-free world of "verition," a term coined by Gebser which is definitely not to be confused with Stephen Colbert's "truthiness."

"Verition, not description is what we experience and know. Philoso-phy is replaced by eteology; that is, the *eteon* or being-in-truth." [200] Eteology is the statement *of* truth rather than a philosophical state-ment *about* truth. This approach goes beyond the limitations of space- and time-perception to a complete and liberating understand-ing of the Whole: Every piece of the Whole is Whole.

Of course, in our attempts to *describe* the Integral structure of consciousness, we fall into the Mental structure's trap of definitions and of creating artificial separations and false dichotomies ...

During his on-camera interview for the companion film to this book, *2012: Science or Superstition*, Graham Hancock appears to understand all of this and he does a commendable job of summing up where we find ourselves today: what is missing and what is not only possible but what is making itself available to us. Through the efforts of people like him and many others, including those cited in this book, we are learning to think and act more independently. With this alternative information about history and technologies—alternatives, across the board, to the currently unsustainable means of production and consumption—we are finding alternative ways of simply *being* to that advertised by modern civilization.

"A NEW BIRTH OF HUMAN CONSCIOUSNESS"

"What the voices of all ancient civilizations say is that our true nature is spiritual, that we are spiritual creatures and that the spirit is expressed through human consciousness. Therefore, I feel worried when I see the extent of materialism in the modern world, and I don't just mean the joy and delight in material things. I mean the philosophy, which holds that there is nothing outside of matter and that there is no meaning or purpose to life beyond the physical manifestation of life that we are expressed within. I think this is a very dangerous system of ideas ...

"The shamans of tribal and hunter-gatherer societies around the world with their systems and techniques for contacting the spirit realm directly ... have a great deal to teach us.

"What I see is that the sensitivity of mankind to the immanence of the spirit realm that surrounds us on all sides and interpenetrates our lives in every way—that we've become ignorant and closed down and shut off from this ... and while we are in that state of somnolence, evil is worked in the world by men of power and wealth.

"I do see a new birth of human consciousness underway. And when these things happen, they can sometimes happen very, very fast. So I do not rule out at all the possibility that all of us are going to be looking at the mystery and meaning of life if a very different way, very soon and that date, 21st of December 2012, sticks in my mind as one that is really worthy of consideration."

—Graham Hancock, On-Camera Interview in *2012: Science or Superstition*

APPENDIX A
PART III OF INTERVIEW WITH MICHAEL CREMO

BRUCE: What have been your own most important findings?

CREMO: Now let's consider a case from the more recent history of archaeology. In 1979, Mary Leakey found dozens of footprints at a place called Laetoli, in the East African country of Tanzania. She said that the footprints were indistinguishable from those of modern human beings. But they were found in layers of solidified volcanic ash that are 3.7 million years old. According to standard views, humans capable of making such prints should not have existed that long ago. So how do scientists explain the Laetoli footprints?

They say that there must have existed in East Africa 3.7 million years ago some kind of ape-man who had feet just like ours. And that is how the footprints were made. That is a very interesting proposal, but unfortunately there is no physical evidence to support it. Scientists already have the skeletons of the ape-men who existed 3.7 million years ago in East Africa. They are called *Australopithecus*. And the foot structure of *Australopithecus* is quite different from that of a modern human being. The only creature known to science that has a foot exactly like a modern human being is in fact, a human being like us. So what did Mary Leakey find? I believe she found evidence that humans like us were existing millions of years ago.

Scientists who find things that should not be found sometimes suffer for it professionally. One such scientist is Dr. Virginia Steen-McIntyre, an American geologist whom I know personally.

In the early 1970s, some American archaeologists discovered some stone tools and weapons at a place called Hueyatlaco, in Mexico. They included arrowheads and spear points. According to archaeologists, such weapons are made and used only by humans like us, not by ape-men.

At Hueyatlaco, the artifacts were found in the bottom layers of the trenches. When archaeologists want to know how old something is, they call in some geologists because the geologists will be able to tell them, "The layer of rock in which you found these objects is so-and-so thousand years old." Among the geologists who came to date the site was Virginia Steen-McIntyre. Using four of the latest geological dating methods, she and her colleagues from the United States Geological Survey determined that the artifact-bearing layer was 300,000 years old. When this information was presented to the chief archaeologist, the chief archaeologist said, "That is impossible. There were no human beings in existence 300,000 years ago anywhere in the world." The current doctrine is that humans did not enter the Americas any earlier than 30,000 years ago. So what happened? The archaeologists refused to publish the date of 300,000 years. Instead they published an age of 20,000 years for the site. And where did they get that date? It came from a carbon-14 date on a piece of shell found 5 km away from the place where the artifacts were found.

Virginia Steen-McIntyre tried to get the true age of the site known. Because of this, she began to get a bad reputation in her profession. She lost a teaching position she held at a university and all of her opportunities for advancement in the United States Geological Survey were blocked. She became so disgusted that she went to live in a small town in

the Rocky Mountains of Colorado and remained silent for ten years—until I found out about her case and wrote about it in *Forbidden Archaeology*, giving her work some of the attention it deserves. Partly because of this, the Hueyatlaco site is now being studied by more open-minded archaeologists, and hopefully before too long, her original conclusions about the age of the site will be reconfirmed.

ON FUNDAMENTALIST MATERIALISTIC EVOLUTIONISTS ...

BRUCE: Have you ever personally experienced suppression of your own work by the mainstream scientific community and by the media? If so, how was the suppression deployed justified and/or propagated?

CREMO: There are many reactions to my work by the mainstream scientific community, because the mainstream scientific community is not monolithic. It is diverse. In practice, I see three main divisions.

The first is what I call the fundamentalist materialistic evolutionists. These are scientists who accept the theory of evolution not for purely scientific reasons but because it supports their prior belief in atheism and materialism. They do not like my work. They do not want to hear it, and they do not want others to hear it. They sometimes try to suppress my work. A few years ago, I was a consultant for a television program called "The Mysterious Origins of Man," produced by Bill Cote of B. C. Video in New York City for NBC. The show included cases from my book *Forbidden Archaeology*, coauthored with Richard Thompson. One of the cases was that of the California gold mine discoveries, which we just discussed.

When evolutionist scientists found out that NBC was going to broadcast a show that challenged the theory of evolution, they were shocked. They were especially shocked when they learned that I had something to do with the show. **They did not like my affiliation with the Hare Krishna movement or my anti-evolutionary views.**

After the show aired they began circulating among scientists proposals for boycotting NBC. They became even angrier when they learned NBC was going to air the show a second time. In response, they organized a letter writing campaign, asking scientists to write letters to the chairman of the General Electric Company, which owns NBC, asking him to stop NBC from showing the program again. This campaign did not succeed, so the pro-evolution scientists tried to get the Federal Communications Commission to censure NBC, to force NBC to broadcast public retractions, and to fine NBC. The FCC did not do these things, but it was interesting to see these kinds of attempts.

Once a scholar named Charles Smith asked me to contribute a chapter to a volume about Alfred Russel Wallace, the co-founder of the theory of evolution by natural selection. I agreed, but he later informed me that the publisher would not accept a chapter by me because of my controversial reputation among mainstream scientists for my anti-evolutionary ideas and my affiliation with the Hare Krishna movement.

So yes, there are attempts at suppression by what I call the fundamentalist Darwinists. But there are other scientists who are more open-minded. They may support the theory of evolution, but they do so for more or less scientific reasons. And they are therefore willing to listen to alternative ideas and evidence that may contradict evolution, if it is presented in a reasonable and intelligent way. So it is scientists and scholars from this group who have invited me to speak at universities, scientific conferences, and scientific institutions (including the Royal Institution in London, the Russian Academy of Sciences in Moscow, etc.). Scientists in this group may not agree with me, but they are willing to listen to me. And that is important. If ideas are going to change, the first step is that scientists have to be willing to listen to new ideas, and fortunately some of them are willing.

And finally there is a third group, the scientists who actually agree with me. They are very small in number at this time, but that is how these things go. It is one reason why I admire Darwin and his early followers. At a time when no one accepted their ideas, they had the courage to stand up and say this is what we think the truth is.

ARCHAEOLOGICAL EVIDENCE FOR EXTREME HUMAN ANTIQUITY: PRESENT IN PROFESSIONAL JOURNALS, ABSENT FROM TEXTBOOKS

BRUCE: By definition, scientific proof begins with a hypothesis of a certain result and the reproducible testing of this hypothesis, proving the result to be a scientific fact.

CREMO: In my works directed toward the scientific community, I try to respect this process. I therefore formulated a hypothesis. If there really does exist in the layers of the Earth, archaeological evidence for extreme human antiquity, then one could predict that the primary scientific literature (reports of primary researchers in professional journals) would contain such discoveries. One could also predict that such reports would be absent from the second literature (text-books, survey studies) because of knowledge filtration by scientists committed to the evolution theory.

I tested this hypothesis. My findings were that the primary scientific literature really does contain reports of archaeological evidence for extreme human antiquity. I also found that such reports are absent from current secondary literature, and that the reasons for this absence is that the reports contradict the theory of evolution.

So my findings are consistent with the idea that archaeological evidence for extreme human antiquity really does exist, and that its absence from the current textbooks can best be explained by a process of knowledge filtration, whereby reports contradicting the theory of evolution are excluded.

BRUCE: Do you consider yourself to be a scientist?

CREMO: I consider myself a scientist in the same sense that Darwin was a scientist. His field of study was theology. He never graduated from a university with an advanced degree. He did not have a Ph.D. Yet he did research and writing and presented his findings to the scientific world and the general public. I do the same thing.

That is one answer to the question. Usually, when people ask this question it is because they think that only professionally trained scientists are scientists, and they also think that science and religion are two different things. So they want to exclude anyone with any religious motivation or inspiration from the category of scientist. But the best historians of science understand that science and religion have always had a relationship.

Another way I answer the question is to say that I consider myself to be neither a scientist nor a religionist. I see myself as a human being looking for truth, and I am prepared to accept truth wherever I find it, be it in what is called science or in what is called religion.

DEVOLUTION: A VEDIC ALTERNATIVE TO DARWIN

BRUCE: Leaving the origin of human beings out of this question for the moment, do you accept the basic precept of evolution that the numerous species living on Earth have evolved into their current state from previous states of adaptation and that they are continuing a constant process of adaptation and evolution, or do you think this is false?

CREMO: My thoughts on this question are influenced by my studies in the ancient Sanskrit writings of India, especially the *Puranas*, or histories, which deal with the history of life in the universe.

Darwin was arguing against the Christian doctrine of special creation, the idea that God created each species individually. Darwin found this idea hard to accept. In *Origin of Species*, he concluded that originally God created one species and then let the rest evolve by natural selection. This basically means that the life forms we see today can all be traced back to a common ancestor through a process of reproduction with modification.

In my book *Human Devolution*, I outline a Vedic alternative to Darwin's theory. According to the Vedic cosmology, all life forms we see around us today can be traced back to a common ancestor. But while Darwin thought the common ancestor was the simplest organism, according to the Vedic cosmology, the first living thing is the most complex, the demigod Brahma.

From Brahma, come *prajapatis*, demigods whose function it is to produce the bodies of living things through reproductive activity. So there are similarities with the ideas of Darwin— common ancestry and reproduction with modification. **But in the case of the Vedic cosmology, the common ancestor is not the one Darwin conceived, and the whole process of re-production with modification is intelligently guided by superior beings (not a purely natural process).**

Also, in the Vedic system, bodies are vehicles for conscious selves, or souls, whereas Darwin did not have any clear idea of a conscious self that is different from the material body.

CLASSIFICATION, SCHMLASSIFICATION ...

BRUCE: What do you make of the massive speciation of life and fos-sil records and the more recent DNA sequencing that sup-ports the scientific taxonomy of the contemporary biological classification system?

CREMO: As I said, the main idea in my system is that bodies are vehi-cles for conscious selves. The conscious selves are normally meant to exist on a level of pure consciousness or spirit.

There they are meant to exist in harmony with the source of all conscious beings and all other conscious beings.

But if a conscious self becomes selfish it can no longer exist in that harmony. So it comes to the world of matter. There it can try to enjoy itself independently, but for that it required a material body. Because different conscious selves have different desires they are provided with different kinds of material bodies, complete with DNA.

As for classification, just because the forms of material bodies can be arranged In sequences and groups does not tell us how the sequences and groups came into being. For example, you can arrange motor vehicles in classes and sequences: motor bikes, small cars, trucks, bigger trucks, etc. But this does not mean that one came from the other. Each of these machines was separately designed and manufactured.

THE ASCENDING & DESCENDING PATHS OF KNOWLEDGE

BRUCE: You are very public about your Hindu faith and your devotion to Krishna. Was your work in *Hidden Archaeology* intended to scientifically prove Vedic cosmology and chronology as fact?

CREMO: Not exactly, although it may seem like that. According to the Vedic epistemology, there are two paths of knowledge. The first is called the "ascending path of knowledge." It is based on sense evidence and logic. This is the path of modern materialistic science. But the conclusions arrived at by this method are not certain, because the senses are limited and imperfect, and the mind that we use for logical inference is also imperfect. It can make mistakes, become deluded, cheat or become the victim of cheating.

Science actually recognizes these problems, and therefore scientists claim that they are giving only provisional knowledge that can change. And if we look at the history of science, we see that in fact scientific ideas always are changing. Practically every scientific theory that has ever been proposed has later been shown wrong. Of course, scientists hope, and sometimes claim, that although their conclusions are provisional, they are gradually approaching the truth. But many philosophers of science have problems with such claims. Such claims are simply based on faith. How do you know you are approaching the truth unless you actually know for certain what the truth is? **According to the scientific method, as it is currently taught, there can be no such certain knowledge of what the actual truth is.**

According to the Vedic epistemology, there is another path of knowledge, called the "descending path of knowledge." It is based on the idea that there is a supreme conscious being who has certain, absolute knowledge and is capable of communicating that knowledge to us. This knowledge is concluded in the Vedic literature. Here I use the term Vedic in its broadest sense to include not just the original four *Vedas* but also the derived literature such as the *Puranas*.

So from this source, it is possible to get certain knowledge. The Vedic literature is thus the highest form of evidence, and is not in need of proof from the material path of knowledge. However, one would expect that if the Vedic literature is giving accurate knowledge, there should be material evidence and logic that are consistent with it. And this is actually the case, as I have shown in archaeology. **I would not say I am trying to prove the Vedic literature. Rather I am showing that there is material evidence that is consistent with the conclusions of the Vedic literature, with the hope that this might draw the interest of scientists to the Vedic literature as a valid source of knowledge about the world.**

THE REASON FOR DEVOLUTION

BRUCE: On the page on your website about your book, *Human Devolution: A Vedic Alternative to Darwin's Theory,* you are quoted in an article as saying "We did not evolve up from matter; instead we devolved, or came down, from the realm of pure consciousness, spirit." This statement brings up a few questions for me. First, would you say that our "devolution" is due to the inexorable cycle of *yugas*? Conversely, would human beings living in the *Satya Yuga* match your description of coming from "the realm of pure consciousness, spirit"?

CREMO: I use the word devolution is several senses. The first and primary sense is "devolution from the realm of pure consciousness to the material world." The original position of the conscious self is in the realm of pure consciousness, existing in loving harmony with the source of all conscious beings and with all other conscious beings. This realm is beyond time, beyond the *yuga* cycles.

The reason for devolution from the eternal realm of pure consciousness to the temporal material realm is misuse of free will. The ruling principle of the realm of pure consciousness is selfless love. When a conscious self refuses to continue selfless love, and develops a desire for selfish love (which means exploiting others for one's own pleasure), then it can no longer exist on the level of pure consciousness. So this primary devolution is not caused by the *yugas*.

THE THREE MODES OF MATERIAL NATURE

CREMO: Once the conscious self has devolved into the material world, it does become influenced by the cycle of *yugas*. The *yugas* are influenced by the modes of material nature. There are three modes of material nature: goodness, passion, and ignorance. The *Satya Yuga* is influenced by the mode of goodness. The mode of goodness is favorable for spiritual existence. It is the position from which one can most easily return to the position of pure consciousness. The material elements exist in more pure and subtle forms in the *Satya Yuga* than in other *yugas*, which are less favorable to the cultivation of pure consciousness.

BRUCE: Following this line of thought, would the relatively dense physical state of modern-day human beings correspond to where we are presently occurring, in the *yugic* cycle?

CREMO: As the *yugas* progress, things become less and less hospitable to the cultivation of pure consciousness. But although the conditions become more difficult, the opportunity is still there. So yes, we are now in a difficult time, the *Kali Yuga*.

MORE ABOUT THE GIANTS ...

BRUCE: Would you agree with H. P. Blavatsky's assertion that modern day humans are the fifth version of the human race on

Earth, as well as the most solidified and dense in structure and if not, what is the secret history of the human race?

CREMO: As I have said, I do not normally get involved in critiquing other researchers in alternative science and cosmology. But if asked directly, I reply to questions. There are perhaps similarities between my work and those of Madame Blavatsky. But there are also differences. The similarities and differences may be traced to the textual sources of our respective inspirations.

There are not any exact correspondences with the information that comes from the *Puranas*, but there are some similarities. According to the *Puranas*, humans in previous *yugas* were taller than humans today. And in the past, humans had bodies more suited for spiritual practice and awareness. I do not accept that humans today are a fifth race, but I would accept the general context that humans in the past, during the previous *yugas*, lived longer and had bodies that were composed of more subtle elements.

BRUCE: Blavatsky claimed that legends about giants, which appear in cultures around the world, are related to ancient fifth race human encounters with surviving members of these gigantic, previous races of mankind.

CREMO: According to the *Puranas*, humans in previous ages were larger than those today. This is also reflected in the Bible, which speaks of larger sized humans existing in the past.

(*We thank Mr. Cremo for the incredible details and the genuine care that he put into his responses for this interview!*)

APPENDIX B

GLOSSARY

Age of the Earth is estimated to be around 4.55 billion years old, according to modern geology and geophysics. This age has been determined by radiometric age dating of meteorite material and is consistent with the ages of the oldest-known terrestrial and lunar samples.

Following the development of radiometric age dating, measurements of lead in uranium-rich minerals showed that the oldest such minerals analyzed to date—small crystals of zircon from the Jack Hills of Western Australia—are at least 4.404 billion years old. Comparing the mass and luminosity of the Sun to the multitudes of other stars, it appears that the solar system cannot be much older than those rocks. Calcium-aluminum-rich minerals found in meteorites are the oldest known solid constituents formed within the solar system at 4.567 billion years old, giving an age for the solar system and an upper limit for the age of Earth.

Because the exact time of Earth's accretion (formation) is not yet known and the predictions from different accretion models range from a few millions up to about 100 million years, the exact age of Earth is difficult to determine.

Age of the universe is the time elapsed between the so-called "big bang" and the present day. Current theory and observations suggest that this is between 13.6 and 13.8 billion years. The uncertainty range has been obtained by the agreement of a number of scientific research projects. Scientific instruments and methods have improved the ability to measure the age of the universe with a great accuracy. These projects include background radiation measurements and more ways to measure the expansion of the universe. Background radiation measurements give the cooling time of the universe since the big bang. Expansion of the universe measurements provide accurate data to calculate the age of the universe, according to our current methods. (See also **Big bang**.)

Ages of Man, according to classical Greek and Roman mythology, are the stages of human existence, which tend to progress from an original, long-gone age in which humans enjoyed a nearly divine existence to the current era, in which humans are beset by innumerable pains and evils. In the two surviving accounts, this degradation of the human condition over time is indicated symbolically with metals of successively decreasing value.

    Golden Age. It is said that men lived among the gods, and freely mingled with them. Peace and harmony prevailed during this age. Humans did not have to work to feed themselves, for the earth provided food in abundance. They lived to a very old age but with a youthful appearance and eventually died peacefully.

Their spirits live on as "guardians."

Silver Age. Humans in this age lived for one hundred years as infants. They lived only a short time as grown adults, and spent that time in strife with one another. During this age humans refused to worship the gods; Zeus destroyed this race for its impiety. After death, these humans became "blessed spirits" of the Underworld.

Men of the **Bronze Age** were hard. War was their purpose and passion. Not only arms and tools, but also their very homes were forged of bronze. The men of this age were undone by their own violent ways and left no named spirits but dwell in the "dank house of Hades."

Heroic Age. The one age that does not correspond with any metal. It is also the only age that improves upon the age it follows. In this period lived noble demigods and heroes. It was the heroes of this age who fought at Thebes and Troy. This race of humans died and went to Elysium.

Iron Age. During this [our current] age, humans live an existence of toil and misery. Children dishonor their parents, brother fights with brother and the social contract between guest and host is forgotten. During this age might makes right, and bad men use lies to be thought good. At the height of this age, humans no longer feel shame or indignation at wrongdoing; babies will be born with gray hair and the gods will have completely forsaken humanity: "There will be no help against evil."

Ahaw or "Ahau" is a Mayan language word for the leader of a city-state or a community.

Anachronism is an error in chronology, especially a chronological misplacing of persons, events, objects, or customs in regard to each other. The item is often an object, but may be a verbal expression, a technology, a philosophical idea, a musical style, a material, a custom, or anything else so closely associated with a particular period in time that it seems odd when placed outside its origins.

An anachronism can be an artifact that appears out of place archaeologically, geologically or temporally. It is sometimes called OOPArt, for "Out Of Place Artifact." Anachronisms usually appear more technologically advanced than is expected for their place and period.

However, an apparent anachronism may reflect our ignorance rather than a genuine chronological anomaly. A popular view of history presents an unfolding of the past in which humanity has a primitive start and progresses toward development of technology. Alleged anachronistic artifacts demonstrate contradictions to this idea. Some archaeologists believe that seeing these artifacts as anachronisms underestimates the technology and creativity available to people at the time, although others believe that these are evidence of alternate or "fringe" timelines of human history (See also **Antikythera mechanism**.)

Ancient astronaut theories are various proposals that intelligent extraterrestrial beings have visited Earth and that this contact is linked to the origins or development of human cultures, technologies and religions. Some of these theories suggest that deities from most—if not all—religions are actually extraterrestrial beings, and their technologies were taken as evidence of their divine status.

Ancient astronaut theories have limited support within the scientific community and have garnered little—if any—attention in peer-reviewed studies from scientific journals. (See also **Däniken, Erich von**, **Sitchin, Zecharia** and **Temple, Robert K. G.**)

Antediluvian ("before the Deluge") is that period in the biblical history between the Creation of the Earth and the Deluge. The story takes up chapters 1–6 of Genesis (excluding the Flood narrative). The antediluvian period begins with the Creation and ends with the destruction of all life on the Earth except those saved with Noah in the Ark, 1,656 years later.

Antikythera mechanism is an ancient mechanical calculator designed to calculate astronomical positions. It was discovered in an ancient sea wreck off the Greek island of Antikythera in 1901. Subsequent investigation, particularly in 2006, dated it to about 150–100 BCE and hypothesized that it was on board a ship that sank going from the Greek island of Rhodes to Rome. The Antikythera mechanism is an anachronistic artifact. Technological artifacts of similar complexity did not reappear until a thousand years later.

The device is on display at the National Archaeological Museum of Athens and reconstructions are on display at the American Computer Museum in Bozeman, Montana and the Children's Museum of Manhattan in New York. (See also **Anachronism**.)

Apocalypse (literally, "revelation" in Greek) in the terminology of early Jewish and Christian literature is a revelation of hidden things revealed by God to a chosen prophet or apostle. The term is often used to describe the written account of such a revelation. Apocalyptic literature is of considerable importance in the history of the Judeo-Christian-Islamic beliefs and traditions, because it makes specific references to beliefs such as the resurrection of the dead, judgment day, eternal life, final judgment and perdition. Apocalyptic beliefs predate Christianity, appear throughout other religions, and have been assimilated into contemporary secular society, especially through popular culture (see also **Apocalypticism**). Apocalyptic beliefs also occur in other religious systems, for example, the Hindu concept of *pralaya*.

Apocalypticism is a worldview based on the idea that civilization as we know it will soon come to a tumultuous end with some sort of global event, usually war. This belief is usually conjoined with esoteric knowledge that will likely be revealed in a major confrontation between good and evil forces, destined to change the course of history. Apocalypticism is often tied to religious views, but there is a non-religious scientific version also. Apocalypses can be viewed as good, evil, ambiguous or neutral, depending on the belief system. They can appear as a personal or group tendency, an outlook or a perceptual frame of reference, or a just rhetorical style. Beliefs in apocalypses can lead people towards: paranoia, relief, hyperactivity, passivity, lethargy or depression while awaiting the perceived or possible end.

Apocalypticism was especially evident with the approach of the millennial year 2000, but it need not be tied to a particular calendar date. The next popularly predicted date for the apocalypse is in 2012, on the basis that this year signifies the end of the Mayan calendar. Many hundreds of books and predictions have been made throughout history about looming apocalypses and none of them have ever come true. Christians, the most popular apocalyptians, have been buzzing with End Times expectations since the Jews returned to Israel in 1948 but arguably, nothing has solidly come true from this yet. When it comes to apocalyptic views and beliefs, only the future seems to be able to tell, and the future seems to be up to us. Still there are no guarantees that unknown forces won't intervene at some point, or that unknown natural cycles won't reassert themselves.

Apogee (See **Apsis**).

Apophis (a.k.a., 99942 Apophis) is a Near-Earth asteroid that caused a brief period of concern in December 2004 because initial observations indicated a significant probability (up to 2.7%) that it would strike Earth in 2029. Additional observations provided improved predictions of a close encounter with Earth in 2029, where the likelihood that Apophis will pass through a "gravitational keyhole," a precise region in space no more than about 600 meters across, may set up its probable future impact on Earth on April 13, 2036. (See also **Extinction event**, **NEOs** and **Toutatis**.)

Apsis. In celestial mechanics an apsis is the point of greatest or least distance of the elliptical orbit of an object from its center of attraction, which is generally the center of mass of the system.

Derivative terms are used to identify the body being orbited. The most common are perigee and apogee, referring to orbits around Earth and perihelion and aphelion, referring to orbits around the Sun. During the Apollo program, the terms pericynthion and apocynthion were used when referring to the Moon.

Arcsecond (See **Minute of arc**).

Armageddon, known in some modern English translations as the Mount of Megiddo, is the site of the final battle between God and Satan (whose name means "Adversary"), also known as the Devil. Satan will operate through the person known as the "Beast" or the Antichrist, written about in the Book of Revelation in the New Testament. More generally, it can also refer to an apocalyptic catastrophe.

Astrology is a group of systems, traditions and beliefs in which knowledge of the apparent relative positions of celestial bodies and related details is held to be useful in understanding, interpreting and organizing information about personality, human affairs and other terrestrial matters. Numerous traditions and applications employing astrological concepts have arisen since its earliest recorded beginnings in the third millennium BCE.

Astrology and astronomy were often indistinguishable before the modern era, with the desire for predictive and divinatory knowledge one of the primary motivating factors for astronomical observation. In Europe, astronomy began to diverge from astrology after a period of gradual separation from the Renaissance up until the 18th century.

Astrology can be defined as the study of the positions of celestial bodies in the belief that their movements either directly influence life on Earth or correspond some-how to events experienced on a human scale. Modern astrologers define astrology as a symbolic language, an art form, and a form of divination. Despite differences of defini-tions, a common assumption of astrology is the use of celestial placements in order to explain past and present events and predict the future. Generally, the scientific com-munity considers astrology a pseudoscience or superstition. Despite its rejection by virtually all scientists, 31% of Americans polled have expressed a belief in astrology.

Modern astrological traditions in use today include Vedic (Hindu), Western and Chinese, which are each quite different from one other. Historical traditions include Persian and Arab (medieval Near East), Babylonian (ancient Near East), ancient Egyp-tian, Hellenistic (ancient Greek) and Maya (ancient Mesoamerican).

Astronomy is the scientific study of celestial objects (such as stars, planets, comets, and galaxies) and phenomena that originate outside Earth's atmosphere. It is concerned with the evolution, physics, chemistry, meteorology, and motion of celestial objects, as well as the formation and development of the universe.

Astronomy is one of the oldest sciences. Astronomers of early civilizations per-formed methodical observations of the night sky, and astronomical artifacts have been found from much earlier periods. However, the invention of the telescope was required before astronomy was able to develop into a modern science. Historically, astronomy has included disciplines as diverse as astrometry, celestial navigation, observational astronomy, the making of calendars and even astrology, but professional astronomy is nowadays often considered to be synonymous with astrophysics.

Since the 20th century, the field of professional astronomy split into observational and theoretical branches. Observational astronomy is focused on acquiring and analyz-ing data, mainly using basic principles of physics. Theoretical astronomy is oriented towards the development of computer or analytical models to describe astronomical objects and phenomena. The two fields complement each other, with theoretical as-tronomy seeking to explain the observational results, and observations being used to confirm theoretical results.

2009 has been declared by the UN to be the International Year of Astronomy 2009 (IYA2009). The focus is on enhancing the public's engagement with and under-standing of astronomy. (See also **Cosmology** and **Plasma cosmology**.)

Astronomical Unit (most commonly abbreviated as AU) is a unit of length based on the distance from Earth to the Sun. The precise value of the AU is currently accepted as 93 million miles (nearly 150 million km).

Astrophysics is the branch of astronomy that deals with the physics of the universe, including the physical properties (luminosity, density, temperature, and chemical composition) of celestial objects such as galaxies, stars, planets, exoplanets, and the interstellar medium, as well as their interactions.

Because astrophysics is a very broad subject, astrophysicists typically apply many disciplines of physics, including mechanics, electromagnetism, statistical mechanics, thermodynamics, quantum mechanics, relativity, nuclear and particle physics, and atomic and molecular physics. In practice, modern astronomical research involves a substantial amount of physics. (See also **Plasma cosmology**.)

Astroturfing is a word in American English describing formal political advertising or public relations campaigns seeking to create the impression of being spontaneous "grassroots" behavior, hence the reference to the artificial grass, AstroTurf®.

The goal of such a campaign is to disguise the efforts of a political or commercial entity to appear to be an independent public reaction to some political entity—a politician, political group, product, service or event. Astroturfers attempt to orchestrate the actions of apparently diverse and geographically distributed individuals, by both overt ("outreach," "awareness," etc.) and covert (disinformation) means.

Astroturfing may be employed by an individual pushing a personal agenda or by highly organized professional groups with financial backing from large corporations, by non-profits or by activist organizations. Political consultants who also specialize in opposition research routinely engage in astroturfing. (See also **Meme**, **Viral marketing** and **Viral phenomena**.)

Atlantis was a legendary ancient culture and island, whose existence and location have never been confirmed. The first mentions we have are from the classical Greek philosopher Plato who said that it was destroyed by a natural disaster (possibly an earthquake or tsunami) about 9,000 years before his own time. Plato did mention it was somewhere near Hyperborea, which is presumed to be near Iceland, though some think the location of Atlantis would have been more suitable in one of the cradles of civilization, the Mediterranean Sea. (See also **Theosophy**.)

Ātman is a philosophical term used within Hinduism and Vedanta to identify the soul. It is one's true self (hence generally translated into English as "Self") beyond identification with the phenomenal reality of worldly existence. (See also **Brahman**.)

Atomic clock is a type of clock that uses an atomic resonance frequency standard as its timekeeping element. They are the most accurate time and frequency standards known, and are used as primary standards for international time distribution services, and to control the frequency of television broadcasts and GPS satellite signals.

Aztec is a term used to refer to certain ethnic groups of central Mexico, particularly those groups who spoke the Nahuatl language and who achieved political and military dominance over large parts of Mesoamerica in the 14th, 15th and 16th centuries, a period referred to as the late post-Classic period in Mesoamerican chronology.

Aztlán is the legendary ancestral home of the Nahua peoples, one of the main cultural groups in Mesoamerica. *Azteca* is the Nahuatl word for "people from Aztlán."

B'ak'tun is 20 *k'atun* cycles of the ancient Mesoamerican or Maya Long Count calendar. It contains 144,000 days or 400 *tuns* or a period of nearly 400 tropical years. The Classic period of Maya civilization occurred during the 8th and 9th *b'ak'tuns* of the current calendrical cycle. According to many Mayanists, on 13.0.0.0.0 (December 21, 2012 using the Gregorian calendar correlation), the current 13th *b'ak'tun* will end or be completed, marking the beginning of the 14th *b'ak'tun*. (See also **Mesoamerican Long Count calendar** and *Pik*.)

Baillie, Mike is a professor emeritus of paleoecology in the School of Archaeology and Paleoecology at Queen's University of Belfast in Northern Ireland. Baillie is a leading expert in dendrochronology, or dating by means of tree-rings. In the 1980s, he was instrumental in building a year-by-year chronology of tree-ring growth reaching 7,400 years into the past.

Upon examining the tree-ring record, he noticed indications of severe environmental downturns around 2354 BCE, 1628 BCE, 1159 BCE, 208 BCE, and 540 CE. The evidence suggests that these environmental downturns were wide-ranging catastrophic events; the 540 CE event in particular is attested in tree-ring chronologies from Siberia through Europe and North and South America. This event coincides with the second largest ammonium signal in the Greenland ice in the last two millennia, the largest occurring in 1014 CE, and both these epochs were accompanied by cometary apparitions. Baillie explains the general absence of mainstream historical references to this event by the fact it was described in terms of biblical metaphors since at that time "Christian beliefs included the dogma that nothing that happens in the heavens could have any conceivable effect on the Earth."

Since then, he has devoted much of his attention to uncovering the causes of these global environmental downturns. He believes that impacts from cometary debris may account for most of the downturns, especially the 540 CE event. This hypothesis is supported in work by British cometary astrophysicists, who find that Earth was at increased risk of bombardment by cometary debris in the 400–600 CE timeframe, based on the frequency of fireball activity in the Taurid meteor streams recorded in Chinese archives.

To provide further support to his cometary debris theory, Dr. Baillie has searched the written record and traditions embodied in myths. There he has found evidence that the dates of the environmental downturns listed above are often associated with collapses of civilizations or turning points in history. The 540 CE event, for example, may have been associated with a catastrophe that ushered in the Dark Ages of Europe.

His book, *Exodus to Arthur: Catastrophic Encounters with Comets* (Batsford, 1999), relates the findings of his tree-ring studies to a series of global environmental traumas over the past 4,400 years that may mark events such as the biblical Exodus, the disasters that befell Egypt, collapses of Chinese dynasties, and the onset of the European Dark Ages. *The Celtic Gods: Comets in Irish Mythology* (Tempus, 2005), co-authored with Patrick McCafferty, focuses on the 540 CE event as recorded in the historical records and myths of Ireland and shows that the imagery in the myths and the times between events are consistent with a comet with an Earth-crossing orbit similar to Encke's Comet, as described by the British astronomers Victor Clube and Bill Napier. His latest book, *New Light on the Black Death: The Cosmic Connection* (Tempus, 2006), shows how the tree-ring and Greenland ice core evidence and descriptions in annals, myths and metaphors adduced in support of the global environmental downturn at 540 CE, which included the Justinian plague, also applies to conditions extant at the time of the Black Death in 1348 CE. (See also **Encke's Comet** and **Taurids**.)

Bhakti is the Sanskrit word for human devotion to the Divine and a philosophy of Hinduism. (See also *Kali Yuga*.)

Big bang theory is the cosmological model of the birth of the universe that has the most support in the scientific community. As used by cosmologists, the term big bang generally refers to the idea that the universe has expanded from a primordial hot and dense initial condition at some finite time in the past, and continues to expand to this day. Georges Lemaître proposed what became known as the big bang theory of the origin of the universe, although he called it his "hypothesis of the primeval atom." The framework for the model relies on Albert Einstein's general relativity as formulated by Alexander Friedmann.

This idea has been considered in detail back in time to extreme densities and temperatures, and large particle accelerators have been built to experiment on and test such conditions, resulting in significant confirmation of the theory, but these accelerators have limited capabilities to probe into such high energy regimes. Without any evidence associated with the earliest instant of the expansion, the big bang theory cannot and does not provide any explanation for such an initial condition; rather, it describes and explains the general evolution of the universe since that instant. (See also **Cosmology** and **Plasma cosmology**.)

Binary star system consists of two stars orbiting around their common center of mass. The brighter star is called the primary and the other is its companion star or secondary. Research between the early 1800s and today suggests that many stars are part of either binary star systems or star systems with more than two stars, called multiple star systems.

Walter Cruttenden at the Binary Research Institute, Professor Richard Muller at UC Berkeley, and Dr. Daniel Whitmire of the University of Louisiana, amongst several others, have long speculated on the possibility that our Sun might have an as-yet undiscovered companion. Most of the evidence has been statistical rather than physical.

The recent discovery of Sedna, a small planet-like object first detected by Cal Tech astronomer Dr. Michael Brown, provides what could be indirect physical evidence of a solar companion. Matching the recent findings by Dr. Brown, showing that Sedna moves in a highly unusual elliptical orbit, Cruttenden has determined that Sedna moves in resonance with previously published orbital data for a hypothetical companion star.[201] However, the scientific currently classes Sedna as a dwarf planet, akin to Pluto, due to its size and spectral analysis of its composition. (See also **Brown dwarf**, **Nibiru**, **Sitchin**, **Zechariah**.)

Blavatsky, Helena Petrovna, (née Helena Petrovna Hahn), (1831–1891), better known as Helena Blavatsky or Madame Blavatsky, was a founder of Theosophy. (See also *Secret Doctrine* and **Theosophy**.)

Brahman is a concept of Hinduism. *Brahman* is the unchanging, infinite, immanent, and transcendent reality, which is the Divine Ground of all matter, energy, time, space, being, and everything beyond in this universe. Different philosophical schools describe *Brahman* as transpersonal, personal and impersonal. (See also *Ātman*.)

Brown dwarfs are sub-stellar objects with a mass below that necessary to maintain hydrogen-burning nuclear fusion reactions in their cores, as do stars on the main sequence, but which have fully convective surfaces and interiors, with no chemical differentiation by depth. Brown dwarfs occupy the mass range between that of large gas giant planets and the lowest mass stars; this upper limit is between 75 and 80 Jupiter masses (M_J). Currently there is some debate as to what criterion to use to define the separation between a brown dwarf from a giant planet at very low brown dwarf masses (~13 M_J), and whether brown dwarfs are required to have experienced fusion at some point in their history. In any event, brown dwarfs heavier than 13 M_J do fuse deuterium and those above ~65 M_J also fuse lithium. Currently, there are only two planets observed to be orbiting brown dwarfs.

Brown dwarfs are hard to find in the sky, as they emit almost no light. Their strongest emissions would be in the infrared (IR) spectrum. Since 1995, when the first brown dwarf was confirmed, hundreds have been identified. Brown dwarfs close to Earth include Epsilon Indi Ba and Bb, a pair of dwarfs gravitationally bound to a sun-like star, around 12 light-years from the Sun.

Burckle crater is an undersea crater likely to have been formed by a very large-scale comet or meteorite impact event. It is located to the east of Madagascar and west of Western Australia in the southern Indian Ocean. Its position was determined in 2006 by the Holocene Impact Working Group using evidence of its existence from prehistoric chevron dune formations in Australia and Madagascar that allowed them to triangulate its location.

The Burckle crater has not yet been dated by radiometric analysis of its sediments. The Holocene Impact Working Group conjectures that it was created about 5,000 years ago during the Holocene epoch when a comet impacted in the ocean, and that enormous megatsunamis created the dune formations, which later allowed the crater to be pin-pointed.

It is possible that legends of a "Great Flood" in the Bible, the *Popul Vuh* and other ancient writings from various cultures are associated with this event.

Cartesian (See **Dualism**).

Catastrophism is the idea that Earth has been affected in the distant past by sudden, short-lived, violent events that were sometimes worldwide in scope.

By contrast, the dominant paradigm of geology has been uniformitarianism (also sometimes described as gradualism), in which slow incremental changes, such as gradual erosion, changed Earth's appearance, a view in which the present is the key to understanding the past. Recently a more inclusive and integrated view of geologic events has developed, changing the scientific consensus to reflect acceptance of some catastrophic events in the geologic past.

Causal determinism expresses the belief that every effect has a cause, and therefore science, pursued diligently enough, will explain all natural phenomena and thus produce a TOE (Theory of Everything).

This idea goes hand in hand with materialism. Scientists and skeptics may implicitly favor causal determinism because it does not allow for any supernatural explanations of reality. (See also **Determinism**, **Fatalism**, **Materialism**, **Predestination** and **Theory of Everything**.)

Celestial sphere is an imaginary rotating spherical bubble, concentric and coaxial with the Earth. All objects in the sky can be thought of as lying upon this spherical bubble. Projected from their corresponding geographic equivalents are the celestial equator and the celestial poles. The celestial sphere projection is a very practical tool for positional astronomy.

Channeling. According to Webster's Dictionary: the practice of professedly entering a meditative or trancelike state in order to convey messages from a spiritual guide.

In the New Age movement, channeling is the claimed receipt of information or commands by a person functioning as a medium or channel for an unknown or divine source, much as a radio receives a signal from a transmitter. Although the term was coined in the 20th century, the concept is quite old and widespread.

Channeling is often believed to entail spiritual possession, where a spiritual being takes control of the receiving person's body. It may also refer to other psychic phenomena where the patient loses only part of his control on his body, as in certain forms of dowsing, or merely acquires new information or ability, as in clairvoyance and telepathy. (See also **New Age movement** and **Shamanism**.)

Chichén Itzá is a large pre-Columbian archaeological site built by the Maya civilization located in the Yucatán state of present-day Mexico.

A major regional focal point in the northern Maya lowlands from the late Classic through the terminal Classic and into the early portion of the early post-Classic period, the site exhibits a multitude of architectural styles, from what is called "Mexicanized" and reminiscent of styles seen in central Mexico to the *Puuc* style found among the *Puuc* Maya of the northern lowlands. The presence of central Mexican styles was once thought to have been representative of direct migration or even conquest from central Mexico, but most contemporary interpretations view the presence of these non-Maya styles more as the result of cultural diffusion.

Cobá is a large ruined city of the pre-Columbian Maya civilization, located in the state of Quintana Roo, Mexico, located about 90 km east of Chichén Itzá. It was at Cobá that an unusual stele was discovered with glyphs representing vast units of time. The shortest named unit represents one day and the longest named unit, the *habla 'tun* represents 460 billion, 800 million days. It is unlikely that this unit was in everyday use by the Maya and many Mayanists regard terms for periods larger than a *k 'atun* (equal to 19.7 years) with a skeptical eye.

It is nonetheless interesting that there are several more unnamed units to be found on this stele that are even larger, which have been lettered A through L.

The longest unit of time on this stele, called the "Cobá number," is equivalent to 10,331,233,010,526,315,789,473,682,240,000 days. In English, that's 10 nonillion, 331 octillion, 233 septillion, 10 sextillion, 526 quintillion, 315 quadrillion, 789 trillion, 473 billion, 240 thousand days. This amount of days is substantially longer than the accepted age of the universe, which was recently calculated to be somewhere between 13.6 and 13.8 billion years old.

Copán, anciently named *Xukpi*, the pre-Columbian city located near to the Guatemalan border in the modern-day Copán department of the western Honduras. It is the site of a major Maya kingdom of the Classic era (5th through 9th centuries) with antecedents going back to at least the 2nd century CE.

The site is known for producing a remarkable series of portrait stele, most of which were placed along processional ways in the central plaza of the city and the adjoining "acropolis" (a large complex of overlapping step-pyramids, plazas, and palaces). The stele and sculptured decorations of the buildings of Copán are some of the very finest surviving art of ancient Mesoamerica.

The site also has a large court for playing the Mesoamerican ballgame. At its height in the late Classic period Copán seems to have had an unusually prosperous class of minor nobility, scribes, and artisans, some of whom had homes of cut stone built for themselves (in most sites a privilege reserved for the rulers and high priests), some of which have carved hieroglyphic texts.

Consciousness is notoriously difficult to define or locate. Many cultures and religious traditions place the seat of consciousness in a soul separate from the body. Conversely, many scientists and philosophers consider consciousness to be intimately linked to the neural functioning of the brain.

Coordinated Universal Time (UTC) from the French name *Temps Universel Coordonné* is a time standard based on International Atomic Time (TAI) with leap seconds added at irregular intervals to compensate for Earth's slowing rotation. Leap seconds are used to allow UTC to closely track UT1, which is mean solar time at the Royal Observatory, Greenwich.

The difference between UTC and UT1 cannot exceed 0.9 seconds, so if high precision is not required the general term Universal Time (UT) (without a suffix) may be used. In casual use, Greenwich Mean Time (GMT) is used to mean either UTC or UT1. Owing to the ambiguity as to whether UTC or UT1 is meant, GMT is generally avoided in technical contexts.

Time zones around the world can be expressed as positive or negative offsets from UTC; UTC replaced GMT as the basis for the main reference time scale or civil time in various regions on January 1, 1972. (See also **Greenwich Mean Time, International Atomic Time, UTC and UT1.**)

Cosmogony is any theory concerning the coming into existence or origin of the universe, or about how reality came to be. Cosmogony can be distinguished from cosmology, which studies the universe at large and throughout its existence, and which technically does not inquire directly into the source of its origins. There is some ambiguity between the two terms; for example, the cosmological argument from theology regarding the existence of God is technically an appeal to cosmogonical rather than cosmological ideas.

Cosmology is the study of the largest-scale structures and dynamics of our universe and is concerned with fundamental questions about its formation and evolution. Cosmology is a branch of astronomy that involves itself with studying the motions of the celestial bodies and the first cause. (See also **Astronomy** and **Plasma cosmology.**)

Cyclopean 1. Often capitalized: of, relating to, or characteristic of a Cyclops; 2. Huge, massive; 3. Of or relating to a style of stone construction marked typically by the use of large irregular blocks without mortar.[202]

Cyclops. In Greek mythology and later Roman mythology, a member of a primordial race of giants, each with a single eye in the middle of its forehead.

Däniken, Erich von (b. Zofingen, Aargau, Switzerland, April 14, 1935) is a controversial Swiss author best known for his books which present claims of evidence for extraterrestrial influences on early human culture, most prominently *Chariots of the Gods?*, published in 1968. Von Däniken is one of the key figures responsible for popularizing the "paleo-contact" and ancient astronaut hypotheses.

Von Däniken is a co-founder of the Archaeology, Astronautics and SETI Research Association (AAS RA). He developed a theme park called Mystery Park in Interlaken, Switzerland, which opened on May 23, 2003 and closed on November 19, 2006.

His 26 books have been translated into more than 20 languages, selling more than 60 million copies worldwide, and his documentary TV shows have been viewed around the world.

Deluge. The story of a Great Flood sent by a deity or deities to destroy civilization as an act of divine retribution is a widespread theme among many cultural myths. Though it is best known in modern times through the biblical story of *Noah's Ark* and in the Hindu Puranic story of *Manu*, it is also known as *Deucalion* in Greek mythology, in the Maya mythology of the *Popol Vuh* and *Utnapishtim* in the Sumerian *Epic of Gilgamesh*.

Determinism is the philosophical conception which claims that every physical event, including human cognition and action, is causally determined by an unbroken chain of prior occurrences. No mysterious miracles or totally random events occur.

The principal consequence of deterministic philosophy is that free will (except as defined in strict compatibilism) becomes an illusion. It is a popular misconception that determinism necessarily entails that all future events have already been determined (a position known as fatalism); this is not obviously the case, and the subject is still debated among metaphysicians. Determinism is associated with, and relies upon, the ideas of materialism and causality. Some of the philosophers who have dealt with this issue are Omar Khayyam, David Hume, Thomas Hobbes, Immanuel Kant, and, more recently, John Searle. (See also **Causal determinism**, **Fatalism**, **Materialism**, **Predestination** and **Theory of Everything**.)

Dogon. A group of people living in the central plateau region of Mali, with a population numbering just under 800,000. The Dogon are best known for their mythology, their mask dances, wooden sculpture and their architecture.

Certain researchers investigating the Dogon have reported that they seem to possess advanced astronomical knowledge, the nature and source of which has subsequently become embroiled in controversy.

From 1931 to 1956, two French anthropologists, Marcel Griaule and Germaine Dieterlen, spent 25 years with the Dogon, during which time they were initiated into the tribe. Griaule and Dieterlen reported that the Dogon appeared to know that the brightest star in the sky, Sirius, has a faint companion, Sirius B, which requires a fairly large telescope to be seen. They also claimed that the Dogon appeared to know of the rings of Saturn, and the moons of Jupiter. Neither Griaule nor Dieterlen ever presented any verifiable evidence for any of these claims.

The idea was made widespread when author Robert K. G. Temple wrote a book suggesting an extra-terrestrial source for the Dogon's knowledge. No additional verifiable evidence was presented. Previously, Griaule and Dieterlen had made no claims on the source of the Dogon's knowledge. (See **Ancient astronaut theories** and **Temple, Robert K. G.**)

Dualism is a set of views about the relationship between mind and matter, which begins with the claim that mental phenomena are, in some respects, non-physical.

Ideas on mind/body dualism originate at least as far back as the Persian prophet Zarathushtra ca. 330 BCE and with the ancient Greek philosophers, Plato and Aristotle, who dealt with speculations as to the existence of an incorporeal soul that bore the faculties of intelligence and wisdom, which could not be explained in terms of the physical body.

A generally well-known version of dualism is attributed to René Descartes (1641), which holds that the mind is a nonphysical substance. Descartes was the first to clearly identify the mind with consciousness and self-awareness and to distinguish this from the brain, which was the seat of intelligence. Hence, he was the first to formulate the Western mind-body problem (a.k.a., "Cartesian split"), in the form in which it exists today. (See also **Non-dualism** and **Shamanism**.)

Eclipse is an astronomical event that occurs when one celestial object moves into the shadow of another. When an eclipse occurs within a stellar system, such as the solar system, it forms a type of syzygy—the alignment of three or more celestial bodies in the same gravitational system along a straight line.

The term eclipse is most often used to describe either a solar eclipse, when the Moon's shadow crosses Earth's surface, or a lunar eclipse, when the Moon moves into the shadow of Earth. However, it can also refer to such events beyond the Earth-Moon system. The very close conjunction of the path of the Sun with the equator of the Milky Way Galaxy at 11:11 a.m. GMT on December 21, 2012 is being referred to by many as an eclipse.

Ecliptic is the apparent path that the Sun traces out in the sky during the year. The name "ecliptic" is derived from its being the area in the sky where eclipses occur.

The ecliptic is the center of a region called the zodiac which constitutes a band of 9° on either side. In Western astrology, this region is divided into 12 signs of 30° longitude each, named after 12 of the 13 constellations straddling the ecliptic.

Up until the 17th century in Europe, star maps and positions in star catalogues were always given in ecliptical coordinates, unlike those of their Chinese counterparts who employed an equatorial system. When astronomers started to use telescopes to measure star positions, equatorial coordinates came into wider use. In modern day astronomy, ecliptical coordinates are no longer used

Ecliptic plane. All planets in our solar system orbit the Sun in essentially the same plane as the Earth and the area of the sky where planets traverse is referred to as the "plane of the ecliptic."

The orbit of the dwarf planet Pluto is exceptional in that it makes an angle of 17° with Earth's orbit. Mercury is the only other planet that moves significantly away from the ecliptic plane (7°).

Empiricism is generally regarded as being at the heart of the modern scientific method, that our theories should be based on our observations of the world rather than on intuition or faith; that is, empirical research and *a posteriori* inductive reasoning rather than purely deductive logic.

Empiricism is contrasted with continental rationalism, epitomized by René Descartes. According to the rationalist, philosophy should be performed via introspection and *a priori* deductive reasoning. Names associated with empiricism include St. Thomas Aquinas, Aristotle, Thomas Hobbes, Francis Bacon, John Locke, George Berkeley, and David Hume. (See also **Shamanism**.)

Encke's Comet is a periodic comet that completes an orbit of the Sun once every three years. It was first recognized as a periodic comet in 1819 by Johann Franz Encke. The diameter of the nucleus of Encke's Comet is 1–3 km.

Comet Encke is believed to be the originator of several related meteor showers known as the Taurids. More than one theory has associated Encke's Comet with impacts of cometary material on Earth and with cultural significance.

Theorists argue that the Bronze Age collapse of several civilizations in the Fertile Crescent was caused by a meteorite impact. Encke's Comet is thought to be the remnant of the breakup of a larger body that caused a crater in Iraq at *Umm al Binni*. A large amount of circumstantial evidence supporting this theory has been published in the literature, including satellite images, but on-site analysis has been hindered due to the war in Iraq.

The Tunguska event of 1908, likely caused by the impact of a cometary body, has also been postulated as a fragment of Comet Encke. (See also **Burckle crater, Taurids** and **Tunguska event**.)

Equinoctial cycle (see **Great year**).

Equinox occurs twice a year, around March 20 and around September 22, when the center of the Sun can be observed to be vertically above Earth's equator. It is experienced as a day and night of equal length. At an equinox, the Sun is at one of two opposite points on the celestial sphere where the celestial equator (i.e., declination zero) and ecliptic intersect. These points of intersection are called equinoctial points— the vernal point and the autumnal point. The term equinox can also be used in a wider sense, as the date (day) that such a passage happens and for the same event happening to other planets.

Eschatology is a part of theology and philosophy concerned with what is believed to be the final events in the history of the world, or the ultimate destiny of humanity, commonly referred to as the end of the world. While in mysticism the phrase refers metaphorically to the end of ordinary reality and reunion with the Divine, in many traditional religions it is taught as an actual future event prophesied in sacred texts or folklore. More broadly, eschatology may encompass related concepts such as the Messiah or Messianic Age, the end time, and the end of days.

The Greek word, "aeon," meaning "century" (connoting "epoch"), may be translated as "end of the age (or historical period)" instead of "end of the world." The time distinction also has theological significance; while the end of time in mystical traditions relates to escaping confinement in the "given" reality, some religions believe and fear it to be the literal destruction of the planet (or of all living things)—with the human race surviving in some new form, ending the current "age" of existence.

Most modern eschatology and apocalypticism, both religious and secular, involves the violent disruption or destruction of the world, whereas Christian and Jewish eschatologies view the End Times as the consummation or perfection of God's creation of the world.

For example, according to ancient Hebrew belief, life takes a linear (and not cyclical) path; the world began with God and is constantly headed toward God's final goal for creation.

Expanding universe (See **Big bang**).

Extinction event, also known as mass extinction, extinction-level event and ELE, is a sharp decrease in the number of species in a relatively short period of time. Mass extinctions affect most major taxonomic groups present at the time—birds, mammals, reptiles, amphibians, fish, invertebrates and other simpler life forms. Over 99% of species that ever lived on Earth are now extinct.

Here are some examples of extinction events:

Present day—the Holocene extinction event. 70% of biologists view the present era as a mass extinction event, possibly one of the fastest ever, according to a 1998 survey by the American Museum of Natural History. Some, such as E. O. Wilson of Harvard University, predict that humanity's destruction of the biosphere could cause the extinction of one-half of all species in the next 100 years. Research and conservation efforts, such as the IUCN's annual "Red List" of threatened species, all point to an ongoing period of enhanced extinction, though some offer much lower rates and hence longer time scales before the onset of catastrophic damage.

65 million years ago—the Cretaceous–Tertiary extinction event. About 17% of all families and 50% of all genera went extinct (75% of all species). It ended the reign of dinosaurs and opened the way for mammals and birds to become the dominant land vertebrates.

205 million years ago—the Triassic-Jurassic extinction event. About 20% of all marine families (55% genera) as well as most non-dinosaurian archosaurs, most therapsids, and the last of the large amphibians were eliminated. 23% of all families and 48% of all genera went extinct.

251 million years ago—the Permian-Triassic extinction event. Killed 53% of marine families, 84% of marine genera, about 96% of all marine species and an estimated 70% of land species (including plants, insects, and vertebrate animals). 57% of all families and 83% of all genera went extinct. The "Great Dying" had enormous evolutionary significance: on land it ended the dominance of mammal-like reptiles and created the opportunity for archosaurs and then dinosaurs to become the dominant land vertebrates; in the seas the percentage of animals that were sessile dropped from 67% to 50%. The whole late Permian was a difficult time for at least marine life—even before the "Great Dying."

360–375 million years ago—Late Devonian extinction. A prolonged series of extinctions eliminated about 70% of all species. This extinction event lasted perhaps as long as 20 million years, and there is evidence for a series of extinction pulses within this period. 19% of all families of life and 50% of all genera went extinct.

440–450 million years ago—the two Ordovician-Silurian extinction events. Together, ranked by many scientists as the second largest of the five major extinctions in Earth's history in terms of percentage of genera that went extinct. 27% of all families and 57% of all genera went extinct.

488 million years ago—the Cambrian-Ordovician extinction events. Eliminated many brachiopods and conodonts and severely reduced the number of trilobite species.

The older the fossil record gets the more difficult to read. This is because:

- Older fossils are harder to find because they are usually buried at a considerable depth in the rock.
- Dating fossils is difficult. Radiocarbon dating, for example, does not work accurately with fossils that are hundreds of millions of years old.
- Productive fossil beds are researched more than unproductive ones, therefore leaving certain periods unresearched.
- Prehistoric environmental disturbances can disturb the deposition process.
- The preservation of fossils varies on land, but marine fossils tend to be better preserved than their sought-after land-based cousins.

Fatalism. While the terms are often used interchangeably, fatalism, determinism, and predestination are discrete in emphasizing different aspects of the futility of human will or the foreordination of destiny. However, all these doctrines share common ground.

Determinists generally agree that human actions affect the future, although that future is predetermined. Their view does not accentuate a "submission" to fate, whereas fatalists stress an acceptance of all events as inevitable. In other words, determinists believe the future is fixed because of action and causality, whereas fatalists and many predestinarians think the future is ineluctable despite causality.

Therefore, in determinism, if the past were different, the present and future would differ also. For fatalists, such a question is negligible, since no other present/future/past could exist except what exists now. (See also **Causal determinism**, **Determinism**, **Materialism**, **Predestination** and **Theory of Everything**.)

Giants. The mythology and legends of many different cultures include primordial monsters of human appearance but prodigious size and strength. "Giant" is the English word commonly used for such beings, derived from one of the most famed examples: the *gigantes* of Greek mythology.

In various Indo-European mythologies, gigantic peoples are featured as primeval creatures associated with chaos and the wild nature, and they are frequently in conflict with the gods, be they Olympian or Norse. There are also other stories featuring giants in the Old Testament, perhaps most famously Goliath. Attributed to them are superhuman strength and physical proportions, a long lifespan, and thus a great deal of knowledge as well.

Geologic time scale is a chronologic schema relating rock strata to time that is used by geologists and other Earth scientists to describe the timing and relationships between events that have occurred during the history of Earth.

Evidence from radiometric dating indicates that Earth is about 4.570 billion years old. The geological or deep time of Earth's past has been organized into various units delimited by major geological or paleontological events, such as mass extinctions. For example, the boundary between the Cretaceous period and the Paleogene period is defined by the Cretaceous–Tertiary extinction event, which marked the demise of the dinosaurs and of many marine species. (See also **Extinction event**.)

Geomagnetic reversal is a change in the orientation of Earth's magnetic field such that the positions of Magnetic North and Magnetic South become interchanged. These events often involve an extended decline in field strength followed by a rapid recovery after the new orientation has been established. These events occur on a scale of thousands of years or longer. (See also **Plate tectonics**, **Pole shift theory** and **True polar wander**.)

God is most often conceived of as the supernatural creator and overseer of the universe. Theologians have ascribed a variety of attributes to the many different conceptions of God. The most common among these include omniscience, omnipotence, omnipresence, omnibenevolence (perfect goodness), divine simplicity, jealousy, and eternal and necessary existence. God has also been conceived as being incorporeal, a personal being, the source of all moral obligation, and the "greatest conceivable existent." These attributes were all supported to varying degrees by the early Jewish, Christian and Muslim theologian philosophers, including Maimonides, Augustine of Hippo, and Al-Ghazali, respectively. Many notable medieval philosophers developed arguments for the existence of God, attempting to wrestle with the apparent contradictions implied by many of these attributes.

Golden Age in Greek mythology and legend can also be found in other ancient cultures. It refers either to the highest age in the Greek spectrum of Iron, Bronze, Silver and Golden Ages, or to a time in the beginnings of humanity which was perceived as an ideal state, or utopia, when mankind was pure and immortal. A "golden age" is known as a period of peace, harmony, stability and prosperity. In literary works, the golden age usually ends with a devastating event, which brings about the Fall of Man. (See **Ages of Man**.)

An analogous idea can be found in the religious and philosophical traditions of the Far East. For example, the Vedic or ancient Hindu culture saw history as cyclical composed of "*yugas*" or eras, whose various characteristics were virtually the same and expressed as metals. The *Kali Yuga* (Iron Age), *Dwapara Yuga* (Bronze Age), *Treta Yuga* (Silver Age) and *Satya Yuga* (Golden Age) correspond to the four Greek ages. Similar beliefs can be found in the ancient Middle East and throughout the ancient world.

According to Giorgio de Santillana, the former professor of history at MIT and co-author of the book *Hamlet's Mill*, there are over 200 myth and folktales from over 30 ancient cultures that spoke of a cycle of the ages tied to the movement of the heavens.

Great Attractor is a gravity anomaly in intergalactic space. The first indications of a deviation from the uniform expansion of the universe were reported in 1973 and the location of the Great Attractor was finally determined in 1986 to be located 250 million light-years from the Milky Way in the direction of the Hydra and Centaurus constellations. This region of space is dominated by the Shapley supercluster, the largest concentration of galaxies in our nearby universe, forming a gravitationally interacting unit that is pulling itself together instead of expanding with the universe. Many of the older galaxies within the Shaply supercluster are colliding with their neighbors, and/or radiating large amounts of radio waves.

Observations of this group of galaxies indicate that they are receding relative to us and to each other. The variations in their speeds cover a range of plus or minus 435 miles per second (+700 km/s to –700 km/s), depending on their angular deviation from their direction to the Great Attractor.

Attempts to study the Great Attractor and other phenomena are hampered due to line-of-sight obstruction by its location in the "zone of avoidance," the part of the night sky obscured by the Milky Way Galaxy. (See also **Big bang**.)

Great year, also known as an equinoctial cycle, is the time required for one complete cycle of the precession of the equinoxes, presently about 25,765 years. (See also **Precession of the equinoxes**.)

Greenwich Mean Time (GMT) is a term originally referring to mean solar time at the Royal Observatory in Greenwich, London. It is now sometimes used to refer to Coordinated Universal Time (UTC) when this is viewed as a time zone, although strictly UTC is an atomic time scale that only approximates GMT in the old sense. It is also used to refer to Universal Time (UT), which is the astronomical concept that directly replaced the original GMT.

Noon Greenwich Mean Time is not necessarily the moment when the Sun crosses the Greenwich meridian (and reaches its highest point in the sky in Greenwich) because of Earth's uneven speed in its elliptic orbit and its axial tilt. This event may be up to 16 minutes away from noon GMT (this discrepancy is known as the equation of time). The fictitious mean Sun is the annual average of this nonuniform motion of the true Sun, necessitating the inclusion of the word "mean" in Greenwich Mean Time.

Gregorian calendar is the most widely used calendar in the world today, decreed by Pope Gregory XIII, after whom it was named, on February 24, 1582. A reform of the Julian calendar, it is a year-numbering system, counting from the traditional year of the birth of Jesus. The years following the date of this event are given the designation "*anno Domini*" (AD, "the year of Our Lord"), or "common era" (CE); years preceding this date are labeled "before Christ" (BC) or "before common era" (BCE).

The Gregorian solar calendar is an arithmetical calendar. It counts days as the basic unit of time, grouping them into years of 365 or 366 days; and repeats completely every 146,097 days, which fill 400 years, and which also happens to be 20,871 seven-day weeks. Of these 400 years, 303 (the "common years") have 365 days, and 97 (the leap years) have 366 days. This gives an average year length of exactly 365.2425 days, or 365 days, 5 hours, 49 minutes and 12 seconds.

Gukumatz, in the highland Mayan language, is the Maya creator god, equivalent to *K'uk'ulkan* in *Yukatek* Mayan and Quetzalcoatl in Aztec. (See also **Quetzalcoatl.**)

Haab' also known as the "Vague Year," was the Maya version of the 365-day calendar which approximated the solar year, known to many of the pre-Columbian cultures of Mesoamerica. According to John Major Jenkins, the *Haab'* was combined with the *T'zolk'in* to create the 52-*Haab'* period called a Calendar Round, which is 13 days less than 52 years because the 365-day *Haab'* is slightly less than the 365.2422-day solar year. This causes New Year's Day to shift slowly backward at the rate of one day every four years. The complete backward transit takes place every 1,507 years and this year-drift formula has its own implications." [203]

Harmonic Convergence is the name given to a worldwide esoteric-religious event, which took place on August 16 and August 17, 1987. The event was centered on a number of "sacred" places throughout the world from Stonehenge to the Golden Gate Bridge where individuals gathered to usher in a new era. The date of the Harmonic Convergence was based to some extent on the Maya calendar, with some consideration also given to European and Asian astrological traditions. The chosen dates have the distinction of marking an alignment of the planets of the solar system.

One of the principal organizers of the Harmonic Convergence event was the academic and author José Argüelles. However the event had been predicted by an author named Tony Shearer in his 1971 book, *Lord of the Dawn.*

Believers of this esoteric prophecy maintain that the Harmonic Convergence ushered in a five-year period of Earth's "cleansing," where many of the planet's "false structures of separation" would collapse. The subsequent events of the late 1980s and early 1990s, including the breakup of the Soviet Union, the reunification of West and East Germany, and the ending of apartheid in South Africa were taken as evidence of the Earth's "cleansing."

According to Argüelles and others, the Harmonic Convergence also began the final 26-year countdown to the end of the Maya Long Count calendar in 2012, which would be the "end of history" and the beginning of a new 5,125-year cycle. All the evils of the modern world—war, materialism, violence, abuses, injustice, governmental abuses of power, etc.—would end with the birth of the 6th Sun and the 5th Earth on December 21, 2012.

The highly publicized event brought the New Age movement into the public eye and contributed to making many esoteric practices and ideas like quartz crystals, channeling, and theories about reincarnation and extraterrestrial life a permanent, if still limited, part of mainstream American culture. (See **New Age movement.**)

Hebrew calendar creates a mathematical resolution for the differences that arise between the solar and lunar years so that all Jewish holidays occur at the same season each year.

Hindu calendar (see *Yuga*).

Hopi mythology. Hopi legend tells that the current Earth is the Fourth World to be inhabited by the creations of the Sun God, Tawa. The story essentially states that in each previous world, the people, though originally happy, became disobedient and lived contrary to Tawa's plan; they engaged in sexual promiscuity, fought one another and would not live in harmony. Thus, the most obedient were led (usually by the goddess, Spider Grandmother) to the next higher world, with physical changes occurring both in the people in the course of their journey, and in the environment of the next world. In some stories, these former worlds were then destroyed along with their wicked inhabitants, whereas in others the good people were simply led away from the chaos, which had been created by their actions.

Two main versions exist as to the Hopi's emergence into the present Fourth World. The more prevalent is that Spider Grandmother caused a hollow reed (or bamboo) to grow into the sky, and the people then climbed up the reed and emerged in the Fourth World at the location known today as the Grand Canyon.

The other version (mainly told in Oraibi, the oldest of the Hopi villages) has it that Tawa destroyed the Third World in a Great Flood. Before the destruction, Spider Grandmother sealed the more righteous people into hollow reeds, which were used as boats. Upon arriving on a small piece of dry land, the people saw nothing around them but more water. Spider Grandmother then told the people to make boats out of more reeds, and using island "stepping-stones" along the way, the people sailed east until they eventually arrived on the mountainous coasts of the Fourth World.

Upon their arrival in the Fourth World, each Hopi clan was to go to the farthest extremity of the land in every direction. Far in the north was a land of snow and ice, which was called the Back Door, but this was closed to the Hopi. However, the Hopi say that other peoples came through the Back Door into the Fourth World. This Back Door could be referring to the Bering land bridge, which connected Asia with present-day Alaska. The Hopi clans also passed through the tropics in the south, and today many Hopis regard the Aztec, Maya, and other Central and South American Indian groups as renegade Hopi clans that never finished their appointed migrations.

The Hopi settled in their desert land in Arizona at the behest of the deity, Masauwu (Master of the Fourth World) so that "they would have to depend upon the scanty rainfall which they must evoke with their power and prayer, and so preserve always that knowledge and faith in the supremacy of their Creator who had brought them to this Fourth World after they had failed in three previous worlds."

Humanism. As a result of the rediscovery and study of the literature, art, and civilization of ancient Greece and Rome cultural and intellectual movement during the European Renaissance between the 14th and 17th centuries, a movement was born which emphasized secular over religious concerns. (See also **Secular humanism.**)[204]

I Ching, also called "Classic of Changes" or "Book of Changes," is one of the oldest of the Chinese classic texts. The book is a symbol system used to identify order in random events.

The text describes an ancient system of cosmology and philosophy that is intrinsic to ancient Chinese cultural beliefs. The cosmology centers on the ideas of the dynamic balance of opposites, the evolution of events as a process, and acceptance of the inevitability of change.

The *I Ching* is a "reflection of the universe in miniature." The word "I" has three meanings: ease and simplicity, change and transformation, and invariability. Thus the three principles underlying the *I Ching* are the following:

1. **Simplicity**—the root of the substance. The fundamental law underlying everything in the universe is utterly plain and simple, no matter how abstruse or complex some things may appear to be.

2. **Variability**—the use of the substance. Everything in the universe is continually changing. By comprehending this one may realize the importance of flexibility in life and may thus cultivate the proper attitude for dealing with a multiplicity of diverse situations.

3. **Persistency**—the essence of the substance. While everything in the universe seems to be changing, among the changing tides there is a persistent principle, a central rule, which does not vary with space and time.

The text of the *I Ching* is a set of oracular statements represented by a set of 64 abstract line arrangements called hexagrams. Each hexagram is a figure composed of six stacked horizontal lines, where each line is either Yang (an unbroken, or solid line), or Yin (broken, an open line with a gap in the center). With six such lines stacked from bottom to top there are 64 possible combinations.

Inflection point. In differential calculus, an inflection point, or point of inflection, is a point on a curve at which the curvature changes sign. The curve changes from being concave upwards (positive curvature) to concave downwards (negative curvature), or vice versa. If one imagines driving a vehicle along the curve, it is a point at which the steering wheel is momentarily "straight," being turned from left to right or vice versa.

International Atomic Time (TAI, from the French, *Temps Atomique International*) is a high-precision atomic coordinate time standard based on the notional passage of proper time on Earth's geoid. It is the principal realization of Terrestrial Time, and the basis for Coordinated Universal Time (UTC), which is used for civil timekeeping all over the Earth's surface.

Time coordinates on the TAI scales are conventionally specified using traditional means of specifying days, carried over from non-uniform time standards based on the rotation of the Earth. Specifically, both the "Julian date" (JD) and Gregorian calendar are used. TAI in this form was synchronized with Universal Time at the beginning of 1958, and the two have drifted apart ever since. (See also **Greenwich Mean Time**, **UT**, **UT1** and **UTC**.)

International System of Units (SI) from the French *Le Système International d' Unités* is the modern form of the metric system and is generally a system devised around the convenience of the number ten. It is the world's most widely used system of measurement, both in everyday commerce and in science.

The SI was developed in 1960 from the old meter-kilogram-second (mks) system, rather than the centimeter-gram-second (cgs) system, which, in turn, had a few variants. Because the SI is not static, units are created and definitions are modified through international agreement among many nations as the technology of measurement progresses, and as the precision of measurements improves.

The system is nearly universally employed, and most countries do not even maintain official definitions of any other units. A notable exception is the United States, which continues to use customary units in addition to SI. In the United Kingdom, conversion to metric units is government policy, but the transition is not quite complete.

Three nations have not officially adopted the International System of Units as their primary or sole system of measurement: Liberia, Myanmar and the United States of America. (See also **Second.**)

Islamic calendar is based on cycles of the phases of the Moon. The only widely-used purely lunar calendar is the Islamic, or *Hijri* calendar whose year always consists of 12 lunar months. A feature of a purely lunar year in the Islamic calendar model is that the calendar ceases to be linked to the seasons and drifts each year by 11 days (or 12 days in leap years), and comes back to the position it had in relation to the solar year approximately every 33 Islamic years. It is used predominantly for religious purposes. In Saudi Arabia it is also used for commercial purposes. Because there are about twelve lunations (synodic months) in a solar year, this period (354.37 days) is sometimes referred to as a "lunar year."

Izapa is a very large pre-Columbian archaeological site located in the Mexican state of Chiapas; it was occupied during the late Formative period. The settlement at Izapa extended over 1.4 miles, making it the largest site in Chiapas. The site reached its apogee between 600 BCE and 100 CE; several archaeologists have theorized that Izapa may have been settled as early as 1500 BCE and remained occupied through the late Classic period. Izapa is thought by some to have originally been an Olmec settlement and renowned archaeologist Michael Coe regards Izapa as the connective link between the Olmec and the Maya. Izapa is noted for having a large amount of preserved stele, some of which depict scenes from the *Popol Vuh*. Independent researcher John Major Jenkins considers Izapa to be the site of the creation of the Long Count calendar, which ends on December 21, 2012. (See also **Mesoamerican Long Count calendar** and *Popol Vuh*.)

Jehovah's Witnesses. The religion emerged from the Bible Student Movement, founded in the late 19th century by Charles Taze Russell. It underwent significant changes between 1917 and the 1940s, having its authority structure centralized and its preaching methods brought under greater regimentation. The religion today claims an active worldwide membership of approximately 7 million people. They are most well known for their door-to-door preaching, and their refusal of military service and blood transfusions.

Since 1876, adherents have believed that they are living in the last days of the present world. In the years leading up to 1925 and 1975, the religion's publications expressed strong expectations that Armageddon would occur in those years, both times resulting in surges in membership and subsequent defections.

The organization's teachings and practices diverge greatly from traditional Christian theology, which has caused several major Christian denominations to denounce the group as either a cult or heretical sect. Medical ethicists have criticized Jehovah's Witnesses as an authoritarian group for coercing members to reject blood transfusions. Former adherents have claimed that the religion demands unquestioning obedience from members, with the consequence of expulsion and shunning facing any who act in disagreement with its doctrines. (See also **Seventh-Day Adventists**.)

Julian calendar, a reform of the Roman calendar, was introduced by Julius Caesar in 46 BCE, and came into force in 45 BCE (or 709 *ab urbe condita*, "after the founding of Rome"). It has a regular year of 365 days divided into 12 months, and a leap day is added to February every four years. Hence the Julian year is on average 365.25 days long. The Julian calendar remained in use into the 20th century in some countries as a national calendar and it is still used by the Berber people of North Africa and by many national Orthodox churches, otherwise, it has been globally replaced by the Gregorian calendar.

Kali Yuga literally "Age of Kali," "Age of Vice" or "Dark Age," is one of the four stages of development that the world undergoes as part of the cycle of *yugas* or ages, as described in Indian scriptures, the others being *Satya* (or *Krita*) *Yuga*, *Treta Yuga* and *Dwapara Yuga*. According to the *Surya Siddhanta*, an astronomical treatise that forms the basis of all Hindu and Buddhist calendars, *Kali Yuga* began at what corresponds with midnight (00:00) on January 23, 3102 BCE.

Adherents of traditional Hinduism believe that the *Kali Yuga* cycle lasts for 432,000 years and that there is a 10,000-year period within the *Kali Yuga*, which began in 1899 CE, where there is increased influence of *bhakti*, the Sanskrit word "for human devotion to the Divine," which affects the manifestation of every day events. (See also *Bhakti* and *Yuga*.)

K'atun is 7,200 days in the Maya calendar.

K'in is one day in the Maya calendar.

K'uk'ulkan (see **Quetzalcoatl**).

Latitude gives the location of a place on Earth (or other planetary body) north or south of the equator. Lines of latitude are the horizontal lines shown running east-to-west on maps. Technically, latitude is an angular measurement in degrees (marked with °)

ranging from 0° at the equator (low latitude) to 90° at the poles (90° N for the North Pole or 90° S for the South Pole; high latitude).

Laws of Manu also known as *Manusmṛti* is the most important and earliest metrical work of the *Dharmaśāstra* textual tradition of Hinduism. Sir William Jones, an English Orientalist and judge of the British Supreme Court in Calcutta, first translated it into English in 1794.

John Major Jenkins claims in his book *Galactic Alignment* that the English translation of the *Laws of Manu* presents updated information about the length of time for each of the *yugas* in the Hindu calendar, such that the total cycle of *yugas* is a mere 12,000 years, as opposed to the traditional 4,320,000 years, and that the *Kali Yuga* is only 1,200 years long, instead of 432,000. Jenkins is unclear as to the exact beginning or end-dates of this latest Dark Age in Hindu calendrics. However, he suggests that the end of the *Kali Yuga* may actually end on or around the end of the Maya Long Count calendar on December 21, 2012.

Leap second is a one-second adjustment that keeps broadcast standards for time of day close to mean solar time. Broadcast standards for civil time are based on Coordinated Universal Time (UTC), a time standard which is maintained using extremely precise atomic clocks. To keep the UTC broadcast standard close to mean solar time, UTC is occasionally corrected by an intercalary adjustment, or "leap," of one second. Over long time periods, leap seconds must be added at an ever increasing rate. The timing of leap seconds is now determined by the International Earth Rotation and Reference Systems Service (IERS). Leap seconds were determined by the Bureau International de l'Heure (BIH) prior to January 1, 1988, when the IERS assumed that responsibility.

When a positive leap second is added at 23:59:60 UTC, it delays the start of the following UTC day (at 00:00:00 UTC) by one second, effectively slowing the UTC clock. (Also see **Atomic clock**, **Greenwich Mean Time**, **International Atomic Time**, **Minute**, **Second**, **UTC**, **UT1**.)

Longitude is the geographic coordinate most commonly used in maps and global navigation for east-west measurement. A line of longitude is a north-south meridian and half of a great circle.

Unlike latitude, which has the equator as a natural starting position, there is no natural starting position for longitude. Therefore, a reference meridian had to be chosen. It was a popular practice to use a nation's capital as the starting point, but other significant locations were also used. British cartographers had long used the Greenwich meridian in London and in 1884, the International Meridian Conference adopted it as the universal prime meridian or zero point of longitude.

Lunar calendar (see **Islamic calendar**).

Maya calendar is a system of distinct calendars and almanacs used by the Maya civilization of pre-Columbian Mesoamerica, and by some modern Maya communities in the Guatemala highlands. These calendars can be synchronized and interlocked, their combinations giving rise to further, more extensive cycles.

Two of the most widely used calendars in pre-Hispanic Mesoamerica were the 365-day solar calendar (*Haab'* in Mayan) and the 260-day ceremonial calendar, which had 20 periods of 13 days (the *T'zolk'in* in Mayan). Because the two calendars were based on 365 days and 260 days respectively, the whole cycle would repeat itself every 52 *Haab'* years exactly. This period is generally known as the Calendar Round. To measure dates over periods longer than 52 years, the Mesoamericans devised the Long Count calendar.

The essentials of the Maya calendric system are based upon a system that had been in common use throughout the region, dating back to at least the 6th century BCE. It shares many aspects with calendars employed by other earlier Mesoamerican civilizations, such as the Zapotec and Olmec, and contemporary or later ones such as the Mixtec and Aztec calendars. Although the Mesoamerican calendar did not originate with the Maya, their subsequent extensions and refinements of it were the most sophisticated. Along with those of the Aztecs, the Maya calendars are the best-documented and most completely understood. (See also **Mesoamerican Long Count calendar**.)

Mayan languages are a language family spoken in Mesoamerica and northern Central America. Mayan languages are spoken by at least 6 million indigenous Maya, primarily in Guatemala, Mexico, and Belize. Guatemala formally recognizes 21 Mayan languages by name and Mexico recognizes 8 more. The Mayan languages with the most speakers are *K'iche'*, from the Guatemalan highlands with 1,000,000 speakers, and *Yucatek* from Mexico's Yucatán Peninsula with 800,000 present-day speakers.

The Mayan language family is one of the best documented and most studied in the Americas. Modern Mayan languages descend from proto-Mayan, a language thought to have been spoken at least 5,000 years ago and which has been partially reconstructed using the comparative method. Mayan languages form part of the Mesoamerican Linguistic Area, an area of linguistic convergence developed throughout millennia of interaction between the peoples of Mesoamerica.

During the pre-Columbian era of Mesoamerican history, some Mayan languages were written in the Maya hieroglyphic script. Its use was particularly widespread during the Classic period of Maya civilization (ca. 250–900 CE). The surviving corpus of over 10,000 known individual Maya inscriptions on buildings, monuments, pottery and bark-paper codices, combined with the rich post-colonial literature in Mayan languages written in the Latin alphabet, provides a basis for the modern understanding of pre-Columbian history unparalleled in the Americas.

Mayanism is a collection of beliefs based on metaphysical speculation about the ancient Maya. It is a term coined to cover a non-codified eclectic collection of New Age beliefs, influenced in part by pre-Columbian Maya mythology and some folk beliefs of the modern Maya peoples. Adherents of this belief system are not to be confused with Mayanists, scholars who research the historical Maya civilization.

Mayanism was most heavily influenced by the 19th century scholarship of French archaeologist Charles Étienne Brasseur de Bourbourg, who made significant academic contributions, including the rediscovery and the translation into French of the Maya creation myth, the *Popol Vuh*.

Towards the end of his career, Brasseur became convinced that the ancient Maya culture could be traced to the lost continent of Atlantis and he influenced works that are today regarded by the scientific community to be pseudoscience and pseudohistory, such as the research of Augustus Le Plongeon, Ignatius L. Donnelly, and James Churchward.

Contemporary Mayanism is additionally characterized by allusions to possible contacts with extraterrestrial life. In the 1970s, ancient astronaut theories relating to the Maya were popularized by Erich von Däniken's book and the Academy Award-nominated documentary based upon it, *Chariots of the Gods?*

Mayanism has been promoted by specific publishing houses, most notably Inner Traditions/Bear & Co., which has produced a number of books on the theme of 2012 by authors such as José Argüelles, John Major Jenkins, Carl Johan Calleman, and Barbara Hand Clow. Daniel Pinchbeck represents a new generation of authors who has contributed to the growing popularity of Mayanism.

Mayanist refers to a scholar who has specialized in research and study of the Central American pre-Columbian Maya civilization. Scholars in this field have drawn upon their expertise in many inter-related disciplines: archaeology, linguistics, epigraphy, ethnology, history, photography, art, architecture, astronomy, ceramics, to name a few. The term has particularly been adopted by those who have studied and contributed to the decipherment of Maya hieroglyphics, the complex and elaborate writing system, which was developed by the ancient Maya.

Materialism is the philosophical view that the only thing that can truly be said to "exist" is matter; that fundamentally, all things are comprised of "material." Materialism has also frequently been understood to designate an entire scientific, "rationalistic" worldview, particularly by religious thinkers opposed to it and also by Marxists. It typically contrasts with dualism and idealism, among others. (See also **Shamanism**.)

Meme. A unit or element of cultural ideas, symbols or practices; such units or elements transmit from one mind to another through speech, gestures, rituals, or other imitable phenomena. It derives from a Greek word for "mimic."

Richard Dawkins coined the word "meme" as a neologism in his book *The Selfish Gene* (1976) to describe how one might extend evolutionary principles to explain the spread of ideas and cultural phenomena. He gave as examples melodies, catchphrases, and beliefs (notably religious belief), clothing/fashion, and the technology of building arches. Memes act as cultural analogues to genes in that they self-replicate and respond to selective pressures.

Meme-theorists contend that memes evolve by natural selection (in a manner similar to that of biological evolution) through the processes of variation, mutation, competition, and inheritance influencing an individual entity's reproductive success. Memes spread through the behaviors that they generate in their hosts. Memes that propagate less prolifically may become extinct, while others may survive, spread, and (for better or for worse) mutate. Theorists point out that memes which replicate the most effectively spread best, and some memes may replicate effectively even when they prove detrimental to the welfare of their hosts. (See also **Astroturfing**, **Viral marketing** and **Viral phenomena**.)

Mesoamerica is a region extending approximately from central Mexico to Honduras and Nicaragua, defined as the cultural area within which a number of pre-Columbian societies flourished before the Spanish colonization of the Americas in the 15th and 16th centuries. Prehistoric groups in this area are characterized by agricultural villages and large ceremonial and politico-religious capitals. This culture area included some of the most complex and advanced cultures of the Americas, including the Olmec, Teotihuacan, the Maya and the Aztec.

Mesoamerican Long Count calendar is a non-repeating, vigesimal (base-20) calendar used by several Mesoamerican cultures, most notably the Maya. For this reason, it is sometimes known as the Maya Long Count calendar. Though no longer in use when discovered by archaeological excavations in the early 20th century, they are thought to have been in use by the Maya as early as 500 BCE. Using a modified vigesimal tally, the Long Count calendar identifies a day by counting the number of days passed since its beginning, which after nearly century of academic trial and tribulation is now generally agreed to have been dated August 11, 3114 BCE in the Gregorian calendar.

Rather than using a base-10 scheme, like Western numbering, the Long Count days were tallied in a base-20 scheme. Thus 0.0.0.1.5 is equal to 25, and 0.0.0.2.0 is equal to 40. However, the Long Count is not consistently base-20, as the second digit rolls over to zero when it reaches 18. Thus 0.0.1.0.0 does not represent 400 days, but rather only 360 days.

The following table shows the period equivalents as well as Maya names for these periods:

Representation	Long Count Subdivisions	Days	~Solar Years
0.0.0.0.1	1 *k'in*	1	1/365
0.0.0.1.0	1 *winal* = 20 *k'in*	20	1/18
0.0.1.0.0	1 *tun* = 18 winal	360	1
0.1.0.0.0	1 *k'atun* = 20 *tun*	7,200	19.7
1.0.0.0.0	1 *b'ak'tun* = 20 *k'atun*	144,000	394

Mesopotamia (see **Sumer**).

Metaphysics. **1.** The branch of philosophy that examines the nature of reality, including the relationship between mind and matter, substance and attribute, fact and value. **2.** (*used with a pl. verb*) The theoretical or first principles of a particular discipline: *the metaphysics of law.* **3.** (*used with a sing. verb*) *A priori* speculation upon questions that are unanswerable to scientific observation, analysis, or experiment. **4.** (*used with a sing. verb*) Excessively subtle or recondite reasoning.[205]

Metonic cycle in astronomy and calendar studies is a particular approximate common multiple of the tropical (solar) year and the synodic (lunar) month. The Greek astronomer Meton of Athens observed that a period of 19 tropical years is almost exactly equal to 235 synodic months, and rounded to full days counts 6,940 days. The difference between the two periods (of 19 tropical years and 235 synodic months) is only 2 hours.

The cycle's most significant contemporary use is to help in trajectory calculations and launch window analysis for lunar spacecraft missions as well as serving as the basis for the Hebrew calendar's 19 year cycle. Another use is in the calculation of the date of the Christian feast of Easter.

Milankovitch cycles are the collective effect of changes in the Earth's movements upon its climate. The eccentricity, axial tilt, and precession of Earth's orbit vary in several patterns, resulting in the 100,000-year Ice Age cycles over the last several million years. The Earth's axis completes one full cycle of precession approximately every 26,000 years. At the same time, the elliptical orbit revolves, more slowly, leading to a 21,000-year cycle between the seasons and the orbit. In addition, the angle between Earth's rotational axis and the normal to the plane of its orbit moves from 22.1 degrees to 24.5 degrees and back again on a 41,000-year cycle. Currently, this angle is 23.44 degrees and is decreasing.

Minute. A unit of measurement of time or of angle. As a unit of time, a minute is equal to 1/60 of an hour or 60 seconds. Some rare minutes have 59 or 61 seconds. (See also **Leap second.**) The fact that an hour contains 60 minutes may be due to influences from the Babylonians, who used a base-60 or sexagesimal counting system. (See also **Second.**)

Minute of arc (MOA or arcminute) is a unit of angular measurement, equal to one sixtieth (1/60) of one degree. Since one degree is defined as one three hundred sixtieth (1/360) of a circle, 1 MOA is 1/21,600 of the amount of arc in a closed circle. It is used in the fields that require a unit for the expression of small angles, such as astronomy or marksmanship. One arcminute is commonly written as 1'. It is also abbreviated as arcmin or amin.

The subdivision of the minute of arc is the second of arc, or arcsecond. There are 60 arcseconds in an arcminute. Therefore, the arcsecond is 1/1,296,000 of a circle. One arcsecond is commonly written as 1". To express even smaller angles, standard metric prefixes can be employed; the milliarcsecond, abbreviated mas, is sometimes used in astronomy.

Myth. A sacred story concerning the origins of the world or how the world and the creatures in it came to have their present form.

Mythomania (See *Pseudologia Fantastica*).

Nadir is the astronomical term for the point directly below the observer, or more precisely, the point with an inclination of −90°. In simple terms, if you are standing on the Earth, it is the direction "down" toward your feet. The point opposite the nadir is the zenith.

Nadir also refers to a downward-facing viewing angle of an orbiting satellite, such as is employed during remote sensing of the atmosphere, as well as when an astronaut faces the Earth while performing an extra-vehicular activity. The word is also used figuratively to mean the lowest point of a person's spirits.

Nahuatl is a group of related languages and dialects of the Aztecan, or Nahuan, branch of the Uto-Aztecan language family. All Nahuan languages are indigenous to Mesoamerica and are spoken by an estimated 1.5 million Nahua people, most of whom live in Central Mexico. Nahuatl has been spoken in Central Mexico since at least the 7th century CE. At the time of the Spanish conquest of Mexico in the early 16th century it was the language of the Aztecs, who dominated central Mexico during the late post-Classic period of Mesoamerican chronology.

Near-Earth Objects (NEOs) are solar system objects whose orbits bring them into close proximity with the Earth. All have a perihelion distance < 1.3 AU. They include a few thousand Near-Earth asteroids (NEAs), Near-Earth comets, a number of solar-orbiting spacecraft, and meteoroids large enough to be tracked in space before striking the Earth. It is now widely accepted that collisions in the past have had a significant role in shaping the geological and biological history of the planet. NEOs have become of increased interest since the 1980s because of increased awareness of the potential danger some of the asteroids or comets pose to the Earth, and active mitigations are being actively pursued.

Some orbits of Near-Earth asteroids intersect Earth's orbit so they pose a collision danger. The United States, European Union and other nations are currently scanning for NEOs in an effort called Spaceguard. In the United States, NASA has a congressional mandate to catalogue all NEOs that are at least 1 km wide, as the impact of such an object would be expected to produce severe to catastrophic effects. As of October 2008, 982 of these mandated NEOs have been detected. It was estimated in 2006 that 20% of the mandated objects have not yet been found. Efforts are under way to use an existing telescope in Australia to cover the ~30% of the sky that has not yet been surveyed. (See also **Apophis** and **Toutakis**.)

Nephilim are beings who appear in the Bible, specifically in the Book of Genesis, and are also mentioned in other biblical texts and in some non-canonical Jewish writings. Genesis Chapter 6, verses 1 through 4 describe the origin of the Nephilim:

Now it came about, when men began to multiply on the face of the land, and daughters were born to them, that the sons of God saw that the daughters of men were beautiful; and they took wives for themselves, whomever they chose ... The Nephilim were on the earth in those days, and also afterward, when the sons of God came in to the daughters of men, and they bore children to them. Those were the mighty men who were of old, men of renown.

Genesis 6:4 implies that the Nephilim have inhabited Earth in at least two different time periods—in antediluvian times "and afterward." If the Nephilim were unearthly beings, it is possible that the "giants of Canaan" in Book of Numbers 13:33 were the direct descendants of the antediluvian Nephilim. An alternate possibility is that the term Nephilim is a generic term for "giants" in general, which is consistent with the Septuagint and Vulgate translations of the word. (See also **Giants**.)

New Age movement describes a broad movement in Western culture characterized by an individual eclectic approach to spiritual exploration. It has some attributes of a new, emerging religion but is currently a loose network of spiritual seekers, teachers, healers and other participants. The name "New Age" also refers to the market segment in which goods and services are sold to people in the movement.

Rather than follow the lead of an organized religion, "New Agers" typically construct their own spiritual journey based on material taken as needed from mystical traditions from all over the world, as well as shamanism, neopaganism and occultism. Participants are likely to dip into many diverse teachings and practices, some mainstream and some fringe, and formulate their own beliefs and practices based on their experiences in each. No clear membership or rigid boundaries actually exist. The movement is most visible where its ideas are traded, for example in alternative bookstores, music stores, and fairs.

Most New Age activity may be characterized as a form of alternative spirituality. Even apparent exceptions (such as alternative health practices) often turn out to have some spiritual dimension (for example, the integration of mind, body, and spirit). "Alternative" here means, with respect to Western Judeo-Christian culture. It is no accident that most New Age ideas and practices seem to contain implicit critiques of mainstream Christianity in particular. An emphasis on meditation suggests that ordinary prayer is insufficient; belief in reincarnation (which not all New Agers accept) challenges familiar Christian doctrines of the afterlife.

New Testament as usually received in the Christian Churches, is made up of twenty-seven different books attributed to eight different authors, six of whom are numbered among the Apostles (Matthew, John, Paul, James, Peter, Jude) and two among their immediate disciples (Mark, Luke) ... These writings ... include historical books (Gospels and Acts), didactic books (Epistles) and a prophetical book (Apocalypse).[206]

The original texts were written in *Koine* Greek by various authors after c. 45 CE. Its 27 books were gradually collected into a single volume over a period of several centuries. Although certain Christian sects differ as to which works are included in the

New Testament, the vast majority of denominations have settled on the same 27-book canon.[207] (See also **Old Testament.**)

Nibiru is a planetary object described by Zecharia Sitchin as having an elongated, elliptical, 3,600-year orbit in Earth's own solar system, which along with his other speculations are entirely discounted by mainstream scientists, historians and archaeologists. (See **Binary star system, Planet X, NEOs, Sitchin, Zechariah.**)

Non-standard cosmology is any physical cosmological model of the universe that has been or still is proposed as an alternative to the big bang model of (standard) physical cosmology. The term "non-standard" is applied to any cosmological theory that does not conform to the scientific consensus. (See also **Astronomy, Cosmology** and **Plasma cosmology.**)

Non-dualism is the understanding or belief that dualism or dichotomy are illusory phenomena. Examples of dualisms include self/other, mind/body, male/female, good/evil, active/passive, dualism/non-dualism and many others. It is accessible as a belief, theory, condition, as part of a tradition, as a practice or as the quality of union with reality.

A non-dual philosophical or religious perspective or theory maintains that there is no fundamental distinction between mind and matter or that the entire phenomenological world is an illusion (with reality being described variously as the "Void," the "Is," "Emptiness," the "mind of God," *Atman* or *Brahman*).

Novelty theory attempts to calculate the ebb and flow of novelty in the universe as an inherent quality of time. It is an idea conceived of and discussed at length by Terence McKenna from the early 1970s until his death in 1999. It is considered to be pseudoscience by the scientific community. Novelty theory involves ontology, morphogenesis, and eschatology. Novelty, in this context, can be thought of as newness, density of complexification, and dynamic change as opposed to static habituation. According to McKenna, when "novelty" is graphed over time, a fractal waveform known as "timewave zero" or simply the timewave results. The graph shows at what times, but never at what locations, novelty is increasing or decreasing. According to the timewave graph, great periods of novelty have occurred:

- about 4 billion years ago when Earth was formed.
- 65 million years ago when dinosaurs became extinct and when mammals expanded.
- around 10,000 years ago after the end of the last Ice Age.
- around the late 18th century when social and scientific revolutions progressed.
- during the 1960s.
- around the time of 9/11.
- novelty periods in November 2008 and October 2010, with novelty progressing towards the infinity on December, 12 2012. (See also **Eshatology** and **Pseudoscience.**)

Oannes was the name given by the Babylonian writer Berossus in the 3rd century BCE to a mythical being who taught mankind wisdom.

Berossus describes Oannes as having the body of a fish but underneath the figure of a man. He is described as dwelling in the Persian Gulf, and rising out of the waters in the daytime and furnishing mankind instruction in writing, the arts and the various sciences.

Once thought to be based on the ancient Babylonian god Ea, it is now known that Oannes is in fact based on Uan (Adapa), the first of the seven antediluvian sages or Abgallu (in Sumerian *Ab* = water, *Gal* = Great, *Lu* = man), who were sent by Ea to deliver the arts of civilization to mankind in ancient Sumerian mythology, at Eridu, the oldest city of Sumer in what is today southern Iraq. (See also **Sumer**.)

Observable universe consists of the galaxies and other matter that we can in principle observe from Earth in the present day, because light or other signals from those objects has had time to reach us since the beginning of the cosmological expansion. The distance to the edge of the observable universe is roughly the same in every direction—that is, the observable universe is a solid sphere (a ball) centered on the Earth, regardless of the shape of the universe as a whole. Every location in the universe has its own observable universe, which may or may not overlap with the one centered around the Earth.

Old Testament. In Western Christianity, the Old Testament refers to the books that form the first of the two-part Christian biblical canon. These works correspond to the Hebrew Bible (*Tanakh*), with some variations and additions. In the Eastern Orthodox Church the comparable texts are known as the Septuagint, from the original Greek translation of the Hebrew scriptures.

Most scholars agree that the Hebrew Bible was composed and compiled between the 12th and the 2nd century BCE. Jesus and his disciples referenced it when discussing Jesus' newer teachings, referring to it as "the law of Moses, the prophets, and the psalms ... the scriptures" (Luke 24:44–45). The accounts of Jesus and his disciples are recorded in the New Testament. (See also **New Testament**.)

Olmec were an ancient pre-Columbian people living in the tropical lowlands of south-central Mexico, in what are roughly the modern-day states of Veracruz and Tabasco. The Olmec flourished during Mesoamerica's Formative period, dating roughly from 1400 BCE to about 400 BCE. They were the first Mesoamerican civilization and are believed to have laid many of the foundations for the civilizations that followed. The Olmecs are speculatively credited with many "firsts," including bloodletting and perhaps human sacrifice, writing and epigraphy, the invention of zero and the Mesoamerican calendar and the Mesoamerican ballgame, hallmarks of nearly all subsequent Mesoamerican societies.

Palenque is a Maya archaeological site in the Mexican state of Chiapas, located about 130 km south of Ciudad del Carmen. It is a medium-sized site, much smaller than such huge sites as Tikal or Copán, but it contains some of the finest architecture, sculpture, roof comb and bas-relief carvings the Maya produced.

The Maya people had abandoned the site of Palenque for several hundreds of years when the Spanish explorers arrived in Chiapas in the 16th century. At that time, the local *Chol* Maya called it *Otolum* meaning "land with strong houses," which was roughly translated into Spanish as *palenque*, meaning "fortification."

An ancient name for the city was *Lakam Ha*, which translates as "Big Water," for the numerous springs and wide cascades that are found within the site. Palenque was the capital of the important Classic period Maya city-state of *B'aakal*.

Parsec ("parallax of one arcsecond," symbol pc) is a unit of length used in astronomy for measuring the distance from a star to the Earth that is based on the distance between the Earth and the Sun (1 AU) and the angle of the star being observed. A parsec is equal to around 19 trillion miles (just under 31 trillion km), or about 3.26 light-years. (See also **Minute of arc** and **Observable universe**.)

Kiloparsecs (kpc), megaparsecs (mpc) and gigaparsecs (gpc) refer to distances measured in units of one thousand, one million and one billion parsecs, respectively.

The nearest known star to Earth, other than the Sun, is Proxima Centauri, 1.29 parsecs away.

The center of the Milky Way is about 8 kpc from Earth, and the Milky Way is about 30 kpc across.

The Andromeda Galaxy, the most distant object visible to the naked eye, is slightly less than 800 kpc away from Earth.

The nearest large galaxy cluster, the Virgo Cluster, is about 18 mpc away.

The observable universe has a radius of about 14 gpc or 46.5 billion light-years.

Perennial philosophy is the notion of the universal recurrence of philosophical insight independent of epoch or culture, including universal truths on the nature of reality, humanity or consciousness (anthropological universals).

The idea was taken up by the German mathematician and philosopher Gottfried Leibniz, who used it to designate the common, eternal philosophy that underlies all religions, and in particular the mystical streams within them. Aldous Huxley popularized the term in more recent times in his 1945 book, *The Perennial Philosophy*.

Perigee (see **Apsis**).

Photon belt is a fringe belief largely linked to some parts of the New Age movement that a belt or ring of photons is going to, depending on the source of the information, fully envelope the Earth in 2011 and possibly cause massive failure of electrical equipment, with 2–3 days of total darkness or total daylight, and/or initiate a spiritual transition. According to some New Age beliefs, Earth will pass though this belt, resulting in either humanity's elevation to a higher plain of existence or the end of the world, or both.

While the concept of the photon belt is a New Age philosophy, some parts of the story can be analyzed scientifically. According to the scientific orthodoxy, there is no evidence for the existence of any sort of "photon belt," as a photon is the elementary particle that makes up light. To the extent that such a thing as a "photon belt" could be accepted as physically possible, it would require the gravitational pull of a black hole, with light rays being bent around the black hole near the event horizon, forming a photon sphere. Barring interaction with gravity or matter, photons otherwise always travel in straight lines. (See also **New Age movement**.)

Pik. Ancient term for *b'ak'tun*. (See also *b'ak'tun*).

Planet X. In the early 2000s, it was widely propagated on the Internet by Nancy Lieder and her online community, Zetatalk, that a planetoid or brown dwarf twin of the Sun was barreling towards the Earth. The predicted effects of this were that local planets and asteroids would be knocked off their orbits "like bowling pins," that the Earth would experience a radical magnetic pole shift, in addition to extreme changes in Earth's crust. Lieder claimed to have "channeled" this information from her extraterrestrial contacts from the Zeta Reticuli star system.

When no such catastrophe occurred, Lieder claimed that the Zeta's May 2003 date was merely a "white lie" to confuse the elites. Lieder insists the Zetas maintain that "Planet X" is coming and that a more specific passage timeline will be forthcoming. Lieder claims that disclosing a date would enable those in power to plan martial law and attempt to trap people in cities during the pole shift, causing their deaths. Lieder regularly claims through her Zetatalk discussions on godlikeproductions.com and other sites that the pole shift will occur before 2012.

It was suggested on Zetatalk that "Planet X" corresponded to "Nibiru," the wandering planetoid described by Zecharia Sitchin in his many books and that it would strike our solar system by May of 2003. However, Sitchin disagreed with Lieder's claim of impending global catastrophe and in 2007, partly in response to Lieder's claims, he published a book, *The End of Days*, which set the time for the last passing of Nibiru by Earth at roughly 600 BCE, which would mean it would be unlikely to return in less than 1,000 years.

Other Internet sites also claim that the orbit of "Planet X," usually identified as "Nibiru," is approaching Earth, which will soon have dramatic effects on Earth's weather patterns, earthquakes, volcanoes, and sea levels. The date most often cited is 2012, which is the end of the current cycle (*b'ak'tun*) in the Maya Long Count calendar.

The website ProjectCamelot.com claims to possess an anonymous letter from a Norwegian politician stating that "Planet X is coming" and describing a secret plan to construct a series of globe-spanning 2012 survival bases. (See also **Binary star system**, **Channeling**, **Nibiru**, **Sitchin, Zecharia**.)

Plasma cosmology is a non-standard cosmology, generally attributed to Nobel Prize winner Hannes Alfvén in the 1960s, that attempts to explain the development of the visible universe through the interaction of electromagnetic forces on astrophysical plasma. Alfvén developed his cosmological ideas based on scaling of observations from terrestrial laboratories and *in situ* space physics experiments to cosmological scales orders-of-magnitude greater. His most famous cosmological proposal was that the universe was an ionized equal mixture of matter and anti-matter in the form of so-called "ambiplasma" that would naturally separate as annihilation reactions occurred, accompanied by a tremendous release of energy.

Plasma cosmology contradicts the current consensus of astrophysicists that Einstein's theory of general relativity explains the origin and evolution of the universe on its largest scales, relying instead on the further development of classical mechanics and electrodynamics in application to astrophysical plasmas. While in the late 1980s to early 1990s there was limited discussion over the merits of plasma cosmology, these ideas have generally been ignored by the mainstream cosmology community. (See also **Astronomy, Cosmology** and **Pseudoscience**.)

Plate tectonics describes the large-scale motions of Earth's lithosphere. The theory encompasses the older concepts of continental drift, developed during the first decades of the 20th century by Alfred Wegener, and seafloor spreading, understood during the 1960s.

The outermost part of Earth's interior is made up of two layers: the lithosphere and the asthenosphere. The lithosphere comprises the crust and the rigid uppermost part of the mantle. Below the lithosphere lies the asthenosphere. Although solid, the asthenosphere has relatively low viscosity and shear strength and can flow like a liquid on geological time scales. The deeper mantle below the asthenosphere is more rigid again due to the higher pressure.

The lithosphere is broken up into what are called tectonic plates. On Earth, there are eight major and many minor plates. The lithospheric plates ride on the asthenosphere. These plates move in relation to one another at one of three types of plate boundaries: convergent, or collisional boundaries; divergent boundaries, also called "spreading centers" and "transform boundaries." Earthquakes, volcanic activity, mountain-building, and oceanic trench formation occur along plate boundaries. The lateral movement of the plates is typically at speeds of 50–100 mm annually. (See also **Geomagnetic reversal, Pole shift theory**, and **True polar wander**.)

Pleiades, also known as M45, the Seven Sisters, *Subaru* (Japan), *Matariki* (New Zealand Maori), *Bitang Skora* (Borneo Bidayuh), *Parvin* (ancient Persians), *Krittika* (ancient Hindus), *Tzab-ek* (the Maya) is an open cluster in the constellation of Taurus. It is among the nearest star clusters, is probably the best known, and is certainly the most obvious to the naked eye. Hot blue stars that have formed within the last 100 million years dominate the cluster.

The Pleiades are a prominent sight in winter in the Northern Hemisphere and in summer in the Southern Hemisphere, and have been known since antiquity to cultures all around the world. They are also mentioned three times in the Bible (Job 9:9, 38:31; Amos 5:8).

Pole shift theory is the hypothesis that the axis of rotation of a planet has not always been at its present-day locations or that the axis will not persist there; in other words, that its physical poles had been or will be shifted. The pole shift hypothesis is almost always discussed in the context of Earth, but other solar system bodies may have experienced axial reorientation during their existences.

Pole shift hypotheses are not to be confused with plate tectonics, the well-accepted geological theory that Earth's surface consists of solid plates which shift over a viscous asthenosphere; nor with continental drift, the corollary to plate tectonics which maintains that locations of the continents have moved slowly over the face of the Earth, resulting in the gradual emerging and breakup of continents and oceans over hundreds of millions of years.

Pole shift hypotheses are also not to be confused with geomagnetic reversal, the periodic reversal of Earth's magnetic field (effectively switching the North and South Magnetic Poles). Geomagnetic reversal has more acceptance in the scientific community than pole shift hypotheses.

It is now established that true polar wander has occurred at various times in the past, but at rates of 1° per million years or less. However, in popular literature many scientifically untenable theories have suggested very rapid polar shift. (See also **Geomagnetic reversal**, **Plate tectonics** and **True polar wander**.)

Popol Vuh is a book compiling details of creation accounts known to the *K'iche'* Maya of the colonial-era highlands of present-day Guatemala.

The Maya equivalent of the Old Testament, the *Popol Vuh* describes how two creator gods, *K'uk'ulkan* (as he was known in *Yucatek* Mayan and variously as *Gucumatz* in highland Mayan and *Quetzalcoatl* to the Aztecs) and *Huracan* (or *Tezcatlipoca* to the Aztecs) first formed men of mud, but in this form man could neither move nor speak and quickly dissolved into nothingness. Next they created men of sculpted wood, which *Huracan* destroyed as the wooden manikins were imperfect, emotionless and showed no praise to the gods. The survivors were then transformed into monkeys and sentenced to live in the wild. The gods were finally successful in their creation by constructing men out of maize. Here the first men were formed: *B'alam Agab, B'alam Quitzé, Iqi B'alam, Mahucatah*. Their sight was far and they understood all. *Gukumatz* and *Huracan* became fearful that these new beings would become as powerful as the gods and limited the eyesight of the first men.

According to the *Popol Vuh*, we are currently living in the "fifth world." In the Maya Long Count, the previous creation ended at the start of a 13th *b'ak'tun*.

The previous creation ended on a Long Count of 12.19.19.17.19. Another 12.19.19.17.19 will occur on December 20, 2012, followed by the start of the fourteenth *b'ak'tun*, 13.0.0.0.0, on December 21, 2012. (Various sources place this on other dates, notably on December 23; see **Schele, Linda**.)

Precession of the equinoxes. Like a wobbling top, the orientation of Earth's axis is slowly but continuously changing, tracing out a conical shape in a cycle of approximately 25,765 years. This movement is widely thought to be caused by the gravitational forces of the Sun and the Moon, and to a lesser extent other bodies on the spinning Earth. One measurable effect of this wobble is the shifting position of the background stars in the zodiac, relative to the fixed stars on the celestial sphere. In ancient times, tracking these changes was a method of keeping time.

The position of the vernal equinox is not fixed among the stars due to this precession, which slowly shifts our view of the sky westwards over the ecliptic at the rate of approximately 1° per 72 years.

Thus, measuring the cycle of seasons in a tropical year (for example, the time from solstice to solstice, or equinox to equinox), is about 20 minutes shorter than the sidereal year, which is measured by the Sun's apparent position relative to the stars.

Twenty minutes per year is approximately equivalent to one year per 25,700 years, so after one full cycle of 25,700 years the positions of the seasons relative to the orbit are "back where they started."

Likewise, the apparent position of the Sun relative to the backdrop of the stars at some seasonally fixed time, say the vernal equinox, slowly regresses a full 360° through all twelve traditional constellations of the zodiac, at the rate of about 50.3 seconds of arc per year (approximately 360 degrees divided by 25,700), or 1 degree every 71.6 years.

Other effects also slowly change the shape and orientation of Earth's orbit, and these, in combination with precession, create various cycles of differing periods. (See also **Milankovitch cycles**.)

Pseudologia Fantastica. Mythomania, or pathological lying, is one of several terms applied by psychiatrists to the behavior of habitual or compulsive lying. The defining characteristics of *pseudologia fantastica* are that first, the stories are not entirely improbable and often have some element of truth. They aren't a manifestation of delusion or some more wider form of psychosis: upon confrontation, the person can acknowledge them to be untrue, even if unwillingly. Second, the fabricative tendency is long lasting; it is not provoked by the immediate situation or social pressure as much as it originates with the person's innate urge to act in accordance. Third, a definitely internal, not an external, motive for the behavior can be clinically discerned, e.g. long lasting extortion or habitual spousal battery might cause a person to lie repeatedly, without the lying being a pathological symptom. Fourth, the stories told tend towards presenting the person in question in a good light. For example, the person might be presented as being fantastically brave, knowing or being related to many famous people.

Pseudoscience is defined as a body of knowledge, methodology, belief, or practice that is claimed to be scientific or made to appear scientific, but does not adhere to the scientific method, lacks supporting evidence or otherwise lacks scientific status. (See also **Scientific method**.)

Quetzalcoatl is an Aztec sky and creator god. The name is a combination of quetzal, a brightly-colored Mesoamerican bird, and coatl, meaning serpent. The name was also taken on by various ancient leaders. Due to their cyclical view of time and the tendency of leaders to revise histories to support their rule, many events and attributes attributed to Quetzalcoatl are exceedingly difficult to separate from the political leaders that took this name on themselves. Quetzalcoatl is often referred to as the

"Feathered Serpent" and was connected to the planet Venus. He was also the patron god of the Aztec priesthood, of learning and knowledge. Today Quetzalcoatl is arguably the best-known Aztec deity.

Several other Mesoamerican cultures are known to have worshipped a feathered serpent god. At Teotihuacan, several monumental structures are adorned with images of a feathered serpent. Such imagery is also prominent at such Maya sites as Chichén Itzá, where there is an enormous pyramid dedicated to him, where he was called *K'uk'ulcan* in the *Yucatek* Maya language.

Rapture is a prophesied event in Christian eschatology, in which Christians are suddenly taken from the Earth to participate in the Second Coming of Christ. Christians who have died are to be resurrected to participate in the coming of Christ along with those who are still living at the time of the event.

The primary passage describing the rapture is 1 Thessalonians 4:15–17, in which Paul cites "the word of the Lord" about the return of Jesus to gather his saints.

Generally, believers in the rapture of the church no longer make predictions regarding the exact timing of the event itself, as any individual or religious group that has dogmatically predicted the day of the rapture has been thoroughly embarrassed and discredited, as the predicted date of fulfillment came and went without event. Some notable rapture date predictions include the following:

- 1792—Shakers calculated this date.
- 1844—William Miller predicted Christ would return between March 21, 1843 and March 21, 1844. He later revised his prediction, claiming to have miscalculated scripture, to October 22, 1844. Miller's theology gave rise to the Advent movement.
- 1977—William M. Branham predicted that the rapture would take place in 1977.
- 1981—Chuck Smith predicted that Jesus would likely return by 1981.
- 1988—Publication of *88 Reasons why the Rapture is in 1988*, by Edgar C. Whisenant.
- 1989—Publication of *The final shout: Rapture report 1989*, by Edgar Whisenant. More predictions by this author appeared for 1992, 1995, and other years.
- 1992—Korean group "Mission for the Coming Days" predicted October 28, 1992 as the date for the rapture.
- 1993—Seven years before the year 2000. The rapture would have to start to allow for seven years of the Tribulation before the Return in 2000. Multiple predictions.
- 1994—Pastor John Hinkle of Christ Church in Los Angeles predicted June 9, 1994. Radio evangelist Harold Camping predicted September 27, 1994.
- 2011—Harold Camping's revised prediction has May 21, 2011 as the date of the rapture.
- 2060—Sir Isaac Newton proposed, based upon his calculations using figures from the Book of Daniel that the rapture could happen no earlier than 2060.

Roman calendar is believed to have originally been a lunar calendar, which may have been based on one of the Greek lunar calendars. As the time between new moons averages 29.5 days, the Romans counted months as alternately "hollow" (29 days) or "full" (30 days). Roman traditions claimed that the calendar was invented by Romulus, the founder of Rome about 753 BCE.

Unlike our dates, which are numbered sequentially from the beginning of the month, the Romans counted backwards from three fixed points—the *Nones*, the *Ides*, and the *Kalends* of the following month. The Roman calendar changed its form several times in the time between the foundation of Rome and the fall of the Roman Empire. The earliest known version contained ten months and started at the vernal equinox however the months by this time were no longer "lunar."

Schele, Linda (October 30, 1942–April 18, 1998) was a noted expert in the field of Maya epigraphy and iconography. She played an invaluable role in the decipherment of much of the Maya hieroglyphics. She produced a massive volume of drawings of stele and inscriptions, which, following her wishes, are free for use to scholars. In 1978, she founded the annual Maya Meetings at the University of Texas at Austin. (See also **Stele**.)

Schoch, Robert M. received his Ph.D. in geology and geophysics from Yale University in 1983, and is best known for his argument that the Great Sphinx of Giza is much older than conventionally thought and that possibly some kind of catastrophe has wiped out other evidence of a significantly older civilization. In 1991 Schoch re-dated the famous monument to 7000–5000 BCE, based on his assertion that its erosion was due mainly to the effects of water, rather than wind and sand and also based on seismic studies around the base of the Sphinx and elsewhere on the plateau.

Schoch's other theories include the belief that possibly all pyramids—in Egypt, Mesoamerica and elsewhere—represent a much older global culture, or at least that there was cultural contact around the world in ancient times, such that the general concept of pyramids was inherited, along with many other cultural commonalities.

Science 1. The observation, identification, description, experimental investigation, and theoretical explanation of phenomena. 2. Such activities restricted to a class of natural phenomena. 3. Such activities applied to an object of inquiry or study.[208]

Scientific method refers to bodies of techniques for investigating phenomena, acquiring new knowledge or correcting and integrating previous knowledge. To be termed scientific, a method of inquiry must be based on gathering observable, empirical and measurable evidence subject to specific principles of reasoning. A scientific method consists of the collection of data through observation and experimentation, and the formulation and testing of hypotheses.

A basic expectation of the scientific method is to document, archive and share all data and methodology so they are available for careful scrutiny by other scientists, thereby allowing other researchers the opportunity to verify results by attempting to reproduce them. This practice, called full disclosure, also allows statistical measures of the reliability of these data to be established.

Second is a unit of measurement of time or of angle. As a measure of time, the second (SI symbol: s), is the name of a unit of time, and is the International System of Units (SI) base unit of time, though it is more commonly encountered within non-SI units of time such as the minute, hour, and day, which increase by multiples of 60 and 24, rather than by powers of ten as in the SI system. (See also **International System of Units**.)

In astronomy, the subdivision of the minute of arc is the second of arc, or arcsecond. There are 60 arcseconds in an arcminute. Therefore, the arcsecond is 1/1,296,000 of a circle.

Secret Doctrine. Book by H. P. Blavatsky, divided into *Cosmogenesis* and *Anthropogenesis* which describe, respectively, the formation of the universe and the creation of successive versions of mankind in deep antiquity. This information is allegedly based on an occult Tibetan Buddhist manuscript to which she claims she was given access.

Blavatsky asserts that modern day humans are the fifth version of the human race, as well as the most solidified and dense in structure. The previous versions of mankind were more ethereal and voluminous and each new version was successively less ethereal and more condensed, as the older versions shrank in size and as each became increasingly "degenerated."

- **First Race of Mankind** on Earth, the "Hyperboreans," were incorporeal with ethereal bodies that, if we could see them would appear to be about 173 ft. (52.73 m) in height.
- **Second Race of Mankind** were in a similarly gaseous but more dense state and approximately 120 ft. (36.6 m) in height at their tallest.
- **Third Race of Mankind**, the "Lemurians," were of a more solidified structure, as the difference between mind and matter became more distinct, according to Blavatsky. The Lemurians were 60 ft. (18 m) tall and their last descendants are said to be represented by the cyclopean statues that remain on Easter Island.
- **Fourth Race of Mankind**, the "Atlanteans" shrank from 30 ft. (9 m) to 15 ft. (4.5 m) over the course of their "degeneration" over several millennia.
- **Fifth Race of Mankind** corresponds to modern day *homo sapiens*.

Blavatasky claimed that representatives of all previous races were carved by Atlantean survivors of the Great Flood, "for the instruction of future generations" [209] into to the cliffs of Bamyan in modern-day Afghanistan. After many attempts over the millennia to destroy these so-called "Buddhas," the Taliban rulers of Afghanistan finally destroyed the statues in March of 2001 in front of international television cameras.

Blavatsky claimed that legends about giants, which appear in cultures around the world concerned ancient fifth race human encounters with surviving members of these gigantic, "degenerated" previous races of mankind.

Secular humanism. An outlook or philosophy that advocates human rather than religious values.[210]

Seventh-Day Adventist is a Christian denomination that is distinguished mainly by its observance of Saturday, the original seventh day of the Judeo-Christian week, as the Sabbath. The denomination grew out of the Millerite movement in the United States during the middle part of the 19th century and was formally established in 1863. Among its founders was Ellen G. White, whose extensive writings are still held in high regard by the church today.

Much of the theology of the Seventh-day Adventist Church corresponds to evangelical teachings such as the Trinity and the infallibility of scripture. Distinctive teachings include the unconscious state of the dead and the doctrine of an investigative judgment. The church is also known for its emphasis on diet and health, its holistic understanding of the person, its promotion of religious liberty, and its conservative principles and lifestyle.

The Seventh-day Adventist Church is the largest of several "Adventist" groups which arose from the Millerite movement of the 1840s, which was part of the wave of revivalism in the United States known as the Second Great Awakening and originated with William Miller, a Baptist preacher from Upstate New York. Miller predicted on the basis of Daniel 8:14 and the "day-year principle" that Jesus Christ would return to Earth on October 22, 1844. When this failed to occur, most of his followers disbanded and returned to their original churches.

Following this "Great Disappointment" (as it came to be known), a small number of Millerites came to believe that Miller's calculations were correct, but that his interpretation of Daniel 8:14 was flawed. Beginning with a vision reported by Hiram Edson on October 23rd, these Adventists arrived at the conviction that Daniel 8:14 foretold Christ's entrance into the "Most Holy Place" of the heavenly sanctuary rather than his Second Coming. Over the next decade this understanding developed into the doctrine of the investigative judgment: an eschatological process commencing in 1844 in which Christians will be judged to verify their eligibility for salvation. The Adventists continued to believe that Christ's Second Coming would be imminent, although they refrained from setting further dates for the event.

As of this writing, a splinter sect of the Adventists called The Church of God— PKG (Preparing for the Kingdom of God) is the biggest buyer of Google Ads for the entry "2012" in the search engine, attracting hapless Internet surfers to their websites that proselytize their faith in hopes converting them to their movement.

The larger church currently has a worldwide membership of over 15 million people, has a missionary presence in over 200 countries and territories and is ethnically and culturally diverse. The church operates numerous schools, hospitals and publishing houses worldwide, as well as a prominent humanitarian aid organization known as the Adventist Development and Relief Agency. (See also **Jehovah's Witnesses.**)

Shamanism is a range of traditional beliefs and practices concerned with communication with the spirit world. A practitioner of shamanism is known as a shaman. There are many variations of shamanism throughout the world; the following are beliefs that are shared by all forms of shamanism:

- Spirits exist and they play important roles both in individual lives and in human society.
- The shaman can communicate with the spirit world.
- Spirits can be good or evil.
- The shaman can treat sickness caused by evil spirits.
- The shaman can employ trance-inducing techniques to incite visionary ecstasy.
- The shaman's spirit can leave the body to enter the supernatural world to search for answers.

The shaman evokes animal images as spirit guides, omens, and message-bearers. Shamans operate outside of established religions and traditionally they operate alone, although they can gather into associations.

Sidereal year is the time taken for the Sun to return to the same position with respect to the stars of the celestial sphere. It is the orbital period of Earth, equal to 365.25636042 mean solar days (31,558,149.540 seconds), that is 366.25636042 Earth rotations or sidereal days. The sidereal year is 20 minutes and 24 seconds longer than the tropical year.

Sirius is the brightest star in the night sky. What the naked eye perceives as a single star is actually a binary star system, consisting of a white main sequence star of spectral type A1V, termed Sirius A, and a faint white dwarf companion of spectral type DA2, termed Sirius B.

Sirius appears bright due to both its intrinsic luminosity and its closeness to Earth. At a distance of 2.6 parsecs (8.6 light-years), the Sirius system is one of our near neighbor stars. Sirius A is about twice as massive as the Sun and is 25 times more luminous but has a significantly lower luminosity than other bright stars such as Canopus or Rigel. The system is between 200 and 300 million years old.

Sirius is also known colloquially as the "Dog Star," reflecting its prominence in its constellation, Canis Major. It is the subject of more myth and folklore than any other star apart from the Sun. The heliacal rising of Sirius marked the flooding of the Nile in Ancient Egypt and the "dog days" of summer for the Ancient Greeks, while to the Polynesians it marked winter and was an important star for navigation around the Pacific Ocean.

Sitchin, Zecharia is an author of books promoting an ancient astronaut theory of human origins. Sitchin claims that many Egyptian, Greek and biblical traditions, even written Chinese, are derived from ancient Sumerian myth and its system of cuneiform script, considered to be one of the earliest known forms of written expression, originating in the 4th and 3rd millennium BCE.

Sitchin claims Sumer was founded by the "Annunaki," which he translates to the Hebrew "Nephilim" and describes as a race of aliens from a planet he calls

Nibiru, which he believes to be in an elongated, elliptical 3,600-year orbit in Earth's own solar system.

He asserts that Sumerian mythology reflects this view, though his speculations are entirely discounted by mainstream scientists, historians, and archaeologists, who see many problems with his translations of ancient texts and with his understanding of physics. (See also **Ancient astronaut theories**, **Nephilim** and **Nibiru**.)

Solar year (see **Tropical year**).

Solstice is an astronomical event that occurs twice a year, when the tilt of Earth's axis is most oriented toward or away from the Sun, causing the Sun to reach its northernmost or southernmost extreme. The term solstice can also be used in a wider sense, as the date (day) that such a passage happens.

Stele is a stone or wooden slab, generally taller than it is wide, erected for funerals or commemorative purposes, most usually decorated with the names and titles of the deceased or living, inscribed, carved in relief (bas-relief, sunken-relief, high-relief, and so forth), or painted onto the slab.

Sumer was a civilization and an historical region located in southern Iraq (Mesopotamia), known as the "cradle of civilization." It lasted from the first settlement of Eridu in the Ubaid period (late 6th millennium BCE) through the Uruk period (4th millennium BCE) and the Dynastic periods (3rd millennium BCE) until the rise of Babylon in the early second millennium BCE. The term "Sumerian" applies to all speakers of the Sumerian language.

Although other cities pre-date Sumer (Jericho, Çatalhöyük and others, either for seasonal protection, or as year-round trading posts) the cities of Sumer were the first to practice intensive year-round agriculture, from ca. 5300 BCE. The surplus of storable food created by this economy allowed the population to settle in one place instead of migrating after crops and grazing land. It also allowed for a much greater population density, and in turn required an extensive labor force and division of labor. This organization led to the necessity of record keeping and the development of writing ca. 3500 BCE. (See also **Oannes** and **Sitchin, Zecharia**.)

Synodic month, is the average period of the Moon's orbit around the Earth with respect to Earth's orbit around the Sun.

Syzygy describes the alignment of three or more celestial bodies in the same gravitational system along a straight line.

Taurids are an annual meteor shower associated with Comet Encke. They are named after their radiant point in the constellation Taurus, where they are seen to come from in the sky.

Encke and the Taurids are believed to be remnants of a much larger comet, which has disintegrated over the past 20,000 to 30,000 years, breaking into several pieces and releasing material by normal cometary activity or perhaps occasionally by close encounters with the gravitational field of Earth or other planets. In total, this stream of matter is the largest in the inner solar system. Due to the stream's size, the Earth takes several weeks to pass through it, causing an extended period of meteor activity, compared with the much smaller periods of activity in other showers. The Taurids are also made up of weightier material, pebbles, instead of dust grains.

Due to the gravitational effect of planets, especially Jupiter, the Taurids have spread out over time, allowing separate segments labeled the Northern Taurids and Southern Taurids to become observable. Essentially these are two cross sections of a single, broad, continuous stream in space. The Beta Taurids, encountered by the Earth in June–July and which many astronomers consider the cause of the Tunguska event, are also a cross section of the stream. Beta Taurids approach from Earth's daytime side; so cannot be observed visually in the way the (night-time) Northern and Southern Taurids of October–November can.

The Taurid stream has a cycle of activity that peaks roughly every 2,500 to 3,000 years, when its core passes nearer to Earth and produces more intense showers. In fact, because of the separate "branches" (night-time in one part of the year and daytime in another; and Northern/Southern in each case) there are two (possibly overlapping) peaks separated by a few centuries, every 3,000 years. Some astronomers note that dates for megalith structures such as Stonehenge are associated with these peaks.

The next peak is expected between 2000–3000 CE, suggesting that the Taurids may also be responsible for the Star of Bethlehem. It has been suggested that in 1 CE, there were Taurid meteor showers due to the Encke tail encountering Earth and breaking up.

Some consider the Bronze Age breakup of the originally larger comet to be responsible for ancient destruction in the Fertile Crescent, perhaps evidenced by a large meteor crater in Iraq. (See also **Encke's Comet** and **Tunguska event**.)

Temple, Robert K. G. is an American author best known for his controversial book *The Sirius Mystery*, which presents the idea that the Dogon people in Mali, Africa preserve the tradition of contact with intelligent extraterrestrial beings from the Sirius star-system. His writings on the Dogon are based on an interpretation of the work of ethnographers Marcel Griaule and Germaine Dieterlen.

Temple attended the University of Pennsylvania in Philadelphia, where in 1965 he received a degree in Oriental studies and Sanskrit. He is a fellow of the Royal Astronomical Society and an occasional broadcaster with the BBC. (See also **Dogon**.)

Teotihuacan is an enormous archaeological site located approximately 40 km (25 mi) northeast of Mexico City. The site covers a total surface area of 83 km², was made a UNESCO World Heritage Site in 1987, and is one of the most visited archaeological sites in Mexico. Containing some of the largest pyramidal structures built in the pre-Columbian Americas, the archaeological site is also known for its large residential complexes and its colorful well-preserved murals.

Teotihuacan was, at its height in the first half of the 1st millennium CE, the largest city in the pre-Columbian Americas with more than 100,000 inhabitants, placing it among the largest cities of the world in this period.

Although it is a subject of debate whether Teotihuacan was the center of an empire, its influence throughout Mesoamerica is well documented; evidence of Teotihuacano presence, if not outright political and economic control, can be seen at numerous sites in Veracruz and the Maya region. The ethnicity of the inhabitants of Teotihuacan is also a subject of debate and possible candidates are the Nahua, Otomi or Totonac ethnic groups. Often it has been suggested that Teotihuacan was in fact a multiethnic state.

Theory of Everything is a goal of theoretical physics and mathematics to fully explain and link together all known physical phenomena (i.e., "everything"). Initially the term was used with an ironical connotation, to refer to various overgeneralized theories. Over time, the term stuck in popularizations of physics to describe a theory that would unify the theories of the four fundamental interactions of nature, possibly due to the influence of a book with material written by Stephen Hawking but later disowned by him called *The Theory of Everything*.

There have been numerous theories of everything proposed by theoretical physicists over the last century, but as yet none has been able to stand up to experimental scrutiny since there is tremendous difficulty in getting such theories to produce even experimentally-testable results. The primary problem in producing a "Theory of Everything" is that quantum mechanics and general relativity have radically different descriptions of the universe, and the ways of combining the two quickly lead to the "renormalization problem," in which the theory does not give the finite results needed for experimentally-testable quantities.

Theosophy is a body of belief, which holds that all religions are attempts by man to ascertain "the Divine," and as such each religion has a portion of the truth. Theosophy, as a coherent belief system, developed from the writings of Helena Petrovna Blavatsky. Together with Henry Steel Olcott, William Quan Judge, and others she founded the Theosophical Society in 1875.

A more formal definition from the *Concise Oxford Dictionary* describes Theosophy as "any of various philosophies professing to achieve a knowledge of God by spiritual ecstasy, direct intuition, or special individual relations, esp. a modern movement following Hindu and Buddhist teachings and seeking universal brotherhood."

Adherents of Theosophy maintain that it is a "body of truth" that forms the basis of all religions. Theosophy, they claim, represents a modern face of Hinduism's *Sanatana Dharma*, the "Eternal Truth," as the proper religion of man. "Christian Theosophy" is a term used to designate the knowledge of God and of Jesus obtained by the direct intuition of the Divine essence.

The five prominent symbols visible in the Seal of the Theosophical Society are the Star of David, the Ankh, the Swastika, the Ouroboros, and above the seal is the Aum. Around the seal are written the words: *There is no religion higher than truth*.

Timewave zero (see **Novelty theory**).

Tikal is one of the largest archaeological sites and urban centers of the pre-Columbian Maya civilization. It is located in the archaeological region of the Petén Basin in what is now modern-day northern Guatemala. The site is part of Guatemala's Tikal National Park and in 1979 was declared a UNESCO World Heritage Site.

Tikal was one of the major cultural and population centers of the Maya civilization. Though monumental architecture at the site dates to the 4th century BCE, Tikal reached its apogee during the Classic period, ca. 200 to 900 CE, during which time the site dominated the Maya region politically, economically, and militarily while interacting with areas throughout Mesoamerica, such as central Mexican center of Teotihuacan. There is also evidence that Tikal was even conquered by Teotihuacan in the 4th century. There was a gradual population decline, culminating with the site's abandonment by the end of the 10th century.

Toltec. In Mesoamerican studies, this designation has been used in different ways by different scholars to refer to actual populations and polities of pre-Columbian central Mexico or to the mythical ancestors mentioned in the mythical/historical narratives of the Aztecs. It is an ongoing debate whether the Toltecs can be understood to have formed an actual ethnic group at any point in Mesoamerican history or if they are mostly or only a product of Aztec myth.

Tonalpohualli is a Nahuatl word, which corresponds with the Mayan word *T'zolk'in* meaning "count of days," referring to the 260-day sacred period (often termed a "year") in use in pre-Columbian Mesoamerica, especially among the Aztecs. This calendrical period is neither solar nor lunar, but rather consists of 20 *trecena*, or 13-day periods. Each *trecena* is dedicated to and under the auspices of a different deity.

Toutatis (a.k.a., 4179 Toutatis) is a Mars-crosser asteroid with a chaotic orbit produced by a 3:1 resonance with the planet Jupiter. Due to its very low orbital inclination (0.47°) and its orbital period of very nearly 4 years, Toutatis makes frequent close approaches to Earth, with a currently minimum orbital intersection distance (MOID) of just 0.006 AU (2.3 times as far as the Moon). The approach on September 29, 2004 was particularly close, at 0.0104 AU (within 4 lunar distances) from Earth, presenting a good opportunity for observation. The most recent close approach (at 0.0502 AU) happened on November 9, 2008 at 12:23 UTC. (See also **Apophis**, **Extinction event** and **NEOs**.)

Trecena is a 13-day period used in pre-Columbian Mesoamerican calendars. The 260-day calendar (called the *T'zolk'in* in Mayan and *tonalpohualli* in Nahuatl) was divided into 20 *trecenas*. Derived from Spanish, *trecena* "a group of thirteen" in the same way that a dozen (or in Spanish a *docena*) relates to the number twelve. It is associated with the Aztecs and is called different names in the calendars of the Maya, Zapotec, Mixtec, and others of the region.

Tropical year (also known as a solar year) is the length of time that the Sun takes to return to the same position in the cycle of seasons, as seen from Earth; for example, the time from vernal equinox to vernal equinox, or from summer solstice to summer solstice.

The length of a tropical year varies slightly, by up to a minute or two, depending on the seasonal starting point. The mean tropical year is calculated by averaging the (slightly differing) tropical years over all possible starting points through the four seasons.

Because of a phenomenon known as the precession of the equinoxes, the tropical year, which is based on the seasonal cycle, is slightly shorter than the sidereal year, which is the time it takes for the Sun to return to the same apparent position relative to the backdrop of stars. This difference was 20.400 minutes in 1900 CE and 20.409 minutes in 2000 CE. Because it is desirable for everyday-use calendars to keep in synchronization with the seasons, it is the tropical year that, in principle, these calendars track. Although the yearly differences are small, they are cumulative, and after many years amount to a very noticeable discrepancy. (See also **Precession of the equinoxes.**)

True polar wander is a phenomenon in which a planet or moon changes its orientation so that different points become the North and South Poles. This can happen when the two larger moments of inertia are near equal. Cases of true polar wander have occurred several times in the course of Earth's history. The speed of rotation (around the axis of lowest inertia) is limited to about 1° per million years.

Polar wander should not be confused with precession, which is where the axis of rotation moves, in other words the North Pole points toward a different star. Precession is caused by the gravitational attraction of the Moon and Sun, and occurs all the time and at a much faster rate than polar wander. It does not result in changes of latitude.

True polar wander is distinct from continental drift, which is where different parts of Earth's crust move in different directions because of circulation in the mantle. (See also **Geomagnetic reversal**, **Plate tectonics** and **Pole shift theory.**)

Tun. The Mayan word for a unit of time in the Long Count calendar, equal to 360 days or 18 *winal*.

Tunguska event was a powerful explosion that occurred near the Tunguska River in what is now Krasnoyarsk Krai of Russia, at around 7:00 a.m. on June 30, 1908.

The explosion was most likely to have been caused by the air burst of a large meteoroid or comet fragment at an altitude of 5–10 km (3–6 miles) above Earth's surface. Different studies have yielded varying estimates for the object's size, with general agreement that it was a few tens of meters across.

Although the meteor or comet burst in the air rather than directly hitting the surface, this event is still referred to as an impact. The most likely estimate of the energy of the blast is 10–15 megatons or about 1,000 times as powerful as the bomb dropped on Hiroshima, Japan. The explosion knocked over an estimated 80 million trees over 2,150 sq km (830 sq. mi.). It is estimated that the earthquake from the blast would have measured 5.0 on the Richter scale, which was not yet developed at the time. An explosion of this magnitude is capable of destroying a large metropolitan area. This possibility has helped to spark discussion of asteroid deflection strategies.

Although the Tunguska event is believed to be the largest impact event on land in Earth's recent history, impacts of similar size in remote ocean areas would have gone unnoticed before the advent of global satellite monitoring in the 1960s and 1970s. (See also **Encke's Comet** and **Taurids**.)

T'zolk'in is a new word in the *Yucatek* Mayan language (spoken in the Yucatán Peninsula, northern Belize and parts of Guatemala), which means "count of days." The words for this that were actually used by pre-Columbian Maya peoples are still debated by scholars. The *T'zolk'in* calendar combines twenty day-names with the thirteen numbers of the *trecena* cycle to produce 260 unique days. It is used to determine the time of religious and ceremonial events and for divination. Each successive day is numbered from 1 up to 13 and then starting again at 1. Separately from this, each day is given a name in sequence from a list of 20-day names. Mayanist Dennis Tedlock translates their meanings as, 1. Lefthanded, 2. *Wind*, 3. Foredawn, 4. Net, 5. Snake, 6. Death, 7. *Deer*, 8. Yellow, 9. Thunder, 10. Dog, 11. Monkey, 12. *Tooth*, 13. Cane, 14. Jaguar, 15. Bird, 16. Sinner, 17. *Thought*, 18. Blade, 19. Rain, 20. Marksman. Four of these signs (italicized) are "year-bearers" and only they can initiate a New Year."[211]

Universal Time (UT) is a timescale based on the rotation of the Earth. It is a modern continuation of Greenwich Mean Time (GMT), i.e., the mean solar time on the meridian of Greenwich, London. GMT is sometimes used loosely as a synonym for UTC. In fact the expression "Universal Time" is ambiguous, as there are several versions of it, the most commonly used being UTC and **UT1** (see below). All of these versions of UT are based on sidereal time, but with a scaling factor and other adjustments to make them closer to solar time.

UT1 is the principal form of Universal Time. It is computed from the raw observed time at an observatory by correcting for the effect of polar motion on the longitude of the observing site. UT1 is the same everywhere on Earth, and is proportional to the true rotation angle of the Earth with respect to a fixed frame of reference (such as from extragalactic radio sources). Since the rotational speed of the Earth is not uniform, UT1 has an uncertainty of plus or minus 3 milliseconds per day. The ratio of UT1 to mean sidereal time is defined to be $0.997269566329084 - 5.8684 \times 10^{-11}T + 5.9 \times 10^{-15}T^2$, where T is the number of "Julian centuries" of 36,525 days each that have elapsed since JD 2451545.0 (J2000).

Vedic calendar (see **Yuga**).

Venus cycle "Venus appears as the morning star every 583.92 days. Five of those Venus cycles equal eight *Haab'*. Thus, Venus traces a five-pointed star around the ecliptic every eight years."[212]

Venus Round equal to "104 *Haab'* (2 Calendar Rounds). This is when the cycles of *T'zolk'in, Haab'* and Venus resynchronize on the *T'zolk'in* day, 1 *Ahau*, the sacred day of Venus. The math: 260 + 146 = 365 × 104 = 584 × 65 = 37,960 days."[213]

Vernal equinox (see **Equinox**).

Vernier scale is a sliding secondary scale that is used to indicate where the measurement lies when it's in-between two of the marks on the main scale. It allows a distance or angle measurement to be read more precisely than directly reading a uniformly-divided straight or circular measurement scale. Verniers are common on sextants used in navigation, scientific instruments used to conduct experiments, machinists' measuring tools (all sorts, but especially calipers and micrometers).

Viral marketing and viral advertising refer to marketing techniques that use pre-existing social networks to produce increases in brand awareness or to achieve product sales through self-replicating viral processes, analogous to the spread of pathological and computer viruses. It can be word-of-mouth delivered or enhanced by the network effects of the Internet. Viral promotions may take the form of video clips, interactive Flash games, advergames, ebooks, brandable software, images, or even text messages. The basic form of viral marketing is not infinitely sustainable.

The goal of marketers interested in creating successful viral marketing programs is to identify individuals with high "social networking potential" (SNP) and create viral messages that appeal to this segment of the population and have a high probability of being passed along.

The term "viral marketing" is also sometimes used pejoratively to refer to stealth marketing campaigns—the use of varied kinds of "astroturfing" both online and offline to create the impression of spontaneous word-of-mouth enthusiasm. (See also **Astroturfing**, **Meme**, and **Viral phenomena**.)

Viral phenomena. The concept of something, other than a biological virus, being "viral" came into vogue just after the Internet became widely popular in the mid-to-late 1990s. An object, even a non-material object, is considered to be viral when it has the ability to spread copies of itself or change other similar objects to become more like itself when those objects are simply exposed to the viral object.

This has become a common way to describe how thoughts, information and trends move into and through a human population. Memes are possibly the best example of viral patterns. "We are all susceptible to the pull of viral ideas. Like mass hysteria. Or a tune that gets into your head that you keep on humming all day until you spread it to someone else. Jokes. Urban legends. Crackpot religions. No matter how smart we get, there is always this deep irrational part that makes us potential hosts for self-replicating information."[214] (See also **Astroturfing**, **Meme** and **Viral marketing**.)

Winal (also spelled "uinal") is a unit of time in the Maya Long Count calendar equal to 20 days (or *k'in*). It is the 4th digit on the Maya Long Count date. For example,

2012

in the Maya Long Count date 12.19.13.15.12 (December 5, 2006), the number 15 is the *winal*.

Y2K (also known as the the "Year 2000 problem" and the "millennium bug") was a notable computer bug resulting from the practice in early computer program design of representing the year with two digits. This caused some date-related processing to operate incorrectly for dates and times on and after January 1, 2000 and on other critical dates, which were billed "event horizons." This fear was fueled by the attendant press coverage and other media speculation, as well as corporate and government reports. People recognized that long-working systems could break down when the "...97, 98, 99..." ascending numbering assumption suddenly became invalid. Companies and organizations worldwide checked and upgraded their computer systems.

While no significant computer failures occurred with global significance when the clocks rolled over into 2000, preparation for the Y2K bug had a significant effect on the computer industry. The fact that countries where very little was spent on tackling the Y2K bug (such as Italy and South Korea) fared just as well as those who spent much more (such as the United Kingdom and the United States) has generated debate on whether the absence of computer failures was the result of the preparation undertaken or whether the significance of the problem had been overstated.

Yuga in Hindu philosophy is the name of an "epoch" or "era" within a cycle of four ages. These are the *Satya Yuga* (or *Krita Yuga*), the *Treta Yuga*, the *Dwapara Yuga* and finally, our present-day *Kali Yuga*.

According to Indian astrology, the world is created, destroyed and recreated every 4,320,000 years (one *Maha Yuga* or "great epoch"). The cycles are said to repeat like the seasons, waxing and waning within a greater time-cycle of the creation and destruction of the universe. Like summer, spring, winter and autumn, each *yuga* involves stages or gradual changes which the Earth and the consciousness of mankind go through as a whole. A complete *yuga* cycle from the high Golden Age of enlightenment of the *Satya Yuga* to the Dark Age of our current *Kali Yuga* and back again is said to be caused by the solar system's motion around a central Sun or galactic center.

The current *Kali Yuga* is believed to have begun in 3102 BCE. Interestingly, this is twelve years before the begin date of the current Maya epoch which ends on December 21, 2012. However, the total duration of the *Kali Yuga* is generally believed to be 432,000 solar years, suggesting that as of 2009 CE, there will be another 426,889 years left of the *Kali Yuga*.

John Major Jenkins counters the standard view in his book *Galactic Alignment*, where he states that Hindu chronology has been grossly manipulated over the millennia. Invoking the works of Sri Yukteswar and the *Laws of Manu*, Jenkins suggests that the *Kali Yuga* ended in 2000 CE. (See also **Laws of Manu**.)

Zapotec civilization was an indigenous pre-Columbian civilization that flourished in the Valley of Oaxaca of southern Mesoamerica. Archaeological evidence shows their culture goes back at least 2,500 years. They left archaeological evidence at the ancient

2

city of Monte Albán in the form of buildings, ball courts, magnificent tombs and grave offerings including finely worked gold jewelry. Monte Albán was one of the first major cities in Mesoamerica and the center of a Zapotec state that dominated much of what we know of as the current state of Oaxaca. The Zapotecs developed a calendar and their writing system is one of several candidates that is debated to have been the predecessor of the writing systems developed by the Maya, Mixtec, and Aztec civilizations.

Zenith is the direction pointing directly above a particular location (perpendicular, orthogonal). Since the concept of being "above" is itself somewhat vague, scientists define the zenith in more rigorous terms. Specifically, in astronomy, geophysics and related sciences (e.g., meteorology), the zenith at a given point is the local vertical direction pointing away from direction of the force of gravity at that location. Zenith is the opposite of nadir, the vertical direction at the given location pointing in the same direction as the gravitational force.

Zodiac denotes an annual cycle of twelve stations along the ecliptic, the apparent path of the Sun across the heavens through the constellations that divide the ecliptic into twelve equal zones of celestial longitude. The zodiac is recognized as the first known celestial coordinate system. Babylonian astronomers developed the zodiac of twelve signs.

The zodiac also means a region of the celestial sphere that includes a band of eight arc degrees above and below the ecliptic, and therefore encompasses the paths of the Moon and the naked eye planets (Mercury, Venus, Mars, Jupiter and Saturn). The classical astronomers called these planets wandering stars to differentiate them from the fixed stars of the celestial sphere. (See also **Astrology**, **Astronomy**, **Celestial sphere** and **Ecliptic**.)

APPENDIX C

FURTHER RESOURCES & BIBLIOGRAPHY

Further Viewing: DVDs

2012: Science Or Superstition
Starring Graham Hancock, Daniel Pinchbeck, John Major Jenkins, Alberto Villoldo, Jim Marrs. Directed by Nimrod Erez Produced by Gary Baddeley. Released by The Disinformation Company on January 27, 2009
1 DVD Run Time: 78 minutes

Terence McKenna: Time Wave Zero
Starring Terence McKenna
Released by Sound Photosynthesis in 1995
1 DVD Run Time: 24 minutes

2012: The Odyssey
Starring Gregg Braden, José Argüelles, Alberto Villoldo, John Major Jenkins, Rick Levine. Directed by Sharron Rose.
Released by Sacred Mysteries Productions on April 25, 2007
1 DVD Run Time: 99 minutes

Timewave 2013: The Future Is Now—The Odyssey II
Starring José Argüelles, Gregg Braden, Riane Eisler, William Henry, Jean Houston. Directed by Sharron Rose
Released by Sacred Mysteries Productions on November 5, 2008
1 DVD Run Time: 88 minutes

Science of Soul: The End-Time Solar Cycle of Chaos in 2012 A.D.
Starring John Jay Harper. Directed by Philip Gardiner
Released by Reality Entertainment on March 15, 2007
1 DVD Run Time: 60 minutes

Nostradamus 2012
A History Channel production
Released by A&E Home Video on June 30, 2009
1 DVD Run Time: 94 minutes

Barbara Hand Clow Presents:
Pleiadian Agenda Activation: The Mayan Calendar Revealed
Starring Barbara Hand Clow
Released by Wise Awakening in 2006
1 DVD Run Time: 73 minutes

The Great Year
Starring Walter Cruttenden, Directed by James Earl Jones
Released by The Yuga Project on August 1, 2003
1 DVD Run Time: 46 minutes

Further Listening

Unlocking the Secrets of 2012
with John Major Jenkins
Released by Sounds True, Inc. on September 1, 2007
3 Audio CDs. Total Run Time: 213 minutes
ISBN 9781591796138

Related Websites

2012: Science or Superstition—Official Movie Website:
http://2012dvd.com

John Major Jenkins' website:
http://www.alignment2012.com/about_jmj.html

Graham Hancock's website:
http://www.grahamhancock.com

MAYACAL: Where Science & Spirituality Meet. Carl Johan Calleman's site devoted to 2012 research:
http://www.calleman.com and http://www.maya-portal.net

Review-Essay Critique of Carl Johan Calleman's *Solving the Greatest Mystery of Our Time: The Mayan Calendar* **by John Major Jenkins:**
http://www.diagnosis2012.co.uk/jmj.htm

Website Devoted to Terence McKenna's Timewave Zero Graph:
http://www.december212012.com/articles/I-Ching/Time-Wave-Zero.htm

Prophet's Manual: Fractal Supersymmetry of Double Helix: Massive site about 2012:
"Solargalactic alignment during solstice/equinox as a cause of polar flip-over and reversal of planetary rotation":
http://www.prophetsmanual.com/content/index.cfm?navID=16&itemID=16

The Living Prophecy: Extensive 2012 site:
http://www.13moon.com/prophecy%20page.htm

Site loaded with 2012 information:
http://2012wiki.com/

Other sites related to 2012:
http://2012base.com/
http://www.december212012.com
http://www.diagnosis2012.co.uk
http://www.sacredmysteries.com
http://www.survive2012.com
http://2012news.com

John Lamb Lash on 2012:
(a favorite writer of mine expounds on this and everything else ...)
http://www.metahistory.org/ENDTIME/Countdown2012.php

Foundation for the Advancement of Mesoamerican Studies:
http://www.famsi.org

Maya Time Units and Associated Glyphs:
http://www.pauahtun.org/Calendar/calglyph.html

Archive of Photographs of Pre-Columbian Sites and Artifacts:
http://www.mayavase.com

The Antiquity of Man:
Exploring human evolution, gender and social organisation
http://www.antiquityofman.com

Flem-Ath Website (authors of *When the Sky Fell: Atlantis at Last*):
Colorful 20-page (linear) article that proposes Antarctica as the site of Atlantis, destroyed by a pole shift. An extension of Hapgood's work
http://www.flem-ath.com

The Holocene Impact Working Group:
http://tsun.sscc.ru/hiwg/members.htm

NASA Report: "Asteroid and Comet Impact Hazards":
Natural Catastrophes During Bronze Age Civilizations
Archaeological, Geological, Astronomical and Cultural Perspectives
http://impact.arc.nasa.gov/news_detail.cfm?ID=79

The Al' Amarah Holocene Impact Structure & Bronze Age Catastrophe:
Umm al Binni Lake, Iraq
http://mcba11.phys.unsw.edu.au/~duane/Al_Amarah.html

Galactic Research Institute:
Site Affiliated with Siberian Physicist/Remote-viewing Researcher Dr. Alexey N.
Dmitriev and with José Argüelles
http://www.lawoftime.org/GRI/noosphere-two/isricapv.html

"Planetophysical State of the Earth and Life":
(Translation from Russian of paper by Dr. Alexey N. Dmitriev)
http://www.tmgnow.com/repository/global/planetophysical.html

Electric Universe:
http://www.holoscience.com

Walter Cruttenden's Website: The Search for Our Sun's Dark Companion
http://www.binaryresearchinstitute.org

Suppressed Science:
http://www.suppressedscience.net

Michael Cremo's Website:
http://www.mcremo.com

An Interdisciplinary Exploration of Myth, Science, and Planetary Catastrophe:
http://www.kronia.com

Illuminations: (Interesting site, page filled with contemporaneous flood myths)
http://www.mystae.com/restricted/streams/science/flood.html

Survivalist sites:
http://www.seedsnc.org
http://www.greenpowerscience.com
http://www.earthbagbuilding.com
http://www.usbunkers.com
http://www.forging.org/facts/faq9.htm
http://www.cabelas.com

Bad Astronomy and Physics Today Chatboard:
http://blogs.discovermagazine.com/badastronomy

Further Reading

More Books Related to 2012

Andrews, Synthia & Colin Andrews. 2008. *The Complete Idiot's Guide to 2012*. Royersford, PA (Alpha). ISBN 9781592578030.

Argüelles, José. 1984. *Earth Ascending: An Illustrated Treatise on Law Governing Whole Systems*. Rochester VT (Bear & Company). ISBN 9780939680450.

Argüelles, José. 1987. *The Mayan Factor: Path Beyond Technology*. Rochester, VT (Bear & Company). ISBN 9780939680382.

Argüelles, José. 1990. *Dreamspell: The Journey of Timeship Earth 2013 Kit*. (Chelsea Pacific).

Argüelles, José. 2002. *Time and the Technosphere: The Law of Time in Human Affairs*. Rochester, VT (Bear & Company). ISBN 9781879181991.

Aveni, Anthony, 2008. *People and the Sky*. London, UK (Thames & Hudson). ISBN 9780500051528.

Braden, Gregg, Russell, Peter, Pinchbeck, Daniel, Jenkins, John Major et al. 2007. *The Mystery of 2012: Predictions, Prophecies & Possibilities*, Boulder. CO (Sounds True, Inc.). ISBN 9781591796114.

Braden, Gregg. 2009. *Fractal Time: The Secret of 2012 and a New World Age*. Carlsbad, CA (Hay House). ISBN 9781401920647.

Clow, Barbara Hand & Calleman, Carl Johan. 2007. *The Mayan Code: Time Acceleration and Awakening the World Mind*. Santa Fe, NM (Inner Traditions-Bear & Co.). ISBN 9781591430704.

Cruttenden, Walter, 2005. *Lost Star of Myth and Time*. Pittsburgh, PA (St. Lynns' Press). ISBN 9780976763116.

De Santillana, Giorgio, and Hertha von Dechend, 1992. *Hamlet's Mill: An Essay Investigating the Origins of Human Knowledge And Its Transmission Through Myth*. Boston, MA (David R. Godine). ISBN 9780879232153.

Endredy, James. 2008. *Beyond 2012: A Shaman's Call to Personal Change and the Transformation of Global Consciousness.* Woodbury, MN (Llewellyn Publications). ISBN 9780738711584.

Flem-Ath, Rand and Rose. 1997. *When the Sky Fell: In Search of Atlantis.* New York, NY (St. Martin's Press). ISBN 9780312964016.

Geryl, Patrick. 2007. *How To Survive 2012.* Kempton, IL (Adventures Unlimited Press). ISBN 9781931882682.

Hancock, Graham, 1996 *Fingerprints of the Gods.* New York, NY (Three Rivers Press). ISBN 9780517887295.

Hancock, Graham, 2006. *Supernatural: Meetings with the Ancient Teachers of Mankind.* New York, NY (Disinformation). ISBN 9781932857849.

Jang, Hwee-Yong. 2007. *The Gaia Project: 2012; The Earth's Coming Great Changes.* Woodbury MN (Llewellyn Publications). ISBN 9780738710426.

Jenkins, John Major. 1998. *Maya Cosmogenesis 2012: The True Meaning of the Maya Calendar End-Date.* Rochester, VT (Bear & Co.). ISBN 9781879181489.

Jenkins, John Major. 2002. *Galactic Alignment: The Transformation of Consciousness According to Mayan, Egyptian, and Vedic Traditions.* Santa Fe, NM (Inner Traditions-Bear & Co.). ISBN 9781879181847.

Jenkins, John Major & Stray, Geoff. 2009. *Beyond 2012: Catastrophe or Awakening?: A Complete Guide to End-of-Time Predictions.* Santa Fe, NM (Inner Traditions-Bear & Co.). ISBN 9781591430971.

Jones, Marie D. 2008. *2013: The End of Days or a New Beginning: Envisioning the World After the Events of 2012.* Franklin Lakes, NJ (New Page Books). ISBN 9781601630070.

Joseph, Lawrence E. 2008. *Apocalypse 2012: An Investigation into Civilization's End.* New York (Morgan Road-Broadway Books). ISBN 9780767924481.

Kaa, Sri Ram & Raa, Kira, 2007. *2012 Atlantean Revelations: Becoming a Mystic in a 9 to 5 World.* Tijeras, NM (TOSA Publishing). ISBN 9780974987231.

Mau, Michael P. 2006. *The Sanctus Germanus Prophecies, Vol. 2: The Lightbearer's Role During the Post-2012 Earth Changes and Reconstruction.* Calgary, AB Canada (The Sanctus Germanus Foundation). ISBN 9780973709216.

McKenna, Terence, 1994. *The Invisible Landscape*. New York, NY (HarperOne). ISBN 9780062506351.

Melchizedek, Drunvalo. 2008. *Serpent of Light Beyond 2012: The Movement of the Earth's Kundalini and the Rise of the Female Light 1949 to 2013*. San Francisco, CA (Red Wheel/Weiser). ISBN 9781578634019.

Page, Christine R. 2008. *2012 and the Galactic Center: The Return of the Great Mother*. Santa Fe, NM (Inner Traditions-Bear & Co.). ISBN 9781591430865.

Petersen, John L. 2008. *A Vision for 2012: Planning for Extraordinary Change*. Golden, CO (Fulcrum Publishing). ISBN 9781555916619.

Pinchbeck, Daniel. 2006. *2012: The Return of Quetzalcoatl*. New York (Jeremy P. Tarcher/Penguin Group). ISBN 9781585425921.

Pinchbeck, Daniel & Jordan, Ken. 2008. *Toward 2012: Perspectives on the Next Age*. New York (Jeremy P. Tarcher/Penguin Group). ISBN 9781585427000.

Plato. 1977. *Timaeus and Critias*. New York, NY (Penguin Classics). ISBN 9780140442618.

Schele, Linda, and Freidel, David. 1992. *A Forest of Kings: The Untold Story of the Ancient Maya*. New York, NY (Harper Perennial). ISBN 9780688112042.

Van der Worp, Jacco & Masters, Marshall. 2007. *Planet X Forecast and 2012 Survival Guide*. Scotts Valley, CA (Your Own World Books). ISBN 9781597720755.

Waters, Frank and Fredericks, Oswald White Bear. 1963. *Book of The Hopi*. New York, NY (Ballantine Books). ISBN 9780140045277.

Yukteswar, Swami Sri. 1894. *The Holy Science*. Los Angeles, CA (Self-Realization Fellowship). ISBN 978087612051.

Popol Vuh

Brasseur de Bourbourg, Charles Étienne. 1861. *Popol Vuh. Le livre sacré*, vol. 1. Paris (Arthus Bertrand). OCLC 7457119.

Chávez, Adrián Inés (ed.) 1981. *Popol Wuj: Poema mito-histórico kí-chè*. Quetzaltenango, Guatemala (Centro Editorial Vile). OCLC 69226261.

Chinchilla Mazariegos, Oswaldo. 2003. *Los dioses del Popol Vuh en el arte maya clásico = Gods of the Popol Vuh in Classic Maya Art*. Guatemala City (Museo Popol Vuh, Universidad Francisco Marroquín). ISBN 9992277513. OCLC 54755323.

Christenson, Allen J. (trans.) 2003. *Popol Vuh: The Sacred Book of the Maya*. (Norman: University of Oklahoma Press). ISBN 9780806138398.

Christenson, Allen J. (trans.) 2004. *Popol Vuh: Literal Poetic Version: Translation and Transcription*. (Norman: University of Oklahoma Press). ISBN 9780806138411.

Colop, Sam; (ed.) 1999. *Popol Wuj: versión poética K'iche'*. Quetzaltenango, Guatemala City (Proyecto de Educación Maya Bilingüe Intercultural Editorial Cholsamaj). ISBN 9992253002. OCLC 43379466.

Edmonson, Munro S.; (ed.) 1971. *The Book of Counsel: The Popol-Vuh of the Quiche Maya of Guatemala*. New Orleans (Middle American Research Institute, Tulane University). OCLC 658606.

Estrada Monroy, Agustín; (ed.) 1973. *Popol Vuh: empiezan las historias del origen de los índios de esta provincia de Guatemala*. Guatemala City (Editorial José de Piñeda Ibarra). OCLC 1926769.

Low, Denise. 1992. *A comparison of the English translations of a Mayan text, the Popol Vuh*. New York (ASAIL (Association for Study of American Indian Literatures)), 4 (2–3): 15–34. ISSN 07303238. OCLC 54533161. Reproduced online, Retrieved on 26 May 2008. http://oncampus.richmond.edu/faculty/ASAIL/SAIL2/42.html

Recinos, Adrián; (ed.) 1985. *Popol Vuh: las antiguas historias del Quiché* (6th ed.). San Salvador, El Salvador (Editorial Universitaria Centroamericana). OCLC 18385790.

Sáenz de Santa María, Carmelo. 1985. *Primera parte del tesoro de las lenguas cakchiquel, quiché y zutuhil, en que las dichal lenguas se traducen a la nuestra, española*. Publ. esp. no. 30. (Academia de Geografía e Historia de Guatemala. Tipografía Nacional, Guatemala).

Schultze Jena, Leonhard (trans.) 1944. *Popol Vuh: das heilige Buch der Quiché-Indianer von Guatemala, nach einer wiedergefundenen alten Handschrift neu übers. und erlautert von Leonhard Schultze*. Stuttgart, Germany (W. Kohlhammer). OCLC 2549190.

Tedlock, Dennis; (trans.) 1985. *Popol Vuh: the Definitive Edition of the Mayan Book of the Dawn of Life and the Glories of Gods and Kings. With commentary based on the ancient knowledge of the modern Quiché Maya*. New York (Simon & Schuster). ISBN 9780684818450. OCLC 11467786.

Ximénez, Francisco. ca. 1701. *Primera parte de el tesoro de las lengvas kakchiqvel, qviche y qutuhil*. Manuscript. Newberry Library, Chicago.

Catastrophism

Find books at this site: http://tsun.sscc.ru/hiwg/members.htm

Allan, D. S. & Delair, J. B. 1994. *When the Earth Nearly Died: Compelling Evidence of a World Cataclysm 11,500 Years Ago*. Gateway Books. ISBN 9781858600086.

Baillie, Mike. 2006. *New Light on the Black Death*. Stroud, UK (Tempus Publishing). ISBN 9780752435985.

Clow, Barbara Hand. 2001. *Catastrophobia: The Truth Behind Earth Changes*. Rochester, VT (Bear & Company). ISBN 9781879181625.

Clube, V. and Napier, W. 1982. *The Cosmic Serpent*. New York, NY (Universe Publishing/Rizzoli). ISBN 9780876633793.

Clube, V. and Napier, W. 1990. *The Cosmic Serpent*. Hoboken, NJ (Blackwell Publishing). ISBN 9780631169536.

Firestone, R., West Al., Warwick-Smith S. 2006. *The Cycle of Cosmic Catastrophes: How a Stone-Age Comet Changed the Course of World Culture*. Santa Fe, NM (Bear & Company). ISBN 9781591430612.

Ath, Flem & Rose. 1997. *When the Sky Fell: In Search of Atlantis*, New York, NY (St. Martin's). ISBN 9780312964016. Updated eBook edition available on website: http://www.flem-ath.com

Hutton, William and Eagle, Jonathan. 2004. *Earth's Catastrophic Past And Future: A Scientific Analysis Of Information Channeled By Edgar Cayce*. (Universal Publishers). ISBN 9781581125177.

LaViolette, Paul A. 2005. *Earth Under Fire: Humanity's Survival of the Ice Age*. Santa Fe, NM (Bear & Company). ISBN 978-1591430520.

Lewis, John S. 1999. *Comet and Asteroid Impact Hazards on a Populated Earth: Computer Modeling*. Burlington, MA (Academic Press). ISBN 9780124467606.

Lewis, John S. 1997, *Rain Of Iron And Ice: The Very Real Threat Of Comet And Asteroid Bombardment*. New York, NY (Basic Books). ISBN 9780201154948.

Talbott, David N. 1980. *The Saturn Myth: A Reinterpretation of Rites and Symbols Illuminating Some of the Dark Corners of Primordial Society*. New York, NY (Doubleday & Company; 1st ed.). ISBN 9780385113762.

Talbott, David N. & Thornhill, Wallace. 2007. *The Electric Universe*. Portland, OR (Mikamar Publishing). ISBN 9780977285136.

Talbott, David N. & Thornhill, Wallace. 2005. *Thunderbolts of the Gods*. Portland, OR (Mikamar Publishing). ISBN 9780977285105.

Tsarion, Michael. 2003. *Atlantis, Alien Visitation & Genetic Manipulation*. (Angels at Work Publishing). ISBN: 9781891962226.

Velikovsky, Immanuel. 1950. *Worlds in Collision*. New York, NY (The Macmillan Company). ISBN 9780385045414.

Crystal Skulls

Morton, Chris & Thomas, Ceri Louise. 2002. *The Mystery of the Crystal Skulls: Unlocking the Secrets of the Past, Present and Future*. Rochester, VT (Bear & Co.). ISBN 9781879181809.

Archaeo-astronomy

Aldana, G. 2007. *The Apotheosis of Janaab' Pakal: Science, History, and Religion at Classic Maya Palenque*. Boulder (University Press of Colorado). ISBN 087081855X.

Aveni, A. F. 1979. "Astronomy in Ancient Mesoamerica" in E. C. Krupp *In Search of Ancient Astronomies*. Chatto and Windus. pp. 154–185. ISBN 0701123141.

Aveni, A. F. 1980. *Skywatchers of Ancient Mexico*. (University of Texas). ISBN 0292775784.

Aveni, A. F. 1989. *World Archaeoastronomy*. (Cambridge University Press). ISBN 0521341809.

Aveni, A. F. 1989. *Empires of Time*. (Basic Books). ISBN 0465019501.

Aveni, A. F. 1997. *Stairways to the Stars: Skywatching in Three Great Ancient Cultures*. Hoboken, NJ (John Wiley and Sons). ISBN 0471329762.

Bahn, P. 1995. *Archaeology: A Very Short Introduction*. (Oxford University Press). ISBN 0192853791.

Bauer, B. & Dearborn, D. 1995. *Astronomy And Empire In The Ancient Andes: The Cultural Origins Of Inca Sky Watching.* (University of Texas). ISBN 0292708378.

Bauval, Robert, 2008. *The Egypt Code.* New York, NY (Disinformation). ISBN 9781934708002.

Cairns, H.C. 2005. "Discoveries in Aboriginal Sky Mapping (Australia)" in John W. Fountain & Rolf M. Sinclair, *Current Studies in Archaeo-astronomy: Conversations Across Time and Space.* Durham, NC. (Carolina Academic Press). pp. 523–538. ISBN 0890897719.

Chamberlain, V. D. & Young, M. J. 2005. "Introduction" in Von Del Chamberlain, John Carlson and M. Jane Young, *Songs from the Sky: Indigenous Astronomical and Cosmological Traditions of the World.* (Ocarina Books). pp. xi–xiv. ISBN 0954086724.

Fountain, J. 2005. "A Database of Rock Art Solar Markers" in John W. Fountain & Rolf M. Sinclair, *Current Studies in Archaeo-astronomy: Conversations Across Time and Space.* Durham, NC. (Carolina Academic Press). ISBN 0890897719.

Freeth, T. et al. November 30, 2006. "Decoding the ancient Greek astronomical calculator known as the Antikythera Mechanism." *Nature* doi:10.1038.

Hawkins, G. 1976. *Stonehenge Decoded.* (Fontana). ISBN 0006323154.

Heggie, D. C. 1982. *Archaeo-astronomy in the Old World.* (Cambridge University Press). ISBN 0521247349.

Hoskin, M. 1999. *The Cambridge Concise History of Astronomy.* (Cambridge University Press). ISBN 0521576008.

Hoskin, M. 2001. *Tombs, Temples, and Their Orientations: A New Perspective on Mediterranean Prehistory.* (Ocarina Books). ISBN 0954086716.

Hugh-Jones, Stephen. 1982. "The Pleiades and Scorpius in Barasana Cosmology" in Anthony F. Aveni and Gary Urton, *Ethno-astronomy and Archaeo-astronomy in the American Tropics.* (Annals of the New York Academy of Sciences). ISBN 0897661605.

Isager, S. and Skydsgaard, J. E. 1992. *Ancient Greek Agriculture.* (Routledge). ISBN 0415001641.

Johnson, W. 1912. *Byways of British Archaeology.* (Cambridge University Press).

Kelley, D. H. & Milone, E. F. 2005. *Exploring Ancient Skies: An Encyclopedic Survey of Archaeo-astronomy.* (Springer-Verlag). ISBN 0387953108.

Krupp, E. C. 1979. *In Search of Ancient Astronomies*. (Chatto and Windus). ISBN 0701123141.

Krupp, E. C. 1988. "Light in the Temples" in C. L. N. Ruggles, *Records in Stone: Papers in Memory of Alexander Thom*. (Cambridge University Press). ISBN 0521333814.

Krupp, E. C. 1997. *Skywatchers, Shamans and Kings*. (John Wiley and Sons). ISBN 0471329754.

McCluskey, S. C. 2005. "Different Astronomies, Different Cultures and the Question of Cultural Relativism" in John W. Fountain and Rolf M. Sinclair, *Current Studies in Archaeo-astronomy: Conversations Across Time and Space*. Carolina Academic Press. pp. 69–79. ISBN 0890897719.

MacKie, E. 1977. *Science and Society in Prehistoric Britain*. Paul Elek. ISBN 023640041X.

MacKie, E. 1997. "Maeshowe and the winter solstice: ceremonial aspects of the Orkney Grooved Ware culture." *Antiquity* 71(272): pp. 338–359.

Michell, J. 2001. *A Little History of Astro-Archaeology*. (Thames & Hudson). ISBN 0500275572.

Milbraith, S. 1988. "Astronomical Images and Orientations in the Architecture of Chichen Itzá" in A. F. Aveni, *New Directions in American Archaeo-astronomy. BAR International Series*. 454. (BAR). ISBN 0360545830.

Milbraith, S. 1999. *Star Gods of the Maya: Astronomy in Art, Folklore and Calendars*. (University of Texas Press). ISBN 0292752261.

O'Kelly, M. J. 1982. *Newgrange: Archaeology, Art and Legend*. (Thames and Hudson). ISBN 0500390150.

Poss, R. L. 2005. "Interpreting Rock Art: European and Anasazi Representations of Spirituality" in John W. Fountain & Rolf M. Sinclair, *Current Studies in Archaeo-astronomy: Conversations Across Time and Space*. Durham, NC (Carolina Academic Press). ISBN 0890897719.

Ruggles, C. L. N. 1993. *Archaeo-astronomy in the 1990s*. (Group D Publications). ISBN 1874152012.

Ruggles, C. L. N. 1999. *Astronomy in Prehistoric Britain and Ireland*. (Yale University Press). ISBN 0300078145.

Ruggles, C. L. N. & Saunders, N. J. 1993. "The Study of Cultural Astronomy" in Clive L. N. Ruggles and Nicholas J. Saunders, *Astronomies and Cultures*. (University Press of Colorado).

Saethre, E. 2007. "Close encounters: UFO beliefs in a remote Australian Aboriginal community." *Journal of the Royal Anthropological Institute* 13(4): 901–915. doi: 10.1111/j.1467-9655.2007.00463.x.

Schaefer, B. E. 2006. "Case Studies of Three of the Most Famous Claimed Archaeo-astronomical Alignments in North America" in Todd W. Bostwick and Bryan Bates, *Viewing the Sky Through Past and Present Cultures: Selected Papers from the Oxford VII International Conference on Archaeo-astronomy*. (Pueblo Grande Museum Anthropological Papers. 15. City of Phoenix Parks and Recreation Department). ISBN 1882572386.

Schlosser, W. 2002. "Zur astronomischen Deuteung der Himmelschreibe vom Nebra." *Archäologie in Sachsen-Anhalt* 1/02: 21–3.

Sofaer, A., ed. 2008. *Chaco Astronomy: An Ancient American Cosmology*. Santa Fe, NM (Ocean Tree Books). ISBN 9780847344460.

Steel, D. June 1999. "Stonehenge and the Terror in the Sky." *British Archaeology* 45. http://www.britarch.ac.uk/BA/ba45/ba45feat.html#steel

Thom, A. 1967. *Megalithic Sites in Britain*. Oxford. (Clarendon Press).

Trotter, A. P. (1927). "Stonehenge as an Astronomical Instrument." *Antiquity* 1:1: 42–53.

Urton, G. 1981. *At The Crossroads Of The Earth And The Sky: An Andean Cosmology*. (University of Texas). ISBN 029270349X.

Witzel, M. May 2001. "Autochthonous Aryans? The Evidence from Old Indian and Iranian Text." *Electronic Journal of Vedic Studies* 7:3: §28–30. http://www.ejvs.laurasianacademy.com/ejvs0703/ejvs0703d.txt

Xu, Z. Pankenier, D. W. and Jiang, Y. 2000. *East Asian Archaeo-astronomy: Historical Records of Astronomical Observations of China, Japan and Korea*. ISBN 905699302X.

Young, M. J. 2005. "Ethno-astronomy and the Problem of Interpretation: A Zuni Example" in Von Del Chamberlain, John Carlson and M. Jane Young, *Songs from the Sky: Indigenous and Cosmological Traditions of the World*. (Ocarina Books). ISBN 0654086724.

Zeilik, M. 1985. "The Ethno-astronomy of the Historic Pueblos, I: Calendrical Sun Watching." *Archaeo-astronomy: Supplement to the Journal for the History of Astronomy* 8 (16): S1–S24.

Zeilik, M. 1986. "The Ethno-astronomy of the Historic Pueblos, II: Moon Watching." *Archaeo-astronomy: Supplement to the Journal for the History of Astronomy* 10 (17): S1–S22.

Further Mesoamerican Studies

Boot, Eric. 2002. "The Dos Pilas-Tikal Wars from the Perspective of Dos Pilas Hieroglyphic Stairway 4." Mesoweb Articles. Retrieved on March 15, 2007. http://www.mesoweb.com/features/boot/dplhs4.pdf

Coe, Michael D. 1999. *Breaking the Maya Code.* London (Thames and Hudson). ISBN 9780500281338.

Coe, Michael D. 1994. *Mexico·from the Olmecs to the Aztecs* (4th ed.). New York (Thames & Hudson). ISBN 0500277222.

Diehl, Richard A. 2004. *The Olmecs: America's First Civilization. Ancient Peoples and Places.* New York (Thames & Hudson). ISBN 0500021198.

Freidel, David & Schele, Linda. 1992. *A Forest of Kings: The Untold Story of the Ancient Maya* (Harper Perennial). ISBN 9780688112042.

Jenkins, John Major & Matz, Martin. 2004. *Pyramid of Fire: The Lost Aztec Codex: Spiritual Ascent at the End of Time.* Rochester, VT (Bear & Company). ISBN 9781591430322.

Gronemeyer, Sven 2006. "Glyphs G and F: Identified as Aspects of the Maize God" (PDF). Wayeb Notes 22: pp.1–23. ISSN 13798286. Retrieved on April 4, 2007. http://www.wayeb.org/notes/wayeb_notes0022.pdf

MacDonald, G. Jeffrey. March 28, 2007. "Does Maya calendar predict apocalypse very soon?" *USA Today.* 11D.

Marcus, Joyce & Flannery, Kent V. 1996. *Zapotec Civilization: How Urban Society Evolved in Mexico's Oaxaca Valley. New aspects of antiquity series.* New York (Thames & Hudson). ISBN 0500050783.

Pérez de Lara, Jorge & Justeson, John. 2005. "Photographic Documentation of Monuments with Epi-Olmec Script/Imagery." The Foundation Granting Department: Reports Submitted to FAMSI. Foundation for the Advancement of Mesoamerican Studies, Inc. (FAMSI). Retrieved on April 4, 2007. http:// www.famsi.org/reports/05084/05084PerezdeLara01.pdf

Thompson, J. Eric S. 1929. "Maya Chronology: Glyph G of the Lunar Series." *American Anthropologist,* New Series 31 (2): pp.223–231. ISSN 0002-7294. OCLC 51205515.

Thompson, J. Eric S. 1971. *Maya Hieroglyphic Writing, an Introduction*. 3rd edition. (Norman: University of Oklahoma Press). ISBN 9780806109589.

Voss, Alexander W. & H. Juergen Kremer. 2000. "K'ak'-u-pakal, Hun-pik-tok' and the Kokom: The Political Organisation of Chichen Itza" (PDF). 3rd European Maya Conference (1998). Retrieved on 2005-10-26.

Wagner, Elizabeth. 2006. "Maya Creation Myths and Cosmology" in Nikolai Grube (ed.), *Maya: Divine Kings of the Rain Forest*. Eva Eggebrecht and Matthias Seidel (assistant eds.). Cologne (Könemann). ISBN 3833119578.

Wikipedia:Text of the GNU Free Documentation License
Version 1.2, November 2002

PREAMBLE

The purpose of this License is to make a manual, textbook, or other functional and useful document "free" in the sense of freedom: to assure everyone the effective freedom to copy and redistribute it, with or without modifying it, either commercially or noncommercially. Secondarily, this License preserves for the author and publisher a way to get credit for their work, while not being considered responsible for modifications made by others.

This License is a kind of "copyleft," which means that derivative works of the document must themselves be free in the same sense. It complements the GNU General Public License, which is a copyleft license designed for free software.

We have designed this License in order to use it for manuals for free software, because free software needs free documentation: a free program should come with manuals providing the same freedoms that the software does. But this License is not limited to software manuals; it can be used for any textual work, regardless of subject matter or whether it is published as a printed book. We recommend this License principally for works whose purpose is instruction or reference.

APPLICABILITY AND DEFINITIONS

This License applies to any manual or other work, in any medium, that contains a notice placed by the copyright holder saying it can be distributed under the terms of this License. Such a notice grants a world-wide, royalty-free license, unlimited in duration, to use that work under the conditions stated herein. The "Document," below, refers to any such manual or work. Any member of the public is a licensee, and is addressed as "you." You accept the license if you copy, modify or distribute the work in a way requiring permission under copyright law.

A "Modified Version" of the Document means any work containing the Document or a portion of it, either copied verbatim, or with modifications and/or translated into another language.

A "Secondary Section" is a named appendix or a front-matter section of the Document that deals exclusively with the relationship of the publishers or authors of the Document to the Document's overall subject (or to related matters) and contains nothing that could fall directly within that overall subject. (Thus, if the Document is in part a textbook of mathematics, a Secondary Section may not explain any mathematics.) The relationship could be a matter of historical connection with the subject or with related matters, or of legal, commercial, philosophical, ethical or political position regarding them.

The "Invariant Sections" are certain Secondary Sections whose titles are designated, as being those of Invariant Sections, in the notice that says that the Document is released under this License. If a section does not fit the above definition of Secondary then it is not allowed to be designated as Invariant. The Document may contain zero Invariant Sections. If the Document does not identify any Invariant Sections then there are none.

The "Cover Texts" are certain short passages of text that are listed, as Front-Cover Texts or Back-Cover Texts, in the notice that says that the Document is released under this License. A Front-Cover Text may be at most 5 words, and a Back-Cover Text may be at most 25 words.

A "Transparent" copy of the Document means a machine-readable copy, represented in a format whose specification is available to the general public, that is suitable for revising the document straightforwardly with generic text editors or (for images composed of pixels) generic paint programs or (for drawings) some widely available drawing editor, and that is suitable for input to text formatters or for automatic translation to a variety of formats suitable for input to text formatters. A copy made in an otherwise Transparent file format whose markup, or absence of markup, has been arranged to thwart or discourage subsequent modification by readers is not Transparent. An image format is not Transparent if used for any substantial amount of text. A copy that is not "Transparent" is called "Opaque."

Examples of suitable formats for Transparent copies include plain ASCII without markup, Texinfo input format, LaTeX input format, SGML or XML using a publicly available DTD, and standard-conforming simple HTML, PostScript or PDF designed for human modification. Examples of transparent image formats include PNG, XCF and JPG. Opaque formats include proprietary formats that can be read and edited only by proprietary word processors, SGML or XML for which the DTD and/or processing tools are not generally available, and the machine-generated HTML, PostScript or PDF produced by some word processors for output purposes only.

The "Title Page" means, for a printed book, the title page itself, plus such following pages as are needed to hold, legibly, the material this License requires to appear in the title page. For works in formats which do not have any title page as such, "Title Page" means the text near the most prominent appearance of the work's title, preceding the beginning of the body of the text.

A section "Entitled XYZ" means a named subunit of the Document whose title either is precisely XYZ or contains XYZ in parentheses following text that translates XYZ in another language. (Here XYZ stands for a specific section name mentioned below, such as "Acknowledgements," "Dedications," "Endorsements," or "History.") To "Preserve the Title" of such a section when you modify the Document means that it remains a section "Entitled XYZ" according to this definition.

The Document may include Warranty Disclaimers next to the notice which states that this License applies to the Document. These Warranty Disclaimers are considered to be included by reference in this License, but only as regards disclaiming warranties: any other implication that these Warranty Disclaimers may have is void and has no effect on the meaning of this License.

VERBATIM COPYING

You may copy and distribute the Document in any medium, either commercially or noncommercially, provided that this License, the copyright notices, and the license notice saying this License applies to the Document are reproduced in all copies, and that you add no other conditions whatsoever to those of this License. You may not use technical measures to obstruct or control the reading or further copying of the copies you make or distribute. However, you may accept compensation in exchange for copies. If you distribute a large enough number of copies you must also follow the conditions in section 3.

You may also lend copies, under the same conditions stated above, and you may publicly display copies.

COPYING IN QUANTITY

If you publish printed copies (or copies in media that commonly have printed covers) of the Document, numbering more than 100, and the Document's license notice requires Cover Texts, you must enclose the copies in covers that carry, clearly and legibly, all these Cover Texts: Front-Cover Texts on the front cover, and Back-Cover Texts on the back cover. Both covers must also clearly and legibly identify you as the publisher of these copies. The front cover must present the full title with all words of the title equally prominent and visible. You may add other material on the covers in addition. Copying with changes limited to the covers, as long as they preserve the title of the Document and satisfy these conditions, can be treated as verbatim copying in other respects.

If the required texts for either cover are too voluminous to fit legibly, you should put the first ones listed (as many as fit reasonably) on the actual cover, and continue the rest onto adjacent pages.

If you publish or distribute Opaque copies of the Document numbering more than 100, you must either include a machine-readable Transparent copy along with each Opaque copy, or state in or with each Opaque copy a computer-network location from which the general network-using public has access to download using public-standard network protocols a complete Transparent copy of the Document, free of added material. If you use the latter option, you must take reasonably prudent steps, when you begin distribution of Opaque copies in quantity, to ensure that this Transparent copy will remain thus accessible at the stated location until at least one year after the last time you distribute an Opaque copy (directly or through your agents or retailers) of that edition to the public.

It is requested, but not required, that you contact the authors of the Document well before redistributing any large number of copies, to give them a chance to provide you with an updated version of the Document.

MODIFICATIONS

You may copy and distribute a Modified Version of the Document under the conditions of sections 2 and 3 above, provided that you release the Modified Version under precisely this License, with the Modified Version filling the role of the Document, thus licensing distribution and modification of the Modified Version to whoever possesses a copy of it. In addition, you must do these things in the Modified Version:

A. Use in the Title Page (and on the covers, if any) a title distinct from that of the Document, and from those of previous versions (which should, if there were any, be listed in the History section of the Document). You may use the same title as a previous version if the original publisher of that version gives permission.

B. List on the Title Page, as authors, one or more persons or entities responsible for authorship of the modifications in the Modified Version, together with at least five of the principal authors of the Document (all of its principal authors, if it has fewer than five), unless they release you from this requirement.

C. State on the Title page the name of the publisher of the Modified Version, as the publisher.

D. Preserve all the copyright notices of the Document.

E. Add an appropriate copyright notice for your modifications adjacent to the other copyright notices.

F. Include, immediately after the copyright notices, a license notice giving the public permission to use the Modified Version under the terms of this License, in the form shown in the Addendum below.

G. Preserve in that license notice the full lists of Invariant Sections and required Cover Texts given in the Document's license notice.

H. Include an unaltered copy of this License.

I. Preserve the section Entitled "History," Preserve its Title, and add to it an item stating at least the title, year, new authors, and publisher of the Modified Version as given on the Title Page. If there is no section Entitled "History" in the Document, create one stating the title, year, authors, and publisher of the Document as given on its Title Page, then add an item describing the Modified Version as stated in the previous sentence.

J. Preserve the network location, if any, given in the Document for public access to a Transparent copy of the Document, and likewise the network locations given in the Document for previous versions it was based on. These may be placed in the "History" section. You may omit a network location for a work that was published at least four years before the Document itself, or if the original publisher of the version it refers to gives permission.

K. For any section Entitled "Acknowledgements" or "Dedications," Preserve the Title of the section, and preserve in the section all the substance and tone of each of the contributor acknowledgements and/or dedications given therein.

L. Preserve all the Invariant Sections of the Document, unaltered in their text and in their titles. Section numbers or the equivalent are not considered part of the section titles.

M. Delete any section Entitled "Endorsements." Such a section may not be included in the Modified Version.

N. Do not retitle any existing section to be Entitled "Endorsements" or to conflict in title with any Invariant Section.

O. Preserve any Warranty Disclaimers.

If the Modified Version includes new front-matter sections or appendices that qualify as Secondary Sections and contain no material copied from the Document, you may at your option designate some or all of these sections as invariant. To do this, add their titles to the list of Invariant Sections in the Modified Version's license notice. These titles must be distinct from any other section titles.

You may add a section Entitled "Endorsements," provided it contains nothing but endorsements of your Modified Version by various parties—for example, statements of peer review or that the text has been approved by an organization as the authoritative definition of a standard.

You may add a passage of up to five words as a Front-Cover Text, and a passage of up to 25 words as a Back-Cover Text, to the end of the list of Cover Texts in the Modified Version. Only one passage of Front-Cover Text and one of Back-Cover Text may be added by (or through arrangements made by) any one entity. If the Document already includes a cover text for the same cover, previously added by you or by arrangement made by the same entity you are acting on behalf of, you may not add another; but you may replace the old one, on explicit permission from the previous publisher that added the old one.

The author(s) and publisher(s) of the Document do not by this License give permission to use their names for publicity for or to assert or imply endorsement of any Modified Version.

COMBINING DOCUMENTS

You may combine the Document with other documents released under this License, under the terms defined in section 4 above for modified versions, provided that you include in the combination all of the Invariant Sections of all of the original documents, unmodified, and list them all as Invariant Sections of your combined work in its license notice, and that you preserve all their Warranty Disclaimers.

The combined work need only contain one copy of this License, and multiple identical Invariant Sections may be replaced with a single copy. If there are multiple Invariant Sections with the same name but different contents, make the title of each such section unique by adding at the end of it, in parentheses, the name of the original author or publisher of that section if known, or else a unique number. Make the same adjustment to the section titles in the list of Invariant Sections in the license notice of the combined work.

In the combination, you must combine any sections Entitled "History" in the various original documents, forming one section Entitled "History"; likewise combine any sections Entitled "Acknowledgements," and any sections Entitled "Dedications." You must delete all sections Entitled "Endorsements."

COLLECTIONS OF DOCUMENTS

You may make a collection consisting of the Document and other documents released under this License, and replace the individual copies of this License in the various documents with a single copy that is included in the collection, provided that you follow the rules of this License for verbatim copying of each of the documents in all other respects.

You may extract a single document from such a collection, and distribute it individually under this License, provided you insert a copy of this License into the extracted document, and follow this License in all other respects regarding verbatim copying of that document.

AGGREGATION WITH INDEPENDENT WORKS

A compilation of the Document or its derivatives with other separate and independent documents or works, in or on a volume of a storage or distribution medium, is called an "aggregate" if the copyright resulting from the compilation is not used to limit the legal rights of the compilation's users beyond what the individual works permit. When the Document is included in an aggregate, this License does not apply to the other works in the aggregate which are not themselves derivative works of the Document.

If the Cover Text requirement of section 3 is applicable to these copies of the Document, then if the Document is less than one half of the entire aggregate, the Document's Cover Texts may be placed on covers that bracket the Document within the aggregate, or the electronic equivalent of covers if the Document is in electronic form. Otherwise they must appear on printed covers that bracket the whole aggregate.

TRANSLATION

Translation is considered a kind of modification, so you may distribute translations of the Document under the terms of section 4. Replacing Invariant Sections with translations requires special permission from their copyright holders, but you may include translations of some or all Invariant Sections in addition to the original versions of these Invariant Sections. You may include a translation of this License, and all the license notices in the Document, and any Warranty Disclaimers, provided that you also include the original English version of this License and the original versions of those notices and disclaimers. In case of a disagreement between the translation and the original version of this License or a notice or disclaimer, the original version will prevail.

If a section in the Document is Entitled "Acknowledgements," "Dedications," or "History," the requirement (section 4) to Preserve its Title (section 1) will typically require changing the actual title.

TERMINATION

You may not copy, modify, sublicense, or distribute the Document except as expressly provided for under this License. Any other attempt to copy, modify, sublicense or distribute the Document is void, and will automatically terminate your rights under this License. However, parties who have received copies, or rights, from you under this License will not have their licenses terminated so long as such parties remain in full compliance.

FUTURE REVISIONS OF THIS LICENSE

The Free Software Foundation may publish new, revised versions of the GNU Free Documentation License from time to time. Such new versions will be similar in spirit to the present version, but may differ in detail to address new problems or concerns. See http://www.gnu.org/copyleft.

Each version of the License is given a distinguishing version number. If the Document specifies that a particular numbered version of this License "or any later version" applies to it, you have the option of following the terms and conditions either of that specified version or of any later version that has been published (not as a draft) by the Free Software Foundation. If the Document does not specify a version number of this License, you may choose any version ever published (not as a draft) by the Free Software Foundation.

ENDNOTES

CHAPTER ONE

1   Garner, Dwight, February 5, 2009. "The End Is Near! Now the Good News: It Could Be Groovy." *New York Times.*

2   Easterbrook, Gregg. June 2008. "The Sky is Falling," *The Atlantic.*

3   http://www.sonypictures.com/movies/2012. The working title of "2012" is alleged to have been "Farewell, Atlantis." See: http://www.imdb.com/title/tt1190080

4   Whewell, William J. 1832. *Principles of Geology,* vol. II, quart. rev., v. 47. London (Charles Leyell).

5   Jenkins, John Major. 2007. "The Origins of the 2012 Revelation" in *The Mystery of 2012: Predictions, Prophecies & Possibilities.* Boulder, CO (Sounds True). ISBN 9781591796114.

6   "2012: Time on Fire—The Prophecy: Recycling the Collapse of Time." http://www.lawoftime.org/content/timeonfire.html

7   Schele, Linda; David Freidel, 1990. *A Forest of Kings: The Untold Story of the Ancient Maya.* New York, NY (HarperCollins). ISBN 9780688112042.

8   Tedlock, Dennis. 1986. *Popol Vuh: the Mayan Book of the Dawn of Life.* New York, NY (Touchstone-Simon & Schuster). ISBN 9780671617714.

9   Sitler, Robert K. 2007. "2012 and the Maya World" in *The Mystery of 2012: Predictions, Prophecies & Possibilities.* Boulder, CO (Sounds True). ISBN 9781591796114.

10   "José Argüelles Speaks Out." http://www.skywebs.com/earthportals/Portal_Messenger/speakout.html

CHAPTER TWO

11   http://en.wikipedia.org/wiki/Timeline_of_environmental_events

12   Conversation between my mother and an archaeologist at a dig in Guatemala in the 1980s.

13 Coe, Michael D. 2005. *The Maya*. (7th Ed.). London, UK (Thames & Hudson). ISBN 9780500285053.

14 http://en.wikipedia.org/wiki/Maya_language

15 Jenkins, John Major. 2007. "The Origins of the 2012 Revelation" in *The Mystery of 2012: Predictions, Prophecies & Possibilities*. Boulder, CO (Sounds True). ISBN 9781591796114.

16 http://alignment2012.com/historychannel.html

17 Shepard, John. 2007. "Christian view of Astrology and Horoscopes." http://www.northforest.org/summary/astrology.html

18 Coe, Michael D. 1966. *The Maya*. Ancient Peoples and Places series (1st ed.). London, UK (Thames & Hudson). ISBN 0500285055.

19 http://en.wikipedia.org/wiki/Comet_Encke & http://en.wikipedia.org/wiki/Taurid

20 Clube, S. V. M.; Napier, W. M. December 1984. "The microstructure of terrestrial catastrophism," *Royal Astronomical Society, Monthly Notices*, vol. 211. Edinburgh, Scotland (Royal Observatory). ISSN 0035-8711. Bibliographic Code: 1984MNRAS.211.953C.

21 Velásquez García, Erik. Summer 2006. "The Maya Flood Myth and the Decapitation of the Cosmic Caiman." *The PARI Journal* Instituto de Investigaciones Estéticas, Universidad Nacional Autónomo de México.

22 Saraswati, Prakashanand. 2002. *The True History and the Religion of India*. New Delhi, India (Motilal Banarsidass). ISBN 9788120817890.

23 Timeline compiled from Wikipedia and from Knight-Jadczyk, Laura. April 2008."THE LIST: Damages, Disasters, Injuries, Deaths, and Very Close Calls." http://laura-knight-jadczyk.blogspot.com/2008/04/meteorites-asteroids-and-comets-damages.html

24 Guatemala-based cultural site: http://www.authenticmaya.com/quirigua1.htm. Note there is some dispute over the exact start-date in the Gregorian calendar, with August 11th, 12th and 13th all being suggested. August 11th is the most commonly used and is the date I refer to in this book.

25 Massachusetts Institute of Technology Classics Department Website & Chatboard: http://classics.mit.edu/Plato/timaeus.html

26   Abbott, Dallas, "Verifying the Sources of Holocene Age Megatsunami Deposits." Earth Institute at Columbia University, 'Last Modified: 12-31-1969' [webpage date appears to be affected by Y2K bug!] http://www.earthinstitute.columbia.edu/eidirectory/displayproject.php?projectid=606

27   Blakeslee, Sandra. November 14, 2006. "Ancient Crash, Epic Wave." *New York Times.* http://www.nytimes.com/2006/11/14/science/14WAVE.html

28   Jenkins, John Major. May 23, 1994. "The How and Why of the Mayan End-date In 2012 A.D." Orig. pub. Dec-Jan 1995 issue of *Mountain Astrologer.* http://alignment2012.com/Why2012.html

29   Jenkins, John Major. 2002. *Galactic Alignment: The Transformation of Consciousness According to Mayan, Egyptian, and Vedic Traditions.* Santa Fe, NM (Inner Traditions-Bear & Co.). ISBN 9781879181847.

30   Sitler, Robert K. 2007. "2012 and the Maya World" in *The Mystery of 2012: Predictions, Prophecies & Possibilities.* Boulder, CO (Sounds True). ISBN 9781591796114.

CHAPTER THREE

31   Jenkins, John Major. 1996. The original working introduction of *Maya Cosmogenesis 2012: The True Meaning of the Maya Calendar End-Date.* Santa Fe, NM (Bear & Co.). ISBN 9781879181489.

32   http://en.wikipedia.org/wiki/Hamlet%27s_Mill

33   Jenkins, John Major. 1996. The original working introduction of *Maya Cosmogenesis 2012: The True Meaning of the Maya Calendar End-Date.* Santa Fe, NM (Bear & Co.). ISBN 9781879181489.

34   Schoch, Robert. 1999. "The Date of the Great Sphinx of Giza." (conference paper). http://www.antiquityofman.com/Schoch_conference.html

35   Fairall, Tony. June 1999, "Precession and the layout of the Ancient Egyptian pyramids." *Journal of the Royal Astronomical Society.*

36   Broadcasting Standards Press Release. Re: Judgment Against BBC2. http://www.grahamhancock.com/horizon/bsc-press_release.htm.

37   Statement by Graham Hancock. November 22, 1999, regarding BBC Horizon: *Atlantis Uncovered and Atlantis Reborn.* http://www.grahamhancock.com/horizon/antarctica.htm

38   Barbiero, Flavio. 2006. "On the Possibility of Instantaneous Shifts of the Poles." http://www.grahamhancock.com/forum/BarbieroF1.php

39   Atlantis in Antarctica page on Flem-Ath.com. http://www.flem-ath.com/?page_id=6

40   Hancock, Graham. Op. cit.

41   Associated Press. July 12, 2007. "Frozen Baby Mammoth Found in Siberia." http://www.foxnews.com/story/0,2933,288975,00.html

42   Clein, A. Robert. April 9, 2009. "Crustal Shift." http://globalwarming-arclein. blogspot.com/2009/04/crustal-shift.html

43   Allan, D. S. & Delair, J. B. 1995. *When the Earth Nearly Died: Compelling Evidence of A Catastrophic World Change 9,500 BC.* Republished in 1997 as *Cataclysm: Compelling Evidence of a Cosmic Catastrophe in 9500 BC.* Santa Fe, NM (Bear & Co.). ISBN 9781879181427.

44   Paul LaViolette's webpage for the Starburst Foundation, a nonprofit research institute based in Schenectady, NY. http://www.etheric.com/Starburst/Starburst.html

45   Paul LaViolette's website. February 20, 2005. "Was the December 26, 2004 Indonesian Earthquake and Tsunami Caused by a Stellar Explosion 26,000 Light Years Away? Sound Crazy? Read Carefully Below." http://www.etheric.com/GalacticCenter/GRB.html

46   Clow, Barbara Hand. 2007. *The Mayan Code: Time Acceleration and Awakening the World Mind.* Rochester, VT (Inner Traditions-Bear & Co.). ISBN 9781591430704.

47   Ibid.

48   Tsarion, Michael. 2003. *Atlantis, Alien Visitation & Genetic Manipulation.* (Angels at Work Publishing). ISBN: 9781891962226.

49   Ibid.

50   Yukteswar, Swami Sri. 1894. *The Holy Science.* Los Angeles, CA (Self-Realization Fellowship). ISBN 9780876120514.

51   Daniel P. Whitmire, Ph.D.'s website. http://www.ucs.louisiana.edu/~dpw9254

52   Walter Cruttenden's website. http//www.binaryresearchinstitute.org

53   Cruttenden, Walter. August 2005. *Atlantis Rising* magazine, Issue 53.

54 Daniel P. Whitmire, Ph.D.'s website. http://www.ucs.louisiana.edu/~dpw9254

CHAPTER FOUR

55 Recinos, Adrián (Author), Goetz, Delia (Translator), Morley, Sylvanus G. (Translator) 1991. *Popol Vuh: The Sacred Book of the Ancient Quiche Maya*. Oklahoma City, OK (University of Oklahoma Press). ISBN 9780806122663.

56 Ibid.

57 Velikovsky, Immanuel. Fall 1979. "On Saturn And The Flood," *Kronos*, vol. V no. 1.

58 The Book of Enoch, Chapter 8. http://reluctant-messenger.com/book_of_enoch.htm

59 http://wiki.answers.com/Q/What_is_the_average_height_of_men_and_women_across_the_world

60 Slightly redacted from glossary for *Blazing Splendor*, the memoirs of Tulku Urgyen Rinpoche. http://www.rangjung.com/blazingsplendor/blazing-glossary.htm

61 Ibid.

62 http://en.wikipedia.org/wiki/The_Voice_of_the_Silence_(Blavatsky

63 http://www.theosociety.org/pasadena/sunrise/50-00-1/as-hpb.htm

64 Blavatsky, Helena Petrovna, December, 1958. "Vaivasvata Manu," *Theosophy*, vol. 47, no. 2, pp. 78–82 (Collated from the writings of H. P. Blavatsky). http://www.blavatsky.net/magazine/theosophy/ww/additional/ListOfCollatedArticles/VaivasvataManu.html#1bottom

65 *The Mahabharata Vana Parva*, Section CLXXXIX. Translated by Sri Kisari Mohan Ganguli.

66 Lash, John Lamb. January 2007. "Countdown to 2012: Reflections on Kali Yuga, the Maya Endtime, and the Western Narrative Spell." http://www.metahistory.org/ENDTIME/Countdown2012.php

67 Cremo, Michael, February 2009. Interview by Alexandra Bruce for this book.

68 Ibid.

69 Jenkins, John Major. 2002. *Galactic Alignment: The Transformation of Consciousness*

According to Mayan, Egyptian, and Vedic Traditions. Santa Fe, NM (Inner Traditions-Bear & Co.). ISBN 9781879181847.

70   Weidner, Jay. 2005. "The Topology of Time: Hyperdimensional Space and the Unfolding of the Four Ages." http://www.jayweidner.com/2012Topology.html

71   Ibid.

72   Van Lysebeth, André, 1995. *TANTRA: The Cult of the Feminine.* York Beach, ME (Samuel Weiser). ISBN 9780877288459.

73   "Kali Yuga" From *The Mahabharata Vana Parva*, Section CLXXXIX. Translated by Sri Kisari Mohan Ganguli.

74   "A few peculiarities of Kali Yuga." Selected texts from Sri Ramacharitamanasa of Sant Tulasidas, Uttar-kanda, verses 96–103.

75   http://en.wikipedia.org/wiki/Kali_Yuga

76   The Church of God—Preparing for the Kingdom of God website. http://www.cog-pkg.org

77   http://en.wikipedia.org/wiki/Left_Behind_(series)

78   Lawrence, Raymond J. September 21, 2008, "Sarah Palin and the Rapture," *CounterPunch.org* http://www.counterpunch.org/lawrence09202008.html

79   http://www.storyofstuff.com

80   http://en.wikipedia.org/wiki/Armageddon

81   Or 51.84 million km. See "Velocity" http://en.wikipedia.org/wiki/Milky_way

82   http://www.astronomy2009.org

83   Miller, D.I. April 4, 2004. "Fred Alan Wolf from 'What the Bleep Do We Know?'" *On Spirituality,* SFGate.com. http://www.sfgate.com/cgi-bin/article.cgi?f=/g/a/2005/04/04/findrelig.DTL

CHAPTER FIVE

84   Testimony by Mr. Russell L. Schweickart to U. S. House of Representatives. http://www.science.house.gov/publications/Testimony.aspx?TID=9743

85   Joseph, Lawrence E. 2008. *Apocalypse 2012: An Investigation into Civilization's End.* New York (Morgan Road-Broadway Books). ISBN 9780767924481.

86   NASA's Asteroid & Impact Hazards page. http://impact.arc.nasa.gov/intro_faq.cfm

87   http://en.wikipedia.org/wiki/Extinction_event

88   Official WISE Mission Statement. http://wise.ssl.berkeley.edu/mission.html

89   Rampino, Michael. 1998. Cambridge Conference Correspondence. http://abob.libs.uga.edu/bobk/ccc/cc020298.html

90   Ibid.

91   http://en.wikipedia.org/wiki/99942_Apophis

92   Reuters. July 7, 2005. "After U.S., China plans 'Deep Impact' mission." http://web.archive.org/web/20050830003558/http://economictimes.indiatimes.com/articleshow/1163067.cms

93   Shiga, David. March 2007. "China and U.S. at highest risk of damage from asteroids," *NewScientist.com.* http://www.newscientist.com/article/dn11467-china-and-us-at-highest-risk-of-damage-from-asteroids.html

94   http://en.wikipedia.org/wiki/Comet_Encke & http://en.wikipedia.org/wiki/Taurid

95   Clube, S. V. M.; Napier, W. M. December 1984. "The microstructure of terrestrial catastrophism," *Royal Astronomical Society, Monthly Notices,* vol. 211, Edinburgh, Scotland (Royal Observatory). ISSN 0035-8711. Bibliographic Code: 1984MNRAS.211.953C.

96   Holocene Impact Working Group Statement of Purpose. http://tsun.sscc.ru/hiwg/purpose.htm

97   King, Thomas F. eds, Bobrowsky, Peter and Rickman, Hans. 2007. "The archaeology and anthropology of Quaternary period cosmic impact," *Comet/Asteroid Impacts and Human Society: An Interdisciplinary Approach.* New York, NY (Springer Press). ISBN 9783540327097.

98   Cochrane, Ev. 1995. "Mars Rocks In Ancient Myth and Modern Science: Part II" *AEON,* vol. IV no. 2, pp. 57–73. http://www.kronia.com/thoth/ThoIII02.txt

99   Köfels impact home page at the University of Bristol. http://www.bris.ac.uk/aerospace/research/dynamicsandsystems/kofels

100 http://en.wikipedia.org/wiki/Extinction_event

101 Myers, Norman. March 8, 2006. http://en.wikinews.org/wiki/Largest_mass_extinction_in_65_million_years_underway,_scientists_say

102 Thousands of megafauna fossils lie directly beneath the City of Los Angeles and are on display at the Page La Brea Tar Pits Museum. http://www.tarpits.org/education/guide/flora/sloth.html

103 Easterbrook, Gregg. June 2008, "The Sky is Falling," *The Atlantic*. See also: Firestone, R. B.; et al. 2007. "Evidence for an extraterrestrial impact 12,900 years ago that contributed to the megafaunal extinctions and the Younger Dryas cooling." PNAS 104 (41): 16016–16021.

104 Press release. January 26, 2009, "Comet impact theory disproved." http://www.bristol.ac.uk/news/2009/6123.html

105 Chang, Kenneth. January 1, 2009. "Diamonds Linked to Quick Cooling Eons Ago." *New York Times*. http://www.nytimes.com/2009/01/02/science/02impact.html

106 http://en.wikipedia.org/wiki/Sun

107 http://en.wikipedia.org/wiki/Critical_ionization_velocity

108 Baker, Daniel et al. January 2008. "Severe Space Weather Events—Understanding Societal and Economic Impacts Workshop Report." Washington, D.C. (The National Academies Press). ISBN 9780309127691. http://www.nap.edu/catalog.php?record_id=12507#description

109 Malik, Tariq. September 19, 2005, "NASA's New Moon Plans: 'Apollo on Steroids.'" http://www.space.com/news/050919_nasa_moon.html

110 Phillips, Dr. Tony. November 8, 2005. "Sickening Solar Flares." http://www.nasa.gov/mission_pages/stereo/news/stereo_astronauts.html

111 Phillips, Dr. Tony. December 16, 2008. "A Giant Breach in the earth's Magnetic Field." http://science.nasa.gov/headlines/y2008/16dec_giantbreach.htm

112 Ibid.

113 http://en.wikipedia.org/wiki/Solar_maximum

114 Haliburton, Mary-Sue. July 12, 2008. "Earth Magnetic Field Reversal." *Pure Energy Systems News*.

115 Personal correspondence with Dr. Bernhard Steinberger. March 13, 2009.

116 Ibid.

117 http://en.wikipedia.org/wiki/Svalbard_Global_Seed_Vault

118 Muller, Richard A. 2002. "Avalanches at the core-mantle boundary." *Geophysical Research Letters*, vol. 29, pp. 41-1 to 41-4.

119 Velikovsky, Immanuel. 1955. *Earth In Upheaval*. New York, NY (Doubleday).

120 Hapgood, Charles H. and Campbell, James H. 1958. *The Earth's Shifting Crust* (Pantheon).

121 Williams, D. M.; Kasting, J. F.; Frakes, L. A. December 1998. "Low-latitude glaciation and rapid changes in the Earth's obliquity explained by obliquity-oblateness feedback." New York, NY. *Nature*, vol. 396, pp. 453–455.

122 November 8, 1901. "Strange Geological Find: Fossils of Tropical Fruits Discovered in Coal from Spitzbergen." *New York Times*. p 1.

123 Steinberger, B., and Torsvik, T. H. 2008, "Absolute plate motions and true polar wander in the absence of hotspot tracks." *Nature*, vol. 452, pp. 620–623.

124 Dmtriev, Alexey N. 1997. "Planetophysical State of the Earth and Life." Published in Russian. IICA Transactions, Volume 4. The Millennium Group. http://www.tmgnow.com

125 Ibid.

126 Wallace Thornhill. On-camera interview in the documentary *Thunderbolts of the Gods*. http://thunderboltsfilm.com

127 Los Alamos National Laboratory website: http://public.lanl.gov/alp/plasma/people/alfven.html

128 Wallace Thornhill. On-camera interview in the documentary *Thunderbolts of the Gods*. http://thunderboltsfilm.com

129 Wallace Thornhill's website. http://www.electric-universe.org

130 The Starburst Foundation website: http://www.etheric.com/Starburst/Starburst.html

131 Christopher C. Sanders' bogus evacuation notice. http://www.earthmountainview. com/yellowstone/yellowstone.htm

132 Yellowstone National Park website. http://www.yellowstonenationalpark.com/ calderas.htm

133 Clube, Victor. February 10, 2008. "Cosmic Winter—A Lecture." kronia.com

CHAPTER SIX

134 McKenna, Terence. 1995. *Terence McKenna: Time Wave Zero.* (Sound Photosynthesis). DVD.

135 McKenna, Terence, February 27, 1993. "Space Time Continuum with Terence McKenna: Archaic Revival." Transcript of live spoken word/multimedia event. *Alien Dreamtime.* Archived by: http://deoxy.org/t_adt.htm

136 Stray, Geoff. 2009. *Beyond 2012: Catastrophe or* Awakening? *A Complete Guide to End-of-Time Predictions.* Rochester VT (Bear & Company). ISBN 9781591430971.

137 McKenna, Terence. 1995. *Terence McKenna: Time Wave Zero.* (Sound Photosynthesis). DVD.

138 Kleiner, Keith. February 27, 2009. "The World's Scariest Techno Prophet." *Rolling Stone.*

139 McKenna, Terence. February 27, 1993. "Space Time Continuum with Terence McKenna: Archaic Revival & Timewave Zero." Transcript of live spoken word/ multimedia event. *Alien Dreamtime.* Archived by: http://deoxy.org/t_adt.htm

140 Chivers, Tom and Highfield, Roger. September 24, 2008. *Time is running out— literally, says scientist.* Telegraph.co.uk

141 Ibid.

142 Argüelles, José. 1984. *Earth Ascending: An Illustrated Treatise on Law Governing Whole Systems.* Rochester VT (Bear & Company). ISBN 9780939680450.

143 Argüelles, José. Spectral Moon 23, Kin 136, Third Year of Prophecy (?). "José Speaks Out." http://www.earthportals.com/Portal_Messenger/speakout.html

144 http://en.wikipedia.org/wiki/Harmonic_Convergence

145 Jenkins, John Major et al. September 1, 2007. *The Mystery of 2012: Predictions, Prophecies & Possibilities*. Boulder, CO (Sounds True). ISBN 9781591796114.

146 Aveni, Anthony. January 2009. Interview transcript of on-camera interview for *2012: Science or Superstition*. New York (Disinformation).

147 Ibid.

148 Vincent H. Malmström's website. http://www.dartmouth.edu/~izapa/index.html

149 Malmström, Vincent H. Undated. "The Astronomical Insignificance of the Maya Date 13.0.0.0.0." http://www.dartmouth.edu/~izapa/M-32.pdf

150 Jardin, Xeni. June 26, 2008. "Josh Harris: 'Pseudo was a fake company.'" http://www.boingboing.net/2008/06/26/josh-harris-pseudo-w.html. Harris is also the subject of the 2009 Sundance award-winning documentary *We Live In Public*.

151 Jenkins, John Major, 2009. "Fear and Lying in 2012-Land," in *You Are Still Being Lied To*. New York, NY (Disinformation). ISBN 9781934708071.

152 Argüelles, José. 2007. "The Mayan Factor," in *The Mystery of 2012: Predictions, Prophecies & Possibilities*. Boulder, CO (Sounds True). ISBN 9781591796114. (Orig. pub. 1987. *Earthshift Series*, interview with Tami Simon).

153 Calleman, Carl Johan et al. 2007. *The Mystery of 2012: Predictions, Prophecies & Possibilities*. Boulder, CO (Sounds True). ISBN 9781591796114.

154 Carl Johan Calleman's website. http://www.calleman.com/ (see "Biography").

155 Clow, Barbara Hand. 2007. *The Mayan Code: Time Acceleration & Awakening the World Mind*. Rochester, VT (Bear & Co.). ISBN: 9781591430704.

156 Braden, Gregg et al. 2007. *The Mystery of 2012: Predictions, Prophecies & Possibilities*. Boulder, CO (Sounds True). ISBN 9781591796114.

157 http://www.diagnosis2012.co.uk/jmj.htm

158 Calleman, Carl Johan. 2007. "The Nine Underworlds: Expanding Levels of Consciousness," in *The Mystery of 2012: Predictions, Prophecies & Possibilities*. Boulder, CO (Sounds True). ISBN 9781591796114.

159 Ibid.

160 Braden, Gregg. 2009. *Fractal Time: The Secret of 2012 and a New World Age*. Carlsbad, CA (Hay House). ISBN 9781401920647.

161 Gregg Braden's webpage with his Time Code Calculator. http://greggbraden.com/calculator

162 Ibid.

163 Braden, Gregg. March 17, 2009. *Fractal Time: The Secret of 2012 and a New World Age*. Carlsbad, CA (Hay House). ISBN 9781401920647.

164 Eden, Dan. Undated. Scientists Now Know: We're Not From Here! http://www.viewzone.com/milkyway.html

165 Braden, Gregg. 2009. *Fractal Time: The Secret of 2012 and a New World Age*. Carlsbad, CA (Hay House). ISBN 9781401920647.

166 Pawlowski, A. January 27, 2009. "Apocalypse in 2012? Date spawns theories, film." CNN. http://www.cnn.com/2009/TECH/science/01/27/2012.maya.calendar.theories

167 http://en.wikipedia.org/wiki/Trans-Neptunian_object

168 Zecharia Sitchin Website. http://www.sitchin.com/adamgene.htm

169 Sitchin, Zecharia. April 2000. "Dialogue in Bellaria: Sitchin and Vatican Theologian Discuss UFOs, Extraterrestrials, Angels, Creation Of Man." http://www.sitchin.com/vatican.htm

170 http://en.wikipedia.org/wiki/Zetatalk

171 Barrios, Carlos. "Mayan Calendar Prophecy: The World Will Not End." Manataka American Indian Council website. http://www.manataka.org/page1578.html

172 Barrios, Carlos. 2004. "The Path of Venus Over the Face of The Sun." http://www.prophecykeepers.com/barrios.html

173 Hall, Molly. *A Mayan Elder Speaks On the Mayan Calendar and 2012*. About.com

CHAPTER SEVEN

174 Aurobindo, Sri. 1970 2nd edition. *The Human Cycle, Ideal of Human Unity, War and Self Determination*. Twin Lakes, WI (Lotus Press). ISBN 9788170580140.

175 Bonillo, Cristina. February 23, 2009. "El viento regirá nuevo año de calendario maya." http://www.prensalibre.com/pl/2009/febrero/23/297290.html

176 Kochkin, Alex & Patricia Van Camp. 2005. *A New America: An Awakened Future on Our Horizon.* Stevensville, MT (Global Awakening Press). ISBN 9781932288001.

177 Kochkin, Alex. March 20, 2009. "Economic Review of Likely Future—CORRECTED VERSION." New Earth Summit Public Online Forum. http://newearthsummit. org/forum/index.php?topic=321.msg4016#msg4016

178 Kochkin, Alex et al. December 21, 2008. "State of the Vision: 2008 Futureviews to 2010 and onwards- Part One." *Global Awakening News* Winter 2008–09 Edition. Stevensville, MT (Global Awakening Press).

179 Ibid.

180 Half-Past Human website. Explanation of methods. http://www.halfpasthuman. com/NuHPHWhatWeDo.htm

181 Half-Past Human website on the Alta Series. http://www.halfpasthuman.com/ NuHPHPastAltaSeries.htm

182 Jones, Troy. September 17, 2008. "Half-Past Human." http://www.realitysandwich.com/half_past_human

183 Kochkin, Alex. March 22, 2009. "Conversations with Clif: Transcript of Radio Interview With Clif From The Web Bot Project (a.k.a., Half-Past Human)." Stevensville, MT (Global Awakening Press).

184 Ure, George. May 25, 2009. http://urbansurvival.com/week.htm

185 High, Clif. "2009 Summary." http://www.halfpasthuman.com and http://www. urbansurvival.com

186 April 25, 2009. *Journeys with Rebecca* (Internet radio show). "Interview with Cliff from the Web Bot Project." http://journeyswithrebecca.com/jwr9/jwr9_april25b.mp3

187 Ibid.

188 Phillips, Dr. Tony. November 19, 2008. "Discovered: Cosmic Rays from a Mysterious, Nearby Object." http://science.nasa.gov/headlines/y2008/19nov_cosmicrays.htm

189 Kochkin, Alex. March 22, 2009. "Conversations with Clif: Transcript of Radio Interview with Clif from The Web Bot Project (a.k.a. Half-Past Human)." Stevensville, MT (Global Awakening Press).

190 Kochkin, Alex. April 25, 2009. "Swine Flu Pandemic? What about existential crisis?" *Global Awakening News* 2008–2009 Winter-Spring Issue. Stevensville, MT (Global Awakening Press).

191 Villoldo, Alberto. May 1, 2008. "*Homo Luminous*: The New Human." http://www.realitysandwich.com/homo_luminous_the_new_human

192 Crawford, John & Kochkin, Alex. April 24, 2009. "Ascension &Transformation: An ongoing discussion about our future-present destiny." *Global Awakening News 2008–2009 Winter-Spring–Part Two–UPDATE SERIES*, Stevensville, MT (Global Awakening Press).

193 Satprem. 1996. *Sri Aurobindo or the Adventure of Consciousness*. Translated from the French. Paris, France & Mysore, India (L'Institut de Recherches Évolutives & Mira Aditi).

194 *Mother's Agenda* is posted online for free at the ashram's website. http://www.auroville.org/vision/maagenda.htm

195 Auroville, In Brief. http://auroville.org/av_brief.htm

196 László, Ervin, 2007, "Birthing of a New World," in *The Mystery of 2012: Predictions, Prophecies & Possibilities*. Boulder, CO (Sounds True). ISBN 9781591796114.

197 Ibid.

198 Ibid.

CONCLUSION

199 Gebser, Jean. 1986. *Ever Present Origin: Part One: Foundations Of The Aperspectival World*. Athens, OH (Ohio University Press). ISBN 9780821407691.

200 Ibid.

GLOSSARY

201 http//www.binaryresearchinstitute.org

202 The American Heritage Dictionary of the English Language: Fourth Edition. 2000.

203 Jenkins, John Major. 2002. *Galactic Alignment: The Transformation of Consciousness According to Mayan, Egyptian, and Vedic Traditions.* Rochester, VT (Bear & Co.). ISBN 9781879181847.

204 The American Heritage Dictionary of the English Language: Fourth Edition. 2000.

205 Ibid.

206 The Catholic Encyclopedia. http://www.newadvent.org/cathen/14530a.htm

207 Wikipedia: http://en.wikipedia.org/wiki/New_Testament

208 Ibid.

209 http://www.theosociety.org/pasadena/sunrise/50-00-1/as-hpb.htm

210 Ibid.

211 Jenkins, John Major. 2002. *Galactic Alignment: The Transformation of Consciousness According to Mayan, Egyptian, and Vedic Traditions.* Santa Fe, NM (Bear & Co.). ISBN 9781879181847.

212 Ibid.

213 Ibid.

214 Stephenson, Neal, 1992. *Snow Crash.* New York, NY (Bantam Spectra). ISBN 9780553380958.

ILLUSTRATION CREDITS

P. 112. This figure was created by Robert A. Rohde from published data and was inspired by a similar figure in Rohde & Muller (2005) supplementary data. This file is licensed under the Creative Commons Attribution ShareAlike 3.0. http://commons.wikimedia.org/wiki/File:Extinction_Intensity.png

P. 115. Illustration by Mario Roberto Duran Ortiz Mariordo, 2008, fair use of public domain info by the B612 Foundation work on Apophis.

P. 121. Painting by Peter Paul Rubens, c. 1604/1605, on display at the National Gallery of Art, Washington, D.C.

P. 132. Still from film *2012: Science or Superstition*. © 2008 The Disinformation Company Ltd.

P. 138. Illustration by Jose F. Vigil. Courtesy of U.S. Geological Survey.

P. 139. Top: Image courtesy of Metrodyne.

P. 139. Bottom: Image courtesy of U.S. Geological Survey.

P. 142. Illustration by Linda Huff and Priscilla Frisch, courtesy of NASA.

P. 149. Illustration by Ben Finney.

P. 150. Screenshot courtesy of Alex Kochkin.

P. 201. Photo by Nimrod Erez. © 2008 Nimrod Erez.

INDEX

ABOUT THE AUTHOR

ALEXANDRA BRUCE is the author of five non-fiction books about popular culture, science and spirituality. This is her third book for The Disinformation Company, following *Beyond The Bleep: The Definitive Unauthorized Guide to 'What The Bleep Do We Know!?'* and *Beyond The Secret: The Definitive Unauthorized Guide to 'The Secret.'* She lives in Los Angeles.

ALSO AVAILABLE

The perfect complement to this book, the documentary film *2012: Science or Superstition* features the leading researchers, authors and scientists in the field.

Available on DVD and as a digital download from iTunes and Amazon.com.

$19.95 (DVD) • $9.99 (iTunes & Amazon VOD)
UPC: 826262005191 • ISBN: 978-1-934708-17-0 • 78 mins. + extras

Featured in the film are Graham Hancock, John Major Jenkins, Daniel Pinchbeck, Alberto Villoldo, Anthony Aveni, Robert Bauval, Jim Marrs, Walter Cruttenden, Lawrence E. Joseph, Alonso Mendez, Douglas Rushkoff, John Anthony West and Benito Vegas Duran.

Find out even more about 2012 at www.2012SOS.com

ALSO FROM **disinformation**®

BEYOND THE BLEEP: The Definitive Unauthorized Guide to *What The Bleep Do We Know!?*

In this book Alexandra Bruce illuminates the personalities and teachings of the physicists, physicians, spiritual teachers, mystics and scholars in the film *What the Bleep Do We Know!?*, helping the reader sort through their wilder theories with simple explanations of the cutting-edge science on which they are based.

Available as a Trade Paperback and an eBook • 4-1/4 x 7 in. • 288 pages • Spirituality / Science • ISBN: 9781932857221

BEYOND THE SECRET: The Definitive Unauthorized Guide to *The Secret*

Alexandra Bruce unveils the truth about the cultural phenomenon that is *The Secret*. Based on a bestselling documentary film of the same name, it presents the "Law of Attraction," which, according to the tagline, "has traveled through centuries to reach you." Also contains the classic self-help book by Wallace D. Wattles, *The Science of Getting Rich*.

Available as a Trade Paperback and an eBook • 4-1/4 x 7 in. • 320 pages • New Age / Self-Actualization & Self Help • ISBN: 9781932857931

Find more disinformation® at http://store.disinfo.com